Using OpenMP—The Next Step

Scientific and Engineering Computation
William Gropp and Ewing Lusk, editors; Janusz Kowalik, founding editor

A complete list of books published in the Scientific and Engineering Computation series appears at the back of this book.

Using OpenMP—The Next Step

Affinity, Accelerators, Tasking, and SIMD

Ruud van der Pas, Eric Stotzer, and Christian Terboven

The MIT Press
Cambridge, Massachusetts
London, England

This book was set in LaTeX by the authors.

Library of Congress Cataloging-in-Publication Data

Names: Pas, Ruud van der.
Title: Using OpenMP—the next step: affinity, accelerators, tasking and
    SIMD / Ruud van der Pas, Eric Stotzer, Christian Terboven.
Description: Cambridge, MA : The MIT Press, [2017] | Series: Scientific and
    engineering computation | Includes bibliographical references and index.
Identifiers: LCCN 2017028107 | ISBN 9780262534789 (pbk. : alk. paper)
Subjects: LCSH: Parallel programming (Computer science) — Application program
    interfaces (Computer software) | OpenMP.
Classification: LCC QA76.642 .P427 2017 | DDC 005.2/75–dc23 LC record available at https://
lccn.loc.gov/2017028107

Dedicated to all the people that continue to use and develop OpenMP.

Contents

Series Foreword

The Scientific and Engineering Computation Series from MIT Press aims to provide practical and immediately usable information to scientists and engineers engaged at the leading edge of modern computing. Aspects of modern computing first presented in research papers and at computer science conferences are presented here with the intention of accelerating the adoption and impact of these ideas in scientific and engineering applications. Such aspects include parallelism, language design and implementation, systems software, numerical libraries, and scientific visualization.

William Gropp and Ewing Lusk, Editors

Foreword

The great paradox of programming languages is that as they become popular and evolve, they become more complex and easier to use, at the same time. Simplicity comes from specialization – features that make some things very natural and easy, e.g., parallelizing a recursive function in OpenMP. Complexity has two sources: needs of expert users for more control to extract the best performance, and just the sheer size of the language as more interdependent features are added. With success comes complexity! Over time, fewer and fewer people understand the fullness and intricacies of each language, yet the language fills the needs of many. It is books that allow this complexity-simplicity contradiction to thrive. It is essential that programming language books focus on the perspective of the language users while providing rationale for the choices made by the language designers. "Using OpenMP—The Next Step" has an ideal set of authors – practitioners, teachers, and language designers who live and breathe OpenMP.

OpenMP is well established as the thread-level language of choice for High Performance Computing. Today, OpenMP and MPI together have become the languages driving scientific discoveries, predictions, and engineering through their use in modeling and simulation. Parallel numerical and computational methods using OpenMP and MPI are used in most, if not all, engineering fields, physical sciences, biological sciences, and even in some arts.

When we embarked on the OpenMP journey in 1996, we could not have envisioned that the language we built, with roots in ANSI X3H5, would be used by so many. After all, parallelism and concurrency are hard! SMP and NUMA systems were commonplace, and x86-based SMP systems were arriving. There were many proprietary languages, each solving similar problems, but none fully. OpenMP 1.0 came into existence to unify the world of proprietary languages into an industry standard to efficiently harness contemporary architectures of the time.

We are at a similar juncture today – a single processor chip contains from tens to hundreds of cores/threads, vector/SIMD systems are back in vogue, accelerators are everywhere, flexible task-based parallelism is needed to support high numbers of hardware threads and heterogeneity, and non-uniform memory is common. It is precisely at this time that a widely implemented language based on a popular standard is most powerful – it offers a unified approach to this diversity so that applications writers with large investments in their code have a clear, dependable, and productive path forward. OpenMP 4.5 addresses exactly these issues, and this book is focused on the features needed to exploit these architectural innovations.

Chapters 5 and 6 are crucial to grasp in order to exploit contemporary processors and accelerators. Almost all processors today have vector units, and chapter 5 on the SIMD construct shows how to use OpenMP to map loops onto these vector units. Chapter 6 shows how to offload code and manage data to run on an accelerator. Programming today's computing systems without a grasp of these constructs will result in sub-optimal performance, frequently by an order of magnitude, and sometimes by multiple orders. They are as fundamental to OpenMP for today's architectures as the "parallel for" construct was in the early years.

Chapter 4 is all about obtaining the highest performance while maintaining data to thread affinity. OpenMP has had affinity support for some time – now, the support is greatly enhanced to allow beginning users much simpler ways to specify affinity, while allowing experts much finer control. Chapter 4 goes into all the gory details to explain how to think about this.

In its early years, OpenMP only supported parallel loops and static blocks of parallel sections. Since then, OpenMP has evolved and now supports while loops and recursion, with features such as dynamic tasking. Such language features are crucial if parallelism with OpenMP is ever going to evolve beyond numerical computing. Chapter 3 covers tasking, intended to handle such flexible control structures for parallelism.

I first met Ruud in the early 2000's. He has passion and a finely crafted skill for teaching, drawn from his experience in working with customers as he helps them add parallelism to and optimize their applications. He co-authored an earlier book on OpenMP 2.5, "Using OpenMP." Eric has an excellent track record in heterogeneous computing and was one of the early proponents to add this support in OpenMP. Eric's ideas and efforts have been instrumental in the design of the target construct for offloading work to accelerators. He continues to drive improvements to OpenMP, fueled by his experience from various tutorials and interactions with users. I met Christian in the late 90's when he was a Ph.D. student at RWTH Aachen University. He was an avid user of OpenMP, with a particularly good understanding of C++, different parallel applications, and how people used different languages. Over the years, he has trained numerous scientists throughout Europe on the intricacies of parallel programming and performance optimization. Christian is one of the proponents and authors of the affinity features in OpenMP 4.5.

OpenMP 4.5 follows the programming language paradox beautifully. "Using OpenMP—The Next Step" will help the paradox thrive! I am thankful to the OpenMP language committee for investing in this language to address the needs of its users.

Sanjiv Shah, 2017
Champaign, IL, and Austin, TX, USA

Sanjiv Shah was a key contributor towards the creation of the first OpenMP specifications, and led the teams who built the wildly successful first OpenMP Fortran and C++ compilers at Kuck and Associates (KAI). He is now employed at Intel as a Software Group Vice President, in charge of software tools for servers. Sanjiv currently serves on OpenMP's Board of Directors.

Preface

This book is a follow-up to "Using OpenMP" [2], a comprehensive tutorial on the widely used OpenMP parallel programming model for shared memory systems. At the time [2] was published, the conventional CPU had already evolved to include multiple cores, but this was not yet mainstream technology.

Nowadays, however, almost all processors have multiple cores and there is a bigger need than ever to use those cores to enhance the performance of applications. We believe that OpenMP is ideally suited for these kinds of systems. It provides a flexible, powerful, and easy-to-use programming model to express the parallelism in an application.

Support for OpenMP is thriving. All major compilers provide full support for OpenMP and continue to implement the latest specifications. The OpenMP language committee is very active in adapting the specifications to the trends in computer systems and applications. Meanwhile, the official list of OpenMP member companies, universities, and research labs continues to grow [20].

Since the first book came out, OpenMP has evolved and expanded in several directions. Major new functionality has been added to better serve certain types of applications, address robustness, keep up with trends in computer architectures, and further enhance performance.

This first book covered OpenMP 2.5 and is still highly recommended for getting started learning OpenMP. It explains the fundamental concepts of parallel computing and presents an extensive and practical overview of all the basic OpenMP constructs and features that most users need to write an OpenMP program.

OpenMP has taken a big step further since OpenMP 2.5. A new task model is provided that is more natural and suitable for unstructured parallelism. New features for specifying thread affinity, vectorization through SIMD instructions, offloading code regions to accelerators, early termination of a parallel construct, and many more are now available.

Readers who bought the first book, or who are already familiar with the topics covered in it, can immediately start using this new book. This book covers OpenMP 4.5 and focuses on what has changed, and what has been added to OpenMP since the 2.5 specifications were released. After reading this book, you should be well equipped to find your way in the specifications, know what is best to use, and how to implement it in your own application.

Given how comprehensive the latest specifications are, it is not possible to discuss every single feature in the same amount of detail. Instead, we want to go beyond the specifications, and show when and how to use a specific feature. Even more than in the first book, the practical usage of OpenMP is emphasized. We try to give as many relevant and different examples as possible. Only where we felt it necessary, are more formal syntax descriptions included.

Another choice we made was to restrict the examples to C and C++, but we believe they are straightforward enough to be useful for Fortran programmers as well. Comments specific to Fortran are included, where relevant.

For ease of reference, Chapter 1 has a brief recap of OpenMP 2.5. This was the last 2.x release before the 3.0 specifications, published in May of 2008, were released. Because the 2.5 specifications are extensively covered in the first book, this overview is kept short. In Chapter 2, many of the enhancements introduced since OpenMP 2.5 are covered, but four of the new features are so extensive that a full chapter has been dedicated to each of these.

Chapter 3 is all about tasking. This is a major functionality enhancement, introduced with OpenMP 3.0 and expanded since then. With tasking, several types of applications, but especially those with less regular parallelism, can be parallelized quite conveniently.

In the early days of OpenMP, the target architecture was an SMP system, but over time, cc-NUMA architectures have become widely available. In contrast with earlier such systems, nowadays even many small two-socket systems have this type of memory architecture. OpenMP 4.0 is the first release to provide support for cc-NUMA, and this has been extended in OpenMP 4.5. This topic is covered in great detail in Chapter 4.

Chapter 5 is dedicated to the support for SIMD. It is an example of parallelism at the instruction level. A SIMD instruction executes the same operation on different data elements at the same time. This is a hardware feature supported by certain processors and although compilers support the generation of such instructions, with the OpenMP support for SIMD, the user can explicitly control the use of these instructions.

Chapter 6 addresses another new trend in computer architecture: heterogeneous systems. The most well-known example is probably the GPU. This is a co-processor, originally designed to accelerate graphics, but nowadays also used to improve the performance of other types of applications. Another example is a DSP, a co-processor that can execute certain operations (for example, FFTs) extremely fast. Because of the massively parallel architecture of these accelerators, a parallel programming model is needed to exploit the hardware parallelism and OpenMP 4.5

provides this. In Chapter 7, we give an outlook towards how OpenMP is expected to evolve.

Acknowledgments

Writing a book like this cannot be done without an army of people to provide assistance where needed and desired. The authors are particularly indebted to the following people.

Susan Stotzer meticulously reviewed numerous draft versions. We want to thank her for her patience and for all the suggestions to improve the style and clarity of the text.

The members of the OpenMP language committee have all been very helpful to explain and clarify questions that came up while writing this book. We especially would like to thank the following members for their help answering our questions: Sergi Mateo Bellido, James Beyer, Nawal Copty, Jim Cownie, Bin Fan, and Thomas R.W. Scogland.

A special word of thanks goes to Bronis R. de Supinski, the long time chairman of the OpenMP language committee. He has been instrumental in expanding OpenMP in multiple dimensions and taking it to the next level. Under his leadership, the sometimes very different opinions have been united. This has resulted in today's extensive support for very complex environments.

Over the years, we have given many tutorials. The discussions with our two co-presenters, Bronis R. de Supinski and Michael Klemm, have helped shape the material presented here.

We are also very grateful to the following people, who all helped to review significant parts of the content: James Beyer, Deepak Eachempati, Alexandre Eichenberger, Michael Klemm, Thomas R.W. Scogland, Xinmin Tian, and Mark Woodyard. Their feedback has been very valuable and a big thank you is in place.

Using OpenMP—The Next Step

1 A Recap of OpenMP 2.5

In [2], OpenMP is covered at great length. At the time that [2] was published, the OpenMP 2.5 specifications were released and that is what that book focused on. Since then, four more specifications have been released. The enhancements and new features they introduced are the major topic of this book. For completeness, this chapter presents a brief recap of OpenMP 2.5. In many cases, the syntax description is informal and not every aspect is covered. For such details, refer to the specifications [20].

1.1 OpenMP Directives and Syntax

OpenMP is an Application Programming Interface (API) for shared memory parallelization, using C, C++, or Fortran. The API consists of compiler directives to specify and control parallelization, augmented with runtime functions, and environment variables. It is incumbent upon the user to identify the parallelism and insert the appropriate control structures in the program. These controls are called *directives*.

In C/C++, the directive is based on the `#pragma omp` construct. This is a regular language pragma and is ignored if it is not recognized by the compiler. This may happen for several reasons: 1) the compiler does not support OpenMP, although that is rare these days, 2) if a typo is made (e.g. `#pragma openmp`), or if the source is not compiled with an option to enable recognition of the directives.

In Fortran, the directive starts with either `!$omp` or `*$omp`/`c$omp` in old-style Fortran programs. To the compiler, this is a regular comment string, unless through the use of a specific option, the compiler is instructed to recognize the special `omp` keyword and generate the corresponding OpenMP code, but also here a typo gives unexpected results.

In C/C++ and Fortran, portability of the code is not violated when using the directives. The source compiles with, or without, OpenMP enabled. If the OpenMP-specific runtime functions are used, but no option to support OpenMP is specified, unresolved references to those functions are reported by the linker. Luckily, there is an easy way around this.

If a source is compiled with OpenMP enabled, the `_OPENMP` macro is guaranteed to be set in C/C++. It is set to the release date of the OpenMP version the compiler supports. Regardless of the value, this macro may be used in conjunction with an `#ifdef` construct to support the runtime functions.

For example, the code fragment below handles the use of the `omp_get_num_-threads()` function and compiles both with and without OpenMP enabled. In the case of the former, the include file `omp.h` is used, exposing all OpenMP function definitions to the compiler. Outside an OpenMP environment, the function is defined to always return 1 for the number of threads.

```
1 #ifdef _OPENMP
2   #include <omp.h>
3 #else
4   #define omp_get_num_threads() 1
5 #endif
```

In Fortran, conditional compilation may be used to handle the use of runtime functions. With this mechanism, the character string `!$` (or `*$` and `c$`) is replaced by two spaces if the source is compiled with OpenMP enabled. Otherwise, it is considered to be a language comment and ignored. This allows for the compile-time activation of executable statements, as demonstrated below:

```
1 !$    use omp_lib
2        ....
3       nthreads = 1
4 !$    nthreads = omp_get_num_threads()
```

If not compiled for OpenMP, the first and third lines in the source snippet are ignored, because they are treated as language comments. If OpenMP is enabled, the `!$` string is replaced by two spaces. This results in the use of module `omp_lib` and the second assignment to variable `nthreads` is activated. The second assignment overrides the first one, and at runtime, the number of active threads is returned.[1]

An additional benefit of the directive-based approach is that compilers have full visibility of the (parallel) code and typically perform many optimizations, as well as issue warning messages. This is much more difficult to do with a programming model based upon function calls.

1.2   Creating a Parallel Program with OpenMP

The user must identify the code part(s) that may be executed in parallel. The parallelism is defined through the addition of the appropriate directives to the

---

[1] Optimizing compilers recognize that the first assignment is redundant and eliminate it.

#pragma omp parallel *[clause[[,] clause]...]* *new-line*   *structured block*
!$omp parallel *[clause[[,] clause]...]*   *structured block* **!$omp end parallel**

Figure 1.1: **Syntax of the parallel construct in C/C++ and Fortran** – The statements within the parallel region are executed by all threads. In C/C++, the parallel region implicitly ends at the end of the structured block.

source code. It is the responsibility of the user to identify which part(s) are selected to run in parallel and use the various constructs to ensure correct results.

The nature (private or shared), or "scoping," of the variables must also be specified, but everything else is handled by the compiler and OpenMP runtime system. This completely eliminates the book-keeping and handling of details found in many other parallel programming models.

In many cases, more control than simply the execution of a block of code in parallel is needed. Extensive additional functionality is available and easy to add to an application. Subsequent sections in this chapter describe the type of building blocks that are available to implement additional functionality.

1.2.1 The Parallel Region

A parallel program in OpenMP starts and ends with the *parallel region*. It is the cornerstone of OpenMP. This is where parallel execution takes place and multiple threads are put to work. The syntax in C/C++ and Fortran is given in Figure 1.1.

There is no limit on the number of parallel regions, but for performance reasons it is best to keep the number of regions to a minimum and make them as large as possible. In C/C++, it is good practice to use a comment string to mark the end of the parallel region. This is less of an issue in Fortran, because it has the mandatory terminating `!$omp end parallel` construct.

The thread that encounters the parallel region is called the *master thread*. It creates the additional threads and is in charge of the overall execution. The threads that are active within a parallel region are referred to as a *thread team*, or "team" for short. Multiple teams may be active simultaneously.

The specifications also distinguish between an *active* and *inactive* parallel region. In the case of the former, the team consists of more than the master thread. This is in contrast with an inactive parallel region, which is executed only by the master thread.

The statements within the parallel region are executed by all threads, unless the optional `if` clause evaluates to `false`. In this case, only one thread executes the region. This implies that it is an inactive parallel region. Outside of the parallel region(s), the master thread executes the serial portions of the application.

All OpenMP directives are to be placed in the *dynamic* extent of a parallel region in order to have an effect. This means that they need not be visible from the parallel region, but must be in the execution path that starts at a parallel region.

An example is a function with OpenMP constructs that is called from within a parallel region. If the same function is called outside of a parallel region, the directives are ignored and only one thread executes the code.

The situation is somewhat different for the OpenMP runtime functions. These may be used anywhere in the program, but some return a meaningful result, only if executed from within a parallel region. Other functions *must* be executed outside of a parallel region. For example, the `omp_set_num_threads()` function is used to set the number of threads. It is illegal to use it within a parallel region, and the runtime behavior is undefined if this rule is violated.

Before discussing the major OpenMP constructs, the execution and memory model are presented. Every user must have a basic understanding of these topics.

1.2.2   The OpenMP Execution Model

The way an OpenMP program executes is defined by the execution model. The OpenMP model is illustrated in Figure 1.2.

An OpenMP program always starts in serial mode. The thread executing the serial parts of the application, that is, the code outside the parallel regions, is called the *master thread*. This thread runs throughout the lifetime of the program.

At some point during the execution, the additional threads are created by the runtime system. When and how this happens is implementation-defined, but the threads are guaranteed to be available when the parallel regions are encountered.[2]

The master thread is included in the total number of active threads in the parallel region. For example, in Figure 1.2, four additional threads are created when the first parallel region is encountered.

---

[2]This assumes nothing unusual has happened, causing one or more threads to be unavailable.

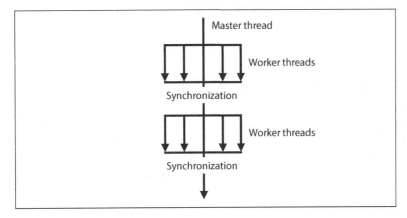

Figure 1.2: **The OpenMP execution model** – The master thread runs from start to finish. When a parallel region is encountered, the additional threads are engaged to perform the work that needs to be done. A barrier at the end of each parallel region synchronizes all threads. Execution continues only after the last thread has arrived at the barrier. After the parallel region exits, the master thread continues, until the next parallel region is encountered.

After this first thread-creation phase, multiple threads are active and within the parallel regions, the program executes in parallel. At the termination of a parallel region, the master thread continues until the next parallel region is encountered. This is called the *fork-join model*.

Until OpenMP 3.0, the user had no control over the behavior of the idle threads in-between the parallel regions, but the newly introduced environment variable `OMP_WAIT_POLICY` sets the behavior of idle threads. For more information on this variable, refer to Section 2.2 on page 53.

There are various ways to control the number of threads executing the parallel region. By default, this value is defined through environment variable `OMP_NUM_-THREADS`. This sets the initial number of threads, but if not set by the user, a system-dependent default is used. Without any other action taken, it remains constant throughout the execution of the program.

If the number of threads needs to be more dynamic, the `omp_set_num_-threads()` runtime function may be used to change the number of threads, while the application executes. This function affects the number of threads used in the next parallel region encountered, as well as all subsequent regions. This function should only be executed *prior* to a parallel region. It is illegal to call it within a parallel region.

An alternative is to use the `num_threads(<nt>)` clause on the directive that defines the parallel region. The OpenMP runtime system uses the value of variable `nt` as the number of threads for the current parallel region, plus all subsequent parallel regions.

A useful feature is that the number of threads may increase, or decrease, on a per-parallel region basis. How this is implemented is transparent to the user and the responsibility of the runtime system. If the thread count shrinks, it is determined by the implementation how to handle the threads no longer needed. A common choice is to keep these threads around and avoid the relatively expensive setup cost of recreating threads in case the number increases again.

Thread synchronization occurs in the implied barrier at the end of the parallel region. The `nowait` clause is not supported on a parallel region. In other words, this barrier is always present and cannot be removed.

For a single-level parallel region this is a not a problem. It makes sense for all threads to finish their work before the master thread continues. With nested parallelism (see also section 1.5), this is not so obvious and the additional barriers may negatively impact performance.

1.2.3   The OpenMP Memory Model

Until now, a very important aspect of shared memory parallel programming has been glossed over: the memory model. It describes what types of memory there are and how threads interact with each of them. It also defines in what way the potentially different views on memory maintain consistency and, most importantly, when.

Until support for heterogeneous computing was introduced in OpenMP 4.0, there was a single address space only. This is still the case for the (host) system where the OpenMP program starts execution, but if accelerators are used, multiple address spaces may exist.

As illustrated in Figure 1.3, an OpenMP program has two different elementary types of memory: *private* and *shared*. To which memory type a variable belongs is defined by default rules, but may also be explicitly controlled through the appropriate clause on a construct.

In the case of the latter, the user must assign the appropriate memory type to variables used in the parallel region. Especially if the `default(none)` clause is

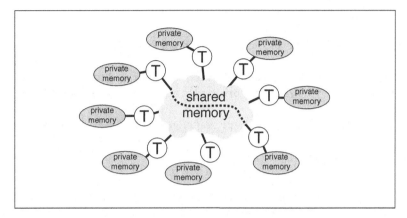

Figure 1.3:   **The OpenMP memory model** – There are two different elementary types of memory: private and shared. Each thread has a private memory. A thread may access, or modify, variables in its own private memory, but not in another thread's private memory. In addition to this, there is a single shared memory. All threads have read and write access to variables stored there.

used, all variables need to be specified. Although more work upfront, it is strongly recommended not to rely on the default rules and explicitly label, or "scope," the variables.

The reason is that the default rules are clearly defined, but not always what one might expect. Knowing the subtleties is one option, but it is still easy to make a mistake. It is also not as difficult as it may seem at first sight to explicitly scope the variables.

There is one exception to this recommendation. In C/C++, variables declared within a code block are automatically made private. This is very convenient, and the next section has more information on this.

Private variables   Each thread has unique access to its private memory and no other thread may interfere. There is never the risk of an access conflict with another thread. Although multiple threads may use the same name for a private variable, these variables are stored in different locations in memory. Modifications apply to the local copy only and a thread can never change the value of a private variable owned by another thread.

```
 1 x = 5;
 2 y = 20;
 3 #pragma omp parallel private(x) firstprivate(y)
 4 {
 5    x = 10;        // x is undefined on entry, but now set to 10
 6    int z = x + y; // y was pre-initialized to a value of 20
 7       ....
 8    y = 30;        // (first)private variables may be modified
 9       ....
10 } // End of parallel region
```

Figure 1.4: **Example of private variables** − Private variables are undefined on
entry to (and exit from) the parallel region. The `firstprivate` clause at line 3 is used to
pre-initialize variable y to 20 and use this value at line 6.

A loop variable is a simple example. If this variable is in private memory, as it
must be, multiple threads may use the *same* variable name to execute a loop. It
is impossible for one thread to modify the loop variable in the private memory of
another thread.

If the same variable name is used outside, and within a parallel region, there
is no risk of a conflict either. The reason is that the variable inside the region is
treated as a different variable (even though it has the same name). For example,
in the code fragment in Figure 1.4, variable x appears both outside, and inside the
parallel region, but there is no conflict.

Although not yet available in OpenMP 2.5, more recent versions of the specifications describe many features in terms of tasks. In Chapter 3, tasking is discussed in great detail, but ahead of this, we need to introduce the concept of an
implicit task. This is a task, generated by an implicit parallel region, or generated
when a parallel construct is encountered during execution. In the context of a
parallel region, or a worksharing construct, an "execution instance" is an implicit
task. When a variable is private, each execution instance refers to its own instance
of that variable. This topic also comes up with the support for SIMD instructions.
See Section 5.2.1 for the definition of an execution instance with `simd` loops.

In OpenMP, the lifetime of a private variable is restricted. It only exists within a parallel region and by default, is undefined on entry to and exit from a construct. If needed, there are ways around this, but this must be explicitly handled through the appropriate constructs.

This is also illustrated in the example. Although variable x has been initialized to 5 by the master thread, its value is undefined within the parallel region. This is not a problem, because it is explicitly set to 10.

How about variable y? The value is needed within the parallel region, but it is not defined. The solution is to declare this variable to be firstprivate, instead of private. This not only guarantees that all threads have a private copy of this variable, but each copy is pre-initialized to the value y had prior to entering the parallel region.

This is also illustrated in the example. Upon executing the parallel region, variable y inherits the original value of 20. This is the value used at line 6. At line 8, it is reset to 30. This variable may actually have a different value within each thread, because it is a private variable.

The firstprivate clause is also supported on some constructs introduced after OpenMP 2.5. This is covered in the respective sections in the remainder of this book.

Variable z is declared within the parallel region. Per the rules of OpenMP, this makes it a private variable. This is a convenient feature and the exception to the recommendation not to rely on the default scoping rules.

In some cases, there is a need to use the value of a private variable after the parallel construct. For this situation, the worksharing loop and sections construct support the lastprivate clause.[3] This makes the value of such variable(s) accessible after the construct.

In a parallel application, it is not always clear what "last" means. For these constructs, this is defined such that the sequential semantics are preserved. For example, on a loop, it is the value as computed for the sequentially last iteration. This convenience comes at a (small) cost in performance, so use it with care.

There is one more thing worth mentioning here. What happens with the value of the original variable if it is also declared to be a private variable within the parallel region? The answer is that it depends on the version of OpenMP used. In OpenMP 2.5 the value is undefined upon exit of the parallel region. This was a

---

[3]This clause is also supported on simd loops, covered in Chapter 5.

highly undesirable limitation and has been lifted. As of OpenMP 3.0, the initial value of this variable is preserved.

Shared variables   In addition to its private memory, each thread has access to the same single shared memory. There are two substantial differences with private memory.

In contrast with a private variable, only one instance of a shared variable exists. All threads "see" the same shared variable(s). In addition to this, each thread may read, as well as write, any shared variable. As long as the variable is within the dynamic extent, there is no constraint as to when this is allowed to occur. It is the responsibility of the user to correctly handle this situation

There is one case that requires extra attention and even warrants a specific directive: global, or static, variables. They are shared by default.

For example, consider the situation where a function uses global data as scratch space that is modified on each function call. If this function is called in parallel, a data race occurs, because multiple threads may modify the same memory address at the same time. A solution is to give each invocation of the function a private copy of the global data. In that way, even if multiple threads modify the data simultaneously, the updates are performed on different memory locations.

This is such a common scenario that, through the `threadprivate` directive, OpenMP provides elegant support for this situation. Each thread uses its private storage for the data that was originally shared. In case such privatized data must be pre-initialized, the `copyin` clause may be used.

The reason to be judicious when using shared variables, especially when they are modified, is performance-related. If multiple threads update the same cache line simultaneously and do this frequently, *false sharing* occurs and this has a negative impact on performance. In the worst case, this may lead to a substantial performance degradation. With private data, this is not an issue, so the recommendation is to use private data as much as possible. Shared variables are indispensable, but only use them if it is necessary to do so.

Memory Consistency Models   The question is what happens when a modification has been made to a shared variable. The thread that made the change has immediate access to the new value, but what about the other threads? Intuitively, one might expect that all the threads see the same change at the same time as the thread that made the modification, but that is not the case.

Consider the following example. A thread initializes, or modifies, the value of two independent shared variables x and y in the order x = ..., y = ... The compiler may decide to interchange the statements and perform the assignment to y first. Unfortunately, such a valid optimization could be an issue if *another* thread assumes the value of x to be available *before* y. That is, the original order should not have been changed. The compiler has no way of knowing this though. It sees only the sequence of statements as executed by one thread and does not know how these statements may interact with other threads.[4]

When do the results of independent store instructions arrive in the main memory system and commit the values? It is not guaranteed that all the bytes of a variable are stored in one atomic transaction and actually may arrive piecemeal. Also, in what order do the variables arrive? Can it be guaranteed that they arrive in the order issued?

The fundamental question is how does one ensure that different threads see the same, consistent, value of a shared variable, and most importantly, when?

This is governed by the *memory consistency model*, or *consistency model* for short [13]. Such a model sets the rules regarding the handling of loads and stores. It defines *when* a thread is guaranteed to read the correct value of a variable after an update.

This is not a new issue. Over time, quite a number of consistency models have been defined, but for our purposes, only two cases are briefly covered. It is important to realize there is no right or wrong when it comes to the choice of a specific model. Performance and ease of use are the main differentiators and trade-offs.

Sequential Memory Consistency - This is defined by Lamport [16] and is intuitively easiest to understand. Each thread performs its loads and stores in the original sequential order, and stores are atomic. The memory operations may be thought of as a set, consisting of the loads and stores performed by this thread in the original sequence. Each of these sets is processed sequentially, but the order in which this happens is arbitrary.

In the code fragment in Figure 1.5, a classical example is shown. There are two threads and two shared variables x and y, both initialized to zero. Because of sequential consistency, either {x,y} = {1,0}, or {x,y} = {0,1}. This means only one thread executes the function call. Without sequential consistency, this is not

---

[4]At the hardware level, there is a potential issue too. Memory operations (among others) could be asynchronous because of caches, store buffers, buffer bypasses, and so on.

```
<Shared variables x and y are initialized to zero>

        Thread 0                 Thread 1

        x = 1;                   y = 1;
        if ( y == 0 )            if ( x == 0 )
           function_call();         function_call();
```

Figure 1.5: **An example of the effect of sequential consistency** – Only one
of the two threads executes the function call.

guaranteed. For example, if the compiler knows the function call has no side effects
regarding x and y, it may decide to move the assignments after the if-statement. If
that is the case, both threads call the function.

Unfortunately, excluding these kinds of optimizations and the imposed severe
restrictions on the hardware regarding the handling of memory operations, reduces
performance significantly. This is why many alternatives to sequential consistency
have been proposed.

Relaxed Memory Consistency - This is not one single model, but a class of models,
with a common goal to improve performance by relaxing the consistency requirements. The models differ in how far they go to relax the rules. The degrees of
freedom are the order of the loads and stores, plus the atomicity.

Some examples of relaxed models are Total Store Order (TSO), Processor Consistency (PC), Relaxed Memory Ordering (RMO), and Release Consistency (RC).
Covering these here is beyond the scope of this book. However, the details of the
underlying memory consistency model need not be known in order to write a correct
and efficient OpenMP program.

Memory Consistency and Cache Coherence - While a consistency model is needed
for shared memory programming, cache coherence is not a necessary feature to
implement OpenMP.

Cache coherence deals with the problem of *how* other cores see memory updates
and does this by tracking changes in cache lines. A software implementation may do
this, but hardware support is needed to make this efficient.[5] This is why hardware
cache coherence has been implemented in shared memory systems for a long time.

---

[5]There are exceptions to this, but mostly in the area of special-purpose processors.

The confusion many users of OpenMP have is that, while cache coherence provides a single system image on a multi-core system, it does not prevent data races. There is no guarantee that a load instruction automatically returns the most recent value of a shared variable. This is defined by the consistency model and for performance reasons, most modern systems use a relaxed model.

The OpenMP View on Memory   OpenMP assumes a relaxed memory consistency model, but does not require a specific implementation. Each thread is allowed to have its own *temporary view* of memory.[6]

As with any relaxed memory model, only at well-defined points, are threads guaranteed to have the same, consistent, view on the value of shared variables. In between such points, the temporary view may be different across the threads. OpenMP defines its own consistency points. At such a point, the temporary views are made consistent again. The question is how that impacts writing OpenMP code.

Read-only shared data is easy, because there are no concerns about consistency. Things get (much) more complicated when shared data is modified. Without precautions, any thread may modify shared data at any time. It is the responsibility of the user to ensure this is handled in the correct way.

As long as different threads write to a different memory location, for example, different elements of the same vector, there is no reason to worry. Problems arise if they simultaneously write to the *same* address in memory. Then, threads may step on each other and generate incorrect results. This is a bug in the code and is called a "data race."

A classical case is the accumulation of partial contributions into a shared variable. This occurs in reduction operations, for example. Each thread computes a contribution and adds it to the final solution, which is stored in a shared variable. This scenario is shown in the code fragment in Figure 1.6.

At line 1, shared variable `sum` is initialized to zero. This is outside the parallel region and performed by one thread only, the master thread. A local variable called `my_contribution` is declared at line 5 and per the rules of OpenMP, it is a private variable. Each thread performs its computations, and at line 7 the result is stored into variable `my_contribution`. In the next step, each thread reads the current

---

[6]The exception is the `seq_cst` clause on the `atomic` construct, which is covered in detail in Section 2.1.6, starting on page 47.

```
 1 sum = 0;
 2 #pragma omp parallel shared(sum)
 3 {
 4
 5   int my_contribution; // Contains the per-thread partial sum
 6   ....
 7   my_contribution = ....  // Thread computes a value
 8
 9   // Without the critical region this code has a data race
10
11   #pragma omp critical
12   {
13       sum += my_contribution;
14   } // End of critical region
15       ....
16 } // End of parallel region
```

Figure 1.6: **Example of the update of a shared variable** – To avoid multiple threads updating shared variable sum at the same time, a critical region is used.

value of variable sum, adds its contribution my_contribution to it, and stores the updated value of sum. This is the update statement at line 13, but without additional controls, this update has a data race on sum and the result is undefined.

The solution is to prevent another thread from reading sum, before the previous update has completed. OpenMP provides constructs like a critical section, or atomic update, to handle this situation. In Figure 1.6, the former is used to guard the update of variable sum. A thread is not allowed to enter a critical region, as long as another thread executes it. As a result, a thread cannot perform the update, while another thread is inside the critical region.

This is, however, not the end of the story. A relaxed memory consistency model is assumed, but what guarantee is there that a thread reads the correct value of sum, as it was recently updated by another thread? The answer is that, without additional measures, there is no such guarantee. Not even the initial value of zero is guaranteed to be available when the first thread performs the update. Unless this happens to be the master thread, but this cannot be counted upon.

This raises a very important question: *how does OpenMP ensure each thread reads the updated value?* This is where the flush construct comes in.

#pragma omp flush [*(flush-set)*] *new-line*
!$omp flush [*(flush-set)*]

Figure 1.7: **Syntax of the flush directive in C/C++ and Fortran** – This directive guarantees that all threads have the same consistent view of shared data.

The Flush Construct   A key element of a relaxed consistency model is that the user needs to know when a shared variable may be read reliably.[7]

To enforce such global consistency, OpenMP provides the `flush` directive. After this directive, and before the next update of shared variables, all threads are guaranteed to have the same global view of all thread-visible variables. The syntax of the `flush` construct in C/C++ and Fortran is given in Figure 1.7.

The *flush-set* consists of a list with all the variables affected by the `flush` directive. Without this optional list, all thread-visible variables are affected. When a list is used, the flush-set consists of the variables in this list only. The recommendation is to *not* use the flush-set feature. It may be extremely difficult to employ correctly. If used incorrectly, optimizing compilers may apply valid code transformations, such that the `flush` does not have the intended effect.

Although compilers are not allowed to move operations on variables in the flush-set, beyond the `flush` directive, they are allowed to move flush constructs relative to each other in case the flush-sets are disjoint. For example, if the list contains variable `a` in one `flush` directive, and variable `b` in another one, both directives may be interchanged. This could result in incorrect values being read. To avoid this, both variables may be put in the same list, but this is also discouraged.

The `flush` directive affects only the thread executing it. The temporary view of other threads is not automatically updated. This implies that, in many cases, *all* threads must execute the same `flush` directive(s) to guarantee consistency.

The `flush` directive may be used explicitly in applications, but for convenience and as a safety net, a flush region is implied in the following situations:

- During a `barrier` region.

- At entry to, and exit from, the `parallel`, `critical`, `target`, and `target data` region.

- At exit from worksharing constructs, unless a `nowait` clause is present.

---

[7]The details depend on the model. Refer to Section 1.2.3 for an explanation of this.

- At entry to, and exit from, an `ordered` region, if a `threads` or `depend` clause is present, or if no clauses are present.

- Immediately before and after every task-scheduling point.

- During the following runtime functions: `omp_set_lock()` and `omp_unset_-lock()`.

- During the following runtime functions, if the region causes the lock to be set or unset:

  - `omp_set_lock()`, `omp_unset_lock()`
  - `omp_test_lock()`, `omp_test_nest_lock()`

- At entry to, and exit from, the atomic operations (`read`, `write`, `update`, or `capture`), performed in a sequentially or non-sequentially consistent atomic region. In the case of the latter, the flush-set must contain the object updated in the construct.

- During a `cancel` or `cancellation point` region, in case cancellation has been enabled and activated.

- At entry to a `target update` region, whose corresponding construct has a `to` clause.

- At exit from a `target update` region, whose corresponding construct has a `from` clause.

- At entry to a `target enter data` region.

- At exit from a `target exit data` region.

The example in Figure 1.6 works correctly, because of the implied flush on the `critical` region. This ensures that the correct value is read before the update. The new value is synchronized, prior to exiting the region. In this case, the latter is not required for correctness, but it won't hurt either.

A flush region is *not* implied at the following locations:

- At entry to a `worksharing` region.

- At entry to, or exit from, a `master` region.

```
1 #pragma omp flush
2
3 while ( execution_state[i] != READ_FINISHED ) {
4
5    <wait for a short while>
6
7    #pragma omp flush
8
9 } // End of while-loop
```

Figure 1.8:   **Example of the use of the flush directive** – The purpose of this while-loop is to wait for element `execution_stats[i]` to be modified.

The `master` construct is different from the `single` construct. Often, such a single thread region is used to initialize shared data. If the `master` construct is used for this, care needs to be taken that the other threads read the correct value(s). Without a `flush` region prior to accessing these variables, this is not guaranteed.

In many situations, the built-in flush operation avoids the need to explicitly use a flush directive. Even when the `nowait` clause is used, a barrier further down the execution path ensures a synchronized view on the shared data again.

This is why most OpenMP applications do not need to use an explicit `flush` construct, but in some cases, it is required for correct execution. An example of this is shown in Figure 1.8.

In this example, it is assumed that the master thread is in control of the value of variable `execution_state[i]`. The threads executing the loop, wait for the value to change. Without the two `flush` directives, there is no guarantee that changes in the value are propagated to the other threads. As a result, they might wait forever to actually see the change, so the program hangs.

The `flush` directive at line 1 is needed to ensure that the first time `execution_state[i]` is read, the correct value is returned at line 3. The second `flush` directive at line 7 guarantees this variable is updated, before it is read again at line 3. Although not shown here, the master thread must use a `flush` directive after setting and changing `execution_state[i]`.

A related, and commonly asked question is about pointers. If a pointer variable is part of a flush-set, *only* the pointer is synchronized, not the block of memory it points to.

The code fragment in Figure 1.8 is taken from the pipeline example presented and discussed in Section 1.3.2. The arrays used there implement dependences between activities. A much more robust and elegant solution, without the need for the `flush` directive, is provided by task dependences. This is discussed extensively in Chapter 3, where the same example is shown, but without explicit flush operations.

1.3 The Worksharing Constructs

A worksharing construct must be placed within a parallel region. Upon encountering a worksharing construct, the runtime system distributes the work to be performed over the threads active in the parallel region.

There are three worksharing constructs in C/C++/Fortran and a fourth one in Fortran. None of the worksharing constructs have a barrier on entry. There is one on exit, but it is omitted when using the `nowait` clause, which also means that there is no implied flush operation.

There are two important restrictions regarding worksharing constructs. First of all, either all threads in the team, or none at all, encounter the construct. As a consequence of this rule, threads are not allowed to skip a worksharing construct. The second rule is that the sequence of worksharing constructs and barriers encountered must be the same for all threads. If an OpenMP program does not comply with these rules, the behavior is undefined.

1.3.1 The Loop Construct

The loop construct provides for a straightforward way to assign the work associated with loop iterations to threads. The syntax for C/C++ and Fortran is shown in Figure 1.9.

The `schedule` clause is optional and may be used to explicitly specify the mapping of loop iterations onto threads. In OpenMP 2.5, there are three different scheduling types: `static`, `dynamic`, and `guided`. All three take an optional `chunk` parameter to control how many iterations are to be processed each time a thread gets assigned new work.

From a runtime overhead point of view, `static` is most efficient. The assignment of work to threads is pre-defined and very easy to determine at runtime. It works best with a regular workload, where each thread roughly gets assigned the same amount of work.

#pragma omp for *[clause[[,] clause]...] new-line*   *for-loop(s)*
!$omp do *[clause[[,] clause]...]*   *do-loop(s)*   **[!$omp end do** *[nowait]*]

Figure 1.9: **Syntax of the parallel loop construct in C/C++ and Fortran**
– The loop iterations are distributed over the threads and executed in parallel. There are
no curly braces in C/C++. The terminating !$omp end do on the Fortran directive is
optional, but is recommended to clearly mark the end of the construct.

The other two types are more suitable in the case of a load imbalance, but they are
more expensive in terms of overhead. The work assignment is handled at runtime
and requires some locking. This is why these scheduling algorithms may not be the
best choice if the imbalance is modest only.

A fourth keyword supported on this clause is `runtime`. As suggested by the
name, the distribution is decided at runtime and controlled through the OMP_-
SCHEDULE environment variable. It is ideally suited to experiment with various
policies and may even make this choice dependent upon the problem size and other
characteristics.

If the schedule clause is not specified, the choice is made by the compiler and is
therefore system-dependent.

OpenMP 3.0 and subsequent releases added more options and features to this
construct. This includes an optional modifier on the `schedule` clause. For this and
more details on the new features, refer to Section 2.1.1, starting on page 41.

1.3.2   The Sections Construct

Parallel sections provide for a very different structure to express and implement
parallelism. Although generally applicable, this feature targets a higher level of
parallelism. In Figure 1.10, the syntax in C/C++ and Fortran is shown for this
directive.

Parallel sections are ideally suited to call different functions in parallel. In [2], it
is explained how this is used to set up a pipeline to overlap I/O with computations.
The assumption is that not all I/O needs to be completed before processing may
start. In Figure 1.11, a code fragment based on this example is given. Three
sections are used to implement the functionality needed.

```
#pragma omp sections [clause[[,] clause]...] new-line
{
      [#pragma omp section ]
        structured block
      [#pragma omp section
        structured block ]
      ...
}
```

```
!$omp sections [clause[[,] clause]...]
      [!$omp section ]
        structured block
      [!$omp section
        structured block ]
      ...
!$omp end sections [nowait]
```

Figure 1.10: **Syntax of the parallel sections construct in C/C++ and Fortran** – The number of sections both controls and limits the amount of parallelism. If there are "n" of these code blocks, at most "n" threads execute in parallel, but if nested parallelism is used, additional threads may be active.

The first section reads a block of data for each loop iteration. After completing the read for iteration i, a notification is posted. This is implemented in function `signal_read()`. Meanwhile, the second thread executes function `wait_read()`. It waits for a ready signal to be set. As soon as this is posted, the computations are performed. Once these have completed, another signal is set through function `signal_processed()`. The thread waiting in the third section picks this up, and starts the post-processing phase.

The threads communicate through flags set in memory and explicit flushes are needed to ensure threads see the modified values of the flags. This is illustrated in the code fragment shown earlier in Figure 1.8, which has been derived from the same pipeline example program.

Parallel sections are straightforward and easy to use, but they are most effective if there are only a relatively small number of sections. In cases where it is unknown upfront how many activities there are, or if the work performed is less regular, OpenMP tasks are more suitable. Tasks are covered extensively in Chapter 3, where this example is revisited. In Section 3.4, starting on page 128, it is shown that in

```
1 #pragma omp parallel sections
2 {
3    #pragma omp section
4    {
5      for (int i=0; i<n; i++) {
6          (void) read_input(i);
7          (void) signal_read(i);
8      }
9    }
10   #pragma omp section
11   {
12     for (int i=0; i<n; i++) {
13         (void) wait_read(i);
14         (void) process_data(i);
15         (void) signal_processed(i);
16     }
17   }
18   #pragma omp section
19   {
20     for (int i=0; i<n; i++) {
21         (void) wait_processed(i);
22         (void) post_process_results(i);
23     }
24   }
25 } // End of parallel sections
```

Figure 1.11: **Example of the use of parallel sections** – A pipeline structure is set up to overlap I/O, computations, and post-processing.

this case, OpenMP tasks provide a more natural and elegant solution, because the arrays used for the signaling are not needed when using tasks. This eliminates the need for the explicit use of the flush construct.

1.3.3   The Single Construct

Sometimes there is a need within a parallel region to perform an activity by one thread only, such as when performing I/O for example.

#pragma omp single *[clause[[,] clause]...] new-line*   *structured block*
!$omp single *[clause[[,] clause]...]*   *structured block* **!$omp end single** *[nowait,[copyprivate]]*

Figure 1.12: **Syntax of the single construct in C/C++ and Fortran** – Only one thread executes the structured block. Unlike with the `master` construct, there is an implied barrier at the end.

The parallel region could be split into two separate regions and the master thread assigned to handle this single thread task, but this is not ideal for performance and requires more coding. The `single` construct is ideally suited for situations like this. It is not known which thread performs the work, which may vary from run to run. This is not an issue because there is no need to distinguish which thread does the work. The syntax in C/C++ and Fortran for this directive is given in Figure 1.12.

What is important, is that there is an implied barrier at the end of this construct. Regardless of which thread executes the code, all other threads wait for this thread. This is why the `nowait` clause may be useful, but be careful not to introduce a data race. If the `single` region is used to initialize data or to read from a file and the `nowait` clause is used, care needs to be taken that the other threads do not use this data before it has been initialized. There is also no implied `flush` construct. If the `nowait` clause is used, an explicit barrier, placed prior to the point where the data is used, guarantees the operations are completed and the data synchronized before execution continues.

This construct has a specific and unique clause called `copyprivate (list)`. This clause ensures all threads have a copy of the variables specified in the list. The values are copied into the private instance of the same variable. All threads wait in the single region until all copies have completed. This is why this clause is not allowed in combination with the `nowait` clause.

Often, the same may be achieved using shared variables. Each thread automatically has access to these, but this clause is more than a convenience. In the case of a recursion, it is more complicated to handle this explicitly, and the `copyprivate` clause provides a convenient solution.

```
!$omp workshare
    structured block
!$omp end workshare  [nowait]
```

Figure 1.13: **Syntax of the workshare construct in Fortran** – This construct is used to parallelize (blocks of) statements using array-syntax.

1.3.4 The Fortran Workshare Construct

The fourth and last worksharing construct is available in Fortran only. This is because it has been designed to parallelize array syntax, a language feature not supported in C/C++. The syntax is shown in Figure 1.13. The only clause supported is the `nowait` clause.

1.3.5 The Combined Worksharing Constructs

The combined constructs are shortcuts and useful in the event there is only a single worksharing construct in a parallel region. The semantics are identical to the version with one worksharing construct within a parallel region. The syntax in C/C++ and Fortran is given in Figures 1.14 and 1.15.

Clauses from both directives may be used, but only if there is no conflict.[8] The application is an illegal OpenMP program if the behavior depends on whether the clause was applied to either the parallel construct, or the worksharing construct.

The combined constructs are not only convenient and easier to read, there is also a (potential) performance difference. To start with, there is only one implied barrier at the end. The compiler may also generate more efficient code. A general parallel region provides significant flexibility, but this may cost some performance. The combined constructs are fairly simple from an OpenMP point of view and this might be exploited by compilers.

Although it may not seem meaningful to embed a single threaded code block in a parallel region, and there is indeed no combined construct for this, this combination actually does have an interpretation in the context of OpenMP tasking. This is explained in detail in Chapter 3.

---

[8]The `if` clause has been extended to support the name of the directive. See also Section 2.1.2.

Full version	Combined construct

#pragma omp parallel
{
  #pragma omp for
    for-loop
}
	#pragma omp parallel for
	  for-loop

#pragma omp parallel
{
  #pragma omp sections
  {
    [#pragma omp section]
      structured block
    [#pragma omp section
      structured block]
    ...
  }
}
	#pragma omp parallel sections
	{
	  [#pragma omp section]
	    structured block
	
	  [#pragma omp section
	    structured block]
	  ...
	}

!$omp parallel
  !$omp do
    do-loop
  [!$omp end do]
!$omp end parallel
	!$omp parallel do
	  do-loop
	!$omp end parallel do

!$omp parallel
  !$omp sections
  [!$omp section]
    structured block
  [!$omp section
    structured block]
  ...
  !$omp end sections
!$omp end parallel
	!$omp parallel sections
	  [!$omp section]
	    structured block
	  [!$omp section
	    structured block]
	  ...
	!$omp end parallel sections

Figure 1.14: **Syntax of the combined worksharing constructs in C/C++ and Fortran** – The combined constructs may have a performance advantage over the more general parallel region with only a single worksharing construct embedded. This is because a parallel region has some overhead the compiler may now eliminate. The Fortran combined workshare construct is listed in Figure 1.15.

Full version	Combined construct
!$omp parallel 　!$omp workshare 　　*structured block* 　!$omp end workshare !$omp end parallel	!$omp parallel workshare 　*structured block* !$omp end parallel workshare

Figure 1.15: **Syntax of the combined workshare construct in Fortran –** The combined construct may have a performance advantage.

#pragma omp master *new-line* 　*structured block*
!$omp master 　*structured block* !$omp end master

Figure 1.16: **Syntax of the master construct in C/C++ and Fortran –** The master thread is guaranteed to execute the structured block.

1.4 The Master Construct

Although not a worksharing construct, the `master` construct is very closely related to the `single` worksharing construct. The syntax in C/C++ and Fortran is shown in Figure 1.16.

As suggested by the name, the master thread is guaranteed to execute this block of code. It may be seen as a special case of the `single` construct, but there is one important difference. In contrast with the `single` construct, the `master` construct does *not* have an implied barrier on exit.

Depending on the operations performed in the master region, this may give rise to a data race. If the master thread initializes or reads shared data, and there is no barrier before the other threads use this data, a data race occurs. This construct does not have an implied `flush` construct either.

1.5 Nested Parallelism

For certain algorithms, it is natural to use *nested parallelism*. With this, each thread within a parallel region initiates a second parallel region. If needed, this repeats to the nesting level desired.

```
1 #pragma omp parallel num_threads(3)
2 {
3     <code in here is executed by 3 threads>
4     #pragma omp parallel num_threads(2)
5     {
6         <code executed by 3x2 = 6 threads>
7     } // End of second level parallel region
8 } // End of first level parallel region
```

Figure 1.17: **Code fragment for a two-level nested parallel region** – There are two parallel regions. Each region may have a different number of threads. In this example, they are set through the **num_threads** clause.

Nested parallelism is achieved by nesting the **parallel** constructs. At runtime, each thread that encounters the next parallel region creates a new parallel region. This happens as often as there are nested parallel region constructs.

In Figure 1.17, the code fragment for a two-level nested parallel region in C/C++ is shown. The dynamic behavior is illustrated in Figure 1.18.

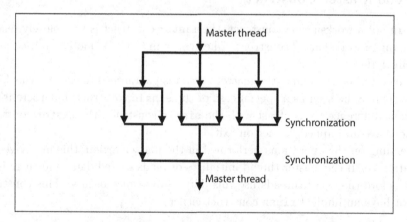

Figure 1.18: **An example of nested parallelism** – The master thread starts the program. Three threads are active in the first parallel region. Each one of these starts a separate parallel region. Because of the **num_threads(2)** clause on the second level parallel region, a total of 6 threads is active at this level.

In the example, three threads are active in the first parallel region. Because the `num_threads(2)` clause is used on the second parallel region, each of these threads creates a parallel region with two threads. At that point, a total of six threads are active.

This also demonstrates that thread teams do not need to be of the same size at every nesting level. A thread initiating another parallel region may set the number of threads through the `omp_set_num_threads()` function, or the `num_threads` clause. In case an `if` clause is used, and it evaluates to `false`, only one thread executes this parallel region.

At each nesting level, all parallel regions have their own master thread. As a consequence, the thread numbers are the same for all parallel regions at the same level. In this example, the second level threads in a team are numbered zero and one.

This is usually not a problem, but if a unique thread number is needed, the new runtime functions related to nested parallelism may be used to construct a thread ID that is unique across all nesting levels. These functions were introduced in OpenMP 3.0 and are discussed in Section 2.3.1 of Chapter 2. In Section 2.3.5, under "Nested Parallelism Revisited," it is shown how to use some of these functions to construct a unique thread ID across all nesting levels.

A common mistake made with nested parallelism is to try to nest *worksharing* constructs, which is not allowed. The nesting is at the level of the parallel region. It is valid to use the combined parallel worksharing constructs and nest them, because these are parallel regions after all. In Figure 1.19, this is illustrated with a parallel section that includes a parallel `for`-loop.

The three parallel sections execute simultaneously, assuming sufficient threads are available. If nested parallelism is enabled, the parallel for-loop at lines $8 - 13$ is executed by four threads and in total, six threads are active then.

Nested parallelism is an optional feature. An implementation is free to not support this, effectively ignoring the nested parallel regions. This feature may also be enabled, or disabled, either from within the application through the `omp_set_nested()` function, or by setting the `OMP_NESTED` environment variable. Keep in mind that the default setting for this variable is implementation-dependent. This means that nested parallelism may be turned off by default.

Nested parallelism definitely has its value, but it is rather rigid and the cost of the implied barrier that comes with each parallel region quickly adds up. In many cases, OpenMP tasks, covered extensively in Chapter 3, provide a much more convenient, flexible, and efficient mechanism.

```
1 pragma omp parallel sections
2 {
3    #pragma omp section
4    { printf("I am section 1\n"); }
5    #pragma omp section
6    {
7        printf("I am section 2\n");
8        #pragma omp parallel for shared(n) num_threads(4)
9        for (int i=0; i<n; i++)
10       {
11           printf("Section 2:\tIteration = %d Thread ID = %d\n",
12                  i, omp_get_thread_num());
13       } // End of parallel for loop
14   }
15   #pragma omp section
16       { printf("I am section 3\n"); }
17
18 } // End of parallel sections
```

Figure 1.19: **Example of nested combined parallel worksharing constructs**
– Three parallel sections are used. If sufficient threads are available, they are executed
simultaneously. The second section includes another parallel region, consisting of a single
for-loop. This loop is executed in parallel, resulting in nested parallelism. In this case
the work in the loop is distributed over four threads.

1.6   Synchronization Constructs

In this section, several synchronization constructs are presented and discussed.
They are used to control the behavior of the threads and it is quite likely an
application needs at least one of them.

1.6.1   The Barrier Construct

The barrier construct forces all threads to wait until all of them have reached the
barrier region in the program. Program execution continues once the last thread
has arrived. The syntax in C/C++ and Fortran is given in Figure 1.20.

The barrier is used, for example, to avoid that a thread prematurely accesses
data that is defined by another thread. This avoids data races and is illustrated in

> **#pragma omp barrier** *new-line*
> **!$omp barrier**

Figure 1.20: **Syntax of the barrier construct in C/C++ and Fortran** – All threads wait in the barrier until the last one has arrived.

```
1 #pragma parallel shared(n,a,b)
2 {
3     #pragma omp for
4     for (int i=0; i<n; i++)
5         a[i] = i;
6
7     // The implied barrier on the for-loop above is needed there
8
9     #pragma omp for nowait
10    for (int i=0; i<n; i++)
11        b[i] += a[i];
12 } // End of parallel region
```

Figure 1.21: **Example to demonstrate the need for a barrier** – The implied barrier on the first loop is needed to avoid a data race on array element a[i].

the code fragment in Figure 1.21. The implied barrier on the first parallel loop is needed to avoid a data race when reading array element a[i] at line 11. Without the implied barrier on the first for-loop, there is no guarantee that the value of a[i], read in the second loop, has been updated.

The parallel region has an implied barrier upon exit. This is why the nowait clause at line 9 may be used to avoid two back-to-back barriers. Although the time spent in the second barrier should be short, there is still an additional cost that is best to avoid.

The implied flush operation that comes with the barrier is essential here. Without this, there is no guarantee that the correct value of a[i] is read in the second loop.

There is another possibility to fine-tune this code. The iteration space of both loops is identical, and the same elements of array a are accessed. Unfortunately in OpenMP 2.5, there is no guarantee that, even with static scheduling on loops with the same iteration space, the same thread operates on the same set of iterations across the loops. A data race may still occur if a nowait clause is used on the first loop.

```
1 #pragma parallel for shared(n,a,b)
2 for (int i=0; i<n; i++)
3 {
4     a[i] = i;
5     b[i] += a[i];
6 } // End of the parallel region
```

Figure 1.22: **Reworked example to eliminate a barrier** – By fusing (or merging) the two loops, one barrier is eliminated. On top of that, a combined worksharing construct is used.

This undesirable situation has been changed as of OpenMP 3.0. The `static` clause may now be used, because the mapping of iterations onto threads is preserved when using this scheduling type. This eliminates the need for the barrier, and a `nowait` clause may be used on the first loop. This is already more efficient, but in this case, another solution is preferred.

In addition to entirely avoid the barrier inside the parallel region, loop fusing creates more work per loop iteration, and cache line reuse improves. By using a combined worksharing construct, the execution time is reduced further. This approach is shown in Figure 1.22.

1.6.2 The Critical Construct

This is probably one of the most commonly used synchronization constructs, because it is ideally suited to avoid a data race when updating a shared variable.

A critical region is a block of code executed by all threads, but it is guaranteed that only one thread at a time may be active in the region. There is no implied

| **#pragma omp critical** *[(name)] new-line* |
| *structured block* |
| **!$omp critical** *[(name)]* |
| *structured block* |
| **!$omp end critical** *[(name)]* |

Figure 1.23: **Syntax of the critical construct in C/C++ and Fortran** – The structured block is executed by all threads, but only one thread at a time executes the block. The construct may have an optional name.

```
1 #pragma parallel
2 {
3               ...
4    #pragma omp critical (c_region1)
5    {
6        sum1 += ...
7    }
8               ...
9    #pragma omp critical (c_region2)
10   {
11       sum2 += ...
12   }
13                  ...
14 } // End of the parallel region
```

Figure 1.24: **An example using named critical regions** – Different threads may be in either one of the two different critical regions at the same time.

barrier on exit from the region, but there is an implied flush construct on entry and exit. The syntax in C/C++ and Fortran is given in Figure 1.23.

The main use of a critical region is to update a shared variable, because with this construct, it can never happen that two or more threads simultaneously update the same variable. This prevents a data race when performing an update.

All critical regions without a name are considered to have the same internal name and are dynamically ordered. Critical regions with different names are allowed to execute in parallel. This allows for advanced synchronization, but care needs to be taken that there are no unwanted side effects when updating shared data. In Figure 1.24, an example with two different critical regions is given.

If multiple named critical regions are used, different threads may simultaneously execute different regions. If a lexically later region uses a variable that is updated in an earlier region, a data race is introduced.

This example produces correct results as long as variable sum1 is not used in the second critical region. If so, both regions should have the same name or no name at all.

In OpenMP 4.5, an optional *hint* is supported. This may be used on the critical construct to allow the implementation to tune the underlying code to the specific

#pragma omp atomic *new-line*   *statement*
!$omp atomic   *statement*

Figure 1.25: **Syntax of the atomic construct in C/C++ and Fortran** – The statement is executed by all threads, but the loads and stores of the updated variable are atomic. There are constraints regarding the type of expression.

access pattern of the critical region. More details are found in Sections 2.1.5 and 2.3.3 on pages 46 and 67, respectively.

1.6.3   The Atomic Construct

The `atomic` construct has been in the specifications from the very first OpenMP 1.0 release. The name is inspired by particle physics and chosen to reflect that an atomic operation cannot be further broken down into sub-operations. It is uninterruptible. The syntax in C/C++ and Fortran is given in Figure 1.25.

The atomic construct can be used to guarantee mutually exclusive access to a specific memory location, represented through a variable. The access to this location is guaranteed to be atomic.

Conceptually, the atomic construct is somewhat similar to a critical region, but the level of atomicity is finer grained: only the load and store instructions are atomic. By restricting the functionality, compilers may generate more efficient code using low-level atomic instructions supported by many processors.

A simple, but typical, example is given in Figure 1.26. Variable x is incremented by 1. While a thread is performing this operation, no other thread can access x. The load and store instructions involved in the update are guaranteed to be atomic. This is to avoid a thread reading variable x before the thread that currently executes the update has completed the write.

In C/C++, the `atomic` construct may be used together with an expression statement to initialize, or update, a single variable, possibly through a simple binary operation. The supported operations are: +, *, -, /, &, ^, |, <<, >>.

In Fortran, the statement must also take the form of an update to a variable. The operator used for the update may be only one of +, *, -, /, .AND., .OR., .EQV., .NEQV., and the intrinsic procedure MAX, MIN, IAND, IOR, or IEOR.

```
1 #pragma omp parallel
2 {
3      ......
4    #pragma omp atomic
5        x += 1;
6      ......
7 } // End of parallel region
```

Figure 1.26: **Example of the atomic construct** – The atomic construct at line 4 guarantees that the load and store instructions related to the update of variable x at line 5 are atomic.

There are several restrictions on the form that the expression may take: for example, it must not involve the variable on the left-hand side of the assignment statement. If the right-hand side includes a function call that is not thread-safe, the result is undefined.

Since OpenMP 3.1, this construct has been extended over the various releases and is quite comprehensive by now. Refer to Section 2.1.6 in Chapter 2 for an overview and more details.

1.6.4   The Ordered Construct

The ordered construct is applicable to parallel loops only. The construct must be placed within the parallel loop. The syntax in C/C++ and Fortran is given in Figure 1.27.

In addition to this construct, the ordered clause must be specified on the loop directive as well. The ordered region within the loop body is guaranteed to be executed in the order of the loop iterations, essentially serializing and ordering execution.

Valid use might be to enforce output to be printed in the original sequential order, or to debug a particular block of code. Because parallel processing changes the order of computations, floating-point round-off behavior could be different compared to the serial code. To verify whether this is the case, the ordered construct may be used. This construct may also be used to isolate a data race by narrowing down the region where this may occur. This construct is expensive and therefore should be used only if no suitable alternative is available.

```
#pragma omp ordered new-line
        structured block
!$omp ordered
        structured block
!$omp end ordered
```

Figure 1.27:   **Syntax of the OpenMP 2.5 ordered construct in C/C++
and Fortran** – This construct is placed within a parallel loop. The structured block is
executed in the sequential order of the loop iterations. As of OpenMP 4.5, this construct
has been enhanced to support additional features.

Function name	Description
OMP_NUM_THREADS	Set the number of threads used.
OMP_SCHEDULE	Set the runtime scheduling type and chunk size.
OMP_DYNAMIC	Enable/disable dynamic thread adjustment.
OMP_NESTED	Enable/disable support for nested parallelism.

Figure 1.28:   **The OpenMP 2.5 environment variables** – These are the four
variables one may set prior to program start up.

As of the OpenMP 4.5 specifications, the `ordered` construct has been enhanced
to support `doacross` and `SIMD` loops. For details refer, to Sections 2.4.4 and 5.2.7,
respectively.

1.7   The OpenMP 2.5 Environment Variables

In OpenMP 2.5, four environment variables are available to initialize the corresponding runtime settings. They are listed in Figure 1.28. If not set by the user,
an implementation-dependent default is used. The exception is nested parallelism.
It is turned off by default and may be activated by setting the `OMP_NESTED` variable
to `true`.

As a general rule, a runtime function with the same functionality as an environment variable takes precedence. For example, by using the `omp_set_num_-`
`threads()` function, the initial value set by `OMP_NUM_THREADS` is overruled.

Since OpenMP 2.5, many new environment variables have been added. These are
introduced and discussed in Section 2.2, starting on page 53. As explained there,
variables `OMP_NUM_THREADS` and `OMP_SCHEDULE` are augmented to better support
nested parallelism and additional workload scheduling features, respectively.

1.8   The OpenMP 2.5 Runtime Functions

Runtime functions may be used to query settings and also override initial values, either set by default or specified through environment variables defined prior to program start-up. Some of the runtime functions may also be used to modify settings while the application executes.

An example is the number of threads used to execute a parallel region. The initial value is implementation-dependent, but through the `OMP_NUM_THREADS` environment variable, this number may be set explicitly before the program starts. During program execution, function `omp_set_num_threads()` may be used to increase, or decrease, the number of threads to be used in the next parallel region(s).

When using the runtime functions in C/C++, file `omp.h` must be included. Fortran programs require either file `omp_lib.h` to be included or a module called `omp_lib` to be used. Either one of these, or both, are guaranteed to be available in Fortran.

Here, and in Section 2.3, the syntax is given for C/C++ only, but the usage in Fortran is very similar. Functions returning, or using, `true` or `false` as a function argument in C/C++, require the `LOGICAL` data type in Fortran. Many C/C++ functions are functions in Fortran as well, but in some cases they are subroutines instead. Refer to the specifications for details.

In Figure 1.29, the functions related to the execution environment are listed. Only the names and a short description are given. Most of these functions are straightforward to use, but there are a few things worth pointing out:

- When the `omp_get_num_threads()` function is used outside of a (nested) parallel region, a value of 1 is returned.

- The value returned by `omp_get_thread_num()` is relative to the parallel region that the thread executing this function is part of. As a result, it always starts at zero upon the execution of a new parallel region or when nested parallelism is used.

- The `omp_get_max_threads()` function returns the number of threads used in the next parallel region (unless the `num_threads` clause is used). This, for example, allows for the allocation of storage based on the number of threads in the parallel region.

Function name	Description
omp_set_num_threads	Set the number of threads.
omp_get_num_threads	Number of threads in the current team.
omp_get_max_threads	Number of threads in the next parallel region.
omp_get_num_procs	Number of processors available to the program.
omp_get_thread_num	Thread number within the parallel region.
omp_in_parallel	Check if within a parallel region.
omp_get_dynamic	Check if thread adjustment is enabled.
omp_set_dynamic	Enable, or disable, thread adjustment.
omp_get_nested	Check if nested parallelism is enabled.
omp_set_nested	Enable, or disable, nested parallelism.

Figure 1.29: **The OpenMP 2.5 runtime functions** – These are the functions to query or change settings related to threads, processors/cores, and the parallel execution environment. The names are the same in C/C++ and Fortran, but the usage follows the language syntax.

Function name	Description
omp_get_wtime	Absolute wall-clock time in seconds.
omp_get_wtick	The number of seconds between successive clock ticks.

Figure 1.30: **The two OpenMP 2.5 timing functions** – The first function is used to time specific portions of the program. The second function returns the clock resolution. It is used to determine what kind of time interval may be measured accurately.

In addition to this functionality, there are two functions to support measuring the execution time. The rationale to include these functions is to provide an accurate, as well as portable, way to measure the execution time of specific parts of the program. Although the specifications do not require this, the expectation is that the OpenMP implementation provides the most accurate timer available on a specific platform.

The two timer functions are listed in Figure 1.30 and are quite straightforward to use. The one thing to remember is that omp_get_wtime() returns the number of wall-clock or "elapsed" seconds. In other words, it returns an absolute value. A meaningful timing value is therefore obtained by taking the difference between two calls. This is illustrated in Figure 1.31.

The third set of runtime functions is related to locks. An overview of the locking functions is given in Figure 1.32. Locks provide a way to avoid that a block of code is executed by multiple threads at the same time. Conceptually this is very simple.

```
1 t_start = omp_get_wtime();
2   <code block to be timed>
3 t_wall_clock = omp_get_wtime() - t_start;
```

Figure 1.31: **An example how to use function omp_get_wtime()** – The value
returned in variable **t_wall_clock** is the wall-clock time of the code block enclosed between
the two calls to this timer function. To obtain accurate measurements, it is highly recommended for this time to significantly exceed the value returned by the **omp_get_wtick()**
function.

A thread tests for the lock to be available. If this is not the case, the application
needs to handle this. In most cases, it waits for the lock to become available but
may also perform some other work and check again later.

Once the lock is owned by the thread, no other thread may access it. This allows
the thread owning the lock to perform its work, without the risk that other threads
execute the same block of code at the same time. When the thread has finished, it
needs to release the lock in order for another thread to gain access to it. Failure to
do so results in a deadlock.

Locking functionality is by no means unique to OpenMP, but by including it in
the specifications, the user has the guarantee that it is available and a natural part
of the OpenMP environment.

Many more runtime functions have been added since OpenMP 2.5. These may
be found in Section 2.3, starting on page 60.

1.9 Internal Control Variables in OpenMP

Internal to the implementation, OpenMP uses a set of *Internal Control Variables*
(*ICVs*) to access and control runtime settings. An example of this is the number of
threads used in the next parallel region. The ICVs are an implementation detail,
but must be mentioned, because in the specifications, some behavior is explained
in terms of ICVs.

The names of the ICVs are given in the specifications, for example **nthreads-var**,
but these are suggestions only. An implementation is free to deviate from this and
by design there is no impact on the user, because an OpenMP application never
uses ICVs directly. Instead, the interaction is through environment variables and
runtime functions.

Function name	Description
omp_init_lock	Initialize a lock variable.
omp_init_nest_lock	Similar, but for a nestable lock.
omp_set_lock	Blocking request to acquire the lock.
omp_set_nest_lock	Similar, but for a nestable lock.
omp_unset_lock	Release the lock.
omp_unset_nest_lock	Similar, but for a nestable lock.
omp_destroy_lock	Change the state of the lock to be unitialized.
omp_destroy_nest_lock	Similar, but for a nestable lock.
omp_test_lock	Non-blocking request to acquire the lock.
omp_test_nest_lock	Similar, but for a nestable lock.

Figure 1.32: **The OpenMP 2.5 locking functions** – These functions define, acquire, and release a lock. A nestable lock may be set multiple times by the same thread.

Initial values are often system-dependent and pre-defined. They may, however, be set by the user through OpenMP environment variables. The corresponding ICV is initialized to this value by the implementation.

The number of threads is again a good example. The default is system-specific and the implementation assigns an initial value to the corresponding ICV. The value set for environment variable OMP_NUM_THREADS overrides this ICV upon program start up.

At runtime, OpenMP runtime functions are available to query the value of a specific ICV (for example, omp_get_num_threads()) and if needed, may be used to change the value. For example, function omp_set_num_threads() changes the number of threads at the user level. The implementation handles this by changing the value of the corresponding ICV.

1.10   Concluding Remarks

This chapter has provided a brief summary of OpenMP 2.5 and has set the foundation for the remainder of this book. At the time this release of OpenMP came out, it was a compact, yet very powerful, parallel programming model for the SMP systems of those days.

Since then, shared memory computer systems have evolved to contain hundreds of cores with multiple threads per core. Most of these systems use a cc-NUMA architecture and optionally support hardware accelerators.

Through the subsequent four releases of the specifications that came out after OpenMP 2.5, these very complex and extremely powerful systems are fully supported in OpenMP. In the remaining chapters, all of the enhancements and new features added are covered in great detail.

2 New Features in OpenMP

In May 2008, the specifications of OpenMP 3.0 were released. This was the first update since the 2.5 release and a major improvement. Many existing features were enhanced, support for C++ was substantially improved, and the concept of tasks was introduced.

Since then, OpenMP has continued to evolve. OpenMP 3.1 was released in July of 2011. This was an update release. Several constructs and features were enhanced, including tasking. The specifications were clarified where needed, but no significant new functionality was added.

New functionality was implemented in OpenMP 4.0. When it was released in July of 2013, OpenMP made a huge step forward. For the first time in the history of OpenMP, support for cc-NUMA architectures became available. Heterogeneous computing support was added also. This integrated very smoothly with the rest of the language and preserved the ease of use of OpenMP. Another noticeable addition was support for handling a failure in a parallel region, or task. In addition, tasking was expanded, vectorization through SIMD instructions was added and User-Defined Reductions (UDRs) were now supported as well.

A little over two years later, in November 2015, OpenMP 4.5 was released. It is another significant step forward with many enhancements to the existing functionality.

In this chapter, most of the features and enhancements, added since the release of OpenMP 2.5, are presented and discussed. The exceptions are tasking, thread affinity, SIMD, and heterogeneous architectures. These are major topics, covered in great detail in the chapters to follow.

2.1 Enhancements to Existing Constructs

In this section, the enhancements to the constructs supported in OpenMP 2.5 and earlier releases are introduced and discussed. Since this release, entirely new concepts and constructs have been introduced as well. An overview of these can be found in Section 2.4.

2.1.1 The Schedule Clause

The `schedule` clause has been extended to support additional functionality. The updated syntax is shown in Figure 2.1.

schedule *([modifier [, modifier]:] kind [, chunk_size])*

Figure 2.1: **Syntax of the extended schedule clause in C/C++ and Fortran** – In addition to the already supported types, the `auto` type for the workload distribution schedule has been added. Another new feature is the support for an optional modifier, or even two, to provide additional details in which way the chunks of work, if applicable, are distributed over the threads.

Modifier	Description
`monotonic`	Each thread executes its chunks in increasing logical iteration order. This is the order the iterations would be executed in if the loop was executed sequentially.
`nonmonotonic`	Chunks are assigned to threads in any order.
`simd`	The new chunk size is set to *chunk_size/simd_width*, with *simd_width* an implementation-defined value.

Figure 2.2: **The three modifiers supported on the schedule clause** – These modifiers specify how the chunks should be distributed over the threads.

As of OpenMP 3.0, in addition to the `static`, `dynamic`, and `guided` options for the workload distribution schedule for parallel loops, a fourth choice is supported. Through the `auto` keyword, the selection of the schedule is determined by the implementation.

In OpenMP 4.5, an optional keyword on the `schedule` clause was introduced to support one, or even two, *modifiers* to specify in which way the chunks should be distributed over the threads. This feature was introduced to resolve an ambiguity in the earlier specifications that could cause applications to make an incorrect assumption of how the work was distributed over the threads. With the introduction of the modifiers, this problem is no longer an issue.

The three new keywords to select the modifier, plus a brief description, are listed in Figure 2.2. If more details are needed, we recommend checking the specifications.

There are several restrictions when using these modifiers:

- The `nonmonotonic` modifier may be used only in combination with the `guided` or `dynamic` scheduling types.

- If the `static` schedule type, or the `ordered` clause, is specified without a modifier, the `monotonic` modifier is assumed. In other words, in these cases, `monotonic` is the default.

Important - With the next release of the OpenMP specifications, this default will change to `nonmonotonic`. Any application relying on the monotonic behavior in these cases should set this explicitly.

- The `monotonic` and `nonmonotonic` modifiers are mutually exclusive. This implies that, when applicable, either one of these may be used in combination with the `simd` modifier only.

- The `nonmonotonic` modifier may not be specified in combination with the `ordered` clause.

2.1.2   The If Clause

With combined constructs, it is not always clear to which part(s) the `if` clause applies. This is why the clause has been extended with an optional name, formally called the *directive-name-modifier*, to specify to which construct it applies.

For example, when using tasking in a combined construct, the following makes it clear the clause applies to the tasking part of the construct: `if(task:  n < 10)`.

2.1.3   The Collapse Clause

A short loop has a downside in a serial program, because the "loop overhead" dominates the performance if there is not much work performed per loop iteration. In a parallel program, the overhead is even worse.

A short loop not only limits the number of threads that may be used, it also easily leads to a load imbalance if the loop trip count is not a multiple of the number of threads. Depending on the amount of work performed per iteration, the parallel overhead may dominate as well.

Consider the serial code fragment in Figure 2.3, where a linearized 2D *mxn* array `a` is initialized. Both loops can be parallelized, but unless nested parallelism is used, only one loop may be selected for parallelization. The inner loop is longest, but for performance reasons it is not a good idea to select it for parallelization, because the parallel loop overhead is incurred "m" times. If the outer loop is parallelized, only two threads may be used.

There does not seem to be an easy way out of this dilemma. The only solution is to merge or "collapse" the two loops into one single and longer loop. This new loop has the length of both loops combined and may be parallelized. This transformation comes at the price of some additional computations to reconstruct the original loop

```
1 int m = 2;
2 int n = 5;
3     ........
4 for (int i=0; i<m; i++)
5   for (int j=0; j<n; j++)
6     a[i*n+j] = i+j+1;
```

Figure 2.3: **Example of a nested loop with short loops** – Both loops can be parallelized, but neither of the choices results in efficient code or substantial speed ups.

```
1 for (int k=0; k<m*n; k++)
2 {
3     int i = (k/n) % m;
4     int j = k % n;
5     a[i*n+j] = i+j+1;
6 }
```

Figure 2.4:   **An example of explicit loop collapsing** – At the cost of some additional book-keeping operations, the two short loops are combined into a single longer loop that can be parallelized and executed more efficiently.

iteration values from the single loop variable. The code fragment that implements this idea is shown in Figure 2.4.

This optimization is not only beneficial in a serial program. Both issues when parallelizing the original loop nest have been eliminated as well. In general, and as demonstrated in this example, loop collapsing provides a good way to deal with short nested parallel loops, but it does not make the code any easier to read and maintain.

This is why the `collapse` clause is useful. It is ideally suited in the event a perfectly nested loop has more than one parallelizable loop, but all of these loops are short. The syntax of the clause is given in Figure 2.5.

Figure 2.6 shows how to use the clause in this example. The compiler first generates code similar to what is shown in Figure 2.4. The resulting single loop is then parallelized.

To demonstrate how this works, we parallelized the outer loop in Figure 2.3 and executed both versions using five threads. The loops were instrumented to print diagnostic information. The results are listed in Figure 2.7.

#pragma omp for collapse *(n) [clause[[,] clause]...] new-line*   *for loop(s)*
!$omp do collapse *(n) [clause[[,] clause]...]*   *do loop(s)* **!$omp end do** *[nowait]*

Figure 2.5: **Syntax of the loop collapse clause in C/C++ and Fortran** – This clause combines multiple loops into a single loop. The length of the resulting parallel loop is the combined length of the loops affected. The parameter **n** is used to specify how many loops should be collapsed.

```
1 #pragma omp parallel for default(none) shared(a,m,n)\
2                              collapse(2)
3 for (int i=0; i<m; i++)
4   for (int j=0; j<n; j++)
5     a[i*n+j] = i+j+1;
```

Figure 2.6: **Example of the collapse clause** – The compiler generates a single loop of length mxn and parallelizes it.

The output lines marked "Outer loop" are from the original loop nest, where the outer loop was parallelized. In this case only two threads may be used, although we requested five threads. This limitation has been lifted for the version that uses the collapse clause. The output lines are marked "Collapse" and clearly all five threads are used now.

There are some things to remember when using the collapse clause:

- This clause is supported on the **worksharing** loop construct, the **simd** construct, and the **distribute** construct.

- The collapsed loops must be perfectly nested.

- The collapsed loops must form a rectangular iteration space.

- The bounds and stride of each loop must be invariant over all the loops.

- Only one collapse clause may be used per loop nest.

- The iterations of the collapsed loop are scheduled according to the **schedule** clause in effect.

```
Outer loop: (0,0) has been initialized to 1 by thread 0
Outer loop: (0,1) has been initialized to 2 by thread 0
Outer loop: (0,2) has been initialized to 3 by thread 0
Outer loop: (0,3) has been initialized to 4 by thread 0
Outer loop: (0,4) has been initialized to 5 by thread 0
Outer loop: (1,0) has been initialized to 2 by thread 1
Outer loop: (1,1) has been initialized to 3 by thread 1
Outer loop: (1,2) has been initialized to 4 by thread 1
Outer loop: (1,3) has been initialized to 5 by thread 1
Outer loop: (1,4) has been initialized to 6 by thread 1

Collapse:   (0,2) has been initialized to 3 by thread 1
Collapse:   (0,3) has been initialized to 4 by thread 1
Collapse:   (0,0) has been initialized to 1 by thread 0
Collapse:   (0,1) has been initialized to 2 by thread 0
Collapse:   (1,3) has been initialized to 5 by thread 4
Collapse:   (1,4) has been initialized to 6 by thread 4
Collapse:   (0,4) has been initialized to 5 by thread 2
Collapse:   (1,0) has been initialized to 2 by thread 2
Collapse:   (1,1) has been initialized to 3 by thread 3
Collapse:   (1,2) has been initialized to 4 by thread 3
```

Figure 2.7: **Output of the original code and the version with the collapse clause** – This example was executed using five threads, but in the first version only two threads may be used. The second version uses all five threads.

2.1.4   The Linear Clause

The linear clause is mentioned here only for the sake of completeness. It is part of the support for SIMD instructions and covered in detail in Section 5.2.4 on page 230.

2.1.5   The Critical Construct

The critical construct has been enhanced with an optional hint. The syntax is given in Figure 2.8.

If a hint is used, the construct *must* have a name and the expression for the hint must evaluate to the same value for all critical regions with the same name.

#pragma omp critical *[(name) [**hint** (hint-expression)]]   new-line*   *structured block*
!$omp critical *[(name) [**hint** (hint-expression)]]*   *structured block* **!$omp end critical** *[(name)]*

Figure 2.8:   **Syntax of the extended critical construct in C/C++ and Fortran** – The hint is optional, but if used, the critical construct must have a name and the expression for the hint must evaluate to the same value for all critical regions with the same name.

The purpose and use of the hint is the same as described in Section 2.3.3 on page 67 and allows an implementation to tailor the code to the expected access pattern of the critical region.

The expression for the hint must be of type `omp_lock_hit_kind` and must evaluate to a scalar value that is a valid lock hint. The supported values are listed in Figure 2.20 on page 68. Without a hint, the effect is as if `hint(omp_lock_hint_none)` was specified.

Because locks and critical regions potentially limit scalability, choosing the correct value for the hint can make a noticeable difference and is certainly worth considering.

2.1.6   The Atomic Construct

In earlier versions of the specifications, the `atomic` construct applied to a single update statement only (see also Section 1.6.3 on page 32), but as of OpenMP 3.1 it has been refined to support several additional access and update patterns. It is now also possible to capture the value of the target variable before, or after an atomic update. The syntax of the extended construct is given in Figure 2.9.

Through the optional *atomic-clause*, the type of modification performed is specified. In absence of a clause, the `update` clause is implied. This is consistent with the earlier definition.

The names of the clauses allude to their respective functionality:

- **Read** - This is an atomic read. The input variable is read atomically and stored into the output variable. This is guaranteed regardless of the size of the variable.

```
#pragma omp atomic [seq_cst [,]] atomic-clause [[,] seq_cst] new-line
    expr. statement
#pragma omp atomic [seq_cst] new-line
    expr. statement
#pragma omp atomic [seq_cst [,]] capture [[,] seq_cst] new-line
    structured block
```
```
!$omp atomic [seq_cst [,]] [read|write|update] [[,] seq_cst]
    capture, write, or update statement respectively
!$omp end atomic
!$omp atomic [seq_cst]
    update statement
!$omp atomic [seq_cst [,]] capture [[,] seq_cst]
    update+capture, capture+update or capture+write statement
!$omp end atomic
```

Figure 2.9: **Syntax of the extended atomic construct in C/C++ and Fortran** – The type of atomic operation performed can be specified. If necessary, sequential consistency may be enforced by using the seq_cst keyword.

- **Write** - This is an atomic write. The output variable is written atomically. This is guaranteed regardless of the size of the variable.

- **Update** - The same variable is both read and written. As before, only the read/write operations are guaranteed to be atomic. If, for example, an expression is used, the evaluation of this need not be atomic. The consequence is that any possible side effect(s) of such an evaluation could lead to an erroneous result. An example is a call to a function that updates a shared variable. If no precautions are taken, a data race may occur. Task scheduling pointss are not allowed between the read and write of the variable. See also page 144 in Section 3.7 for more information on task scheduling points.

- **Capture** - In addition to an update, the value of the modified variable is saved *atomically* either before or after the update.

  There is a subtle, but important, distinction between the two forms of the capture clause in C/C++. The first form supports a single statement only, while the second form is somewhat more general and not only supports the atomic update, but also a (simple) statement to capture the value of the variable modified. The details for this are given in Figure 2.11.

Clause	Expr. STMT (C/C++)	Expr. STMT (Fortran)
read	v = x;	v = x
write	x = *expr*;	x = *expr*
update	x++;	x = x *operator expr*
	++x;	x = *expr operator* x
	x--;	x = *intrinsic_func*(x,*expr_list*)
	--x;	x = *intrinsic_func*(*expr_list*,x)
	x *binop* = *expr*;	
	x = x *binop expr*;	
	x = *expr binop* x;	

Figure 2.10: **Clauses and expression statements supported on the atomic construct** – This table lists the various combinations of clauses and statements one can use with the **read**, **write**, and **update** clauses. The **capture** clause is covered separately.

In Figure 2.10, the expression statements in C/C++ and Fortran supported with the **read**, **write** and **update** clauses are given. In this Figure, *binop* is one of the following operators: +,-,*,/, &,^, |, <<, or >>.

In C++, binop, binop =, ++, and -- cannot be overloaded operators. In Fortran, the operator is +, -, *, /, .AND., .OR., .EQV., or .NEQV.. The intrinsic function is one of MAX, MIN, IAND, IOR, or IEOR.

The fine-print in the specifications on the combined use of an operator and an expression is not always easy to digest. With the following simple observation in mind, it is however hopefully easier to use this construct correctly.

All one needs to remember is that the loads and stores are executed atomically and whatever is contributed to the target variable should have no side effects regarding this variable. Whether it is a function call or an expression, evaluating this should not have an impact on the value of the variable to be updated.

Either the standard precedence rules apply, or parentheses may be used to enforce that the expression is evaluated prior to the update. For example, a statement of the form x = x binop expr must be equivalent to x = x binop (expr).

The following example illustrates this: x = x + y*y. Because the multiplication is guaranteed to be performed prior to the addition, there is no parentheses. If this is not the case, or when in doubt, parentheses may be used to eliminate any ambiguity. For example, in an update of this type, the parentheses enforce the precedence: x = x + (z + y*y).

Clause	Expr. STMT (C/C++)	Structured Block (C/C++)
capture	`v = x++;`	`{v = x; x `*`binop`*` = `*`expr`*`;}`
	`v = ++x;`	`{x `*`binop`*` = `*`expr`*`; v = x;}`
	`v = x--;`	`{v = x; x = x `*`binop`*` `*`expr`*`;}`
	`v = --x;`	`{v = x; x = `*`expr`*` `*`binop`*` x;}`
	`v = x `*`binop`*` = `*`expr`*`;`	`{x = x `*`binop`*` `*`expr`*`; v = x;}`
	`v = x = x `*`binop`*` `*`expr`*`;`	`{x = `*`expr`*` `*`binop`*` x; v = x;}`
	`v = x = `*`expr`*` `*`binop`*` x;`	`{v = x; x = `*`expr`*`;}`
		`{v = x; x++;}`
		`{v = x; ++x;}`
		`{++x; v = x;}`
		`{x++; v = x;}`
		`{v = x; x--;}`
		`{v = x; --x;}`
		`{--x; v = x;}`
		`{x--; v = x;}`

Figure 2.11: **Expression statements and structured blocks supported on the capture clause in C/C++** – With this construct, the value of the target variable is saved into another variable, either before or after the update.

While the other three clauses are refinements on the `atomic` construct prior to the OpenMP 3.1 specifications, the `capture` clause *extends* the functionality. With this clause, the value of the target variable may be saved into another variable before, or after, the update.

Due to syntactical differences between C/C++ and Fortran, the overview for the `capture` clause is split. In Figure 2.11, the supported statements and structured blocks for C/C++ are given. In Figures 2.12 and 2.13, the Fortran case is covered.

Why was there a need for the `capture` clause? Prior to the introduction of this feature there was no way to *atomically* intercept the value of the target variable. This could easily lead to a data race. If one thread accesses this variable outside the atomic construct, while another thread performs the atomic update, the result is undefined.

The example in Figure 2.14 shows such a case and demonstrates how to use the `capture` clause to avoid this problem. In this program, function `update` adds a certain contribution to a shared variable. We want to preserve the previous value and use it as the return value of this function.

Clause	Update STMT (Fortran)
capture	x = x *operator expr*
	x = *expr operator* x
	x = *intrinsic_function* (x,*expr_list*)
	x = *intrinsic_function* (*expr_list*,x)

Figure 2.12: **The update statements supported on the capture clause in Fortran** – The intrinsic function is one of the following: min, max, iand, ior, or ieor.

Clause	Capture STMT (Fortran)	Write STMT (Fortran)
capture	v = x	x = *expr*

Figure 2.13: **The capture and write statement supported on the capture clause in Fortran** – These are the various possibilities to choose from when using this clause.

The main program calls this function from within a parallel region and sets the contribution to the thread ID plus 1. The addition of 1 makes the output in Figure 2.15 easier to follow. The final result should be $1+2+\ldots+NT+(NT+1) = NT*(NT+1)/2$ if NT threads are used.

The output in Figure 2.15 demonstrates how the value is carried over from one thread to another.

Note there is one issue here. Printing variable new_value within the parallel region introduces a data race, because the value as modified by one thread could have been modified by another thread before the print statement is executed. There is no such risk with the old value, because it is stored in a private variable and performs an atomic read of the new value.

There is one feature that has not been discussed so far: the seq_cst clause. This has mainly been introduced to provide the same semantics as the memory_order_- seq_cst and memory_order_relaxed atomic operations in the C11 and C++11 standards [4, 5].

In OpenMP, adding the seq_cst clause to the atomic construct implies a flush operation without a list. This guarantees sequential consistency but comes at a price. As discussed in section 1.2.3 on page 11, this consistency model limits potentially significant compiler optimizations and most likely negatively impacts performance.

```
1   int main(int argc, char *argv[])
2   {
3     int new_value = 0;
4
5     #pragma omp parallel shared(new_value)
6     {
7         int TID       = omp_get_thread_num();
8         int old_value = update(&new_value, TID+1);
9
10        printf("TID = %4d: old_value = %4d\n",TID,old_value);
11
12    } // End of parallel region
13
14    printf("Final value is %4d\n",new_value);
15
16    return(0);
17  }
18  int update (int *new_value, int contribution)
19  {
20      int return_value;
21
22      #pragma omp atomic capture
23      {
24          return_value = *new_value;
25          *new_value  += contribution;
26      } // End of atomic capture
27
28      return(return_value);
29  }
```

Figure 2.14: **Example of the capture clause on the atomic construct** –
Prior to OpenMP 3.1 it was not possible to reliably save the old value before the update.
The **capture** clause used at line 22 addresses this issue. Before variable **new_value** is
updated at line 25, its value is stored into variable **return_value** (line 24). These are
atomic operations, so no other thread may interfere. The final result of this program is
NT*(NT+1)/2 if NT threads are used.

```
TID =      0: old_value =     5
TID =      1: old_value =     0
TID =      2: old_value =     2
TID =      3: old_value =    11
TID =      4: old_value =     6
TID =      5: old_value =    15
TID =      6: old_value =    29
TID =      7: old_value =    21
Final value is    36
```

Figure 2.15: **Sorted output of the update function that uses the atomic capture** – This result was obtained using 8 threads. Thread 1 happens to be the first one to perform the update. It adds 2 to it, and this new value is then picked up by thread 2, which adds 3 to it. The value is then subsequently updated by threads $0, 4, 3, 5, 7$ and 6. The final result is indeed $8 * 9/2 = 36$.

Hence the recommendation to use this clause only if really needed and no suitable alternative is available.

Many aspects of the `atomic` construct have been covered here, but there are some things glossed over. We recommend checking the specifications for all details.

2.2   New Environment Variables

In OpenMP 2.5 there were only four environment variables. Since then, the list given in Figure 1.28 on page 34 has been significantly expanded. These new variables standardize the typical extensions that most compiler vendors have provided already and also support the new functionality introduced since OpenMP 2.5.

In addition to this, the already existing variables `OMP_NUM_THREADS` and `OMP_-SCHEDULE` are extended to support additional functionality.

These two, plus all additional environment variables supported in OpenMP 4.5, are listed in Figure 2.16.

Below, these new environment variables are covered in more detail. As before, the names must be in uppercase, but the value(s) assigned are case-insensitive. In our examples, we use lowercase for the values.

Please keep in mind that, in all cases, the default is system-dependent. Also, as with any environment variable, the way to set these depends on the Operating System used and/or the specific (Unix) shell.

Function name	Description
OMP_DISPLAY_ENV	If set, displays the OpenMP version number and ICV values. In verbose mode, more information is shown.
OMP_NUM_THREADS	Set the number of threads for (nested) parallel regions.
OMP_SCHEDULE	Set the workload distribution schedule for parallel loops.
OMP_STACKSIZE	Set the size of the stack for the threads.
OMP_WAIT_POLICY	Specify the behavior of idle threads.
OMP_MAX_ACTIVE_LEVELS	Set the maximum number of nested active parallel regions.
OMP_THREAD_LIMIT	Set the maximum number of threads to be created in a contention group.
OMP_MAX_TASK_PRIORITY	Set the maximum value that can be used in the priority clause on the task construct.
OMP_PROC_BIND	Set and control thread affinity.
OMP_PLACES	Define where threads are allowed to execute.
OMP_CANCELLATION	Enable or disable cancellation.
OMP_DEFAULT_DEVICE	Set the default device number.

Figure 2.16: **The additional OpenMP 4.5 environment variables** – These are the environment variables changed or added since OpenMP 2.5.

- OMP_DISPLAY_ENV - This is a very useful variable to verify the settings and check the defaults. Each environment variable and macro is printed in the format ENV_VAR_NAME = 'value'. Optionally a line starts with [device-id].

  The information is printed after the environment variables have been processed, but before any of the corresponding ICVs are modified. The information is enclosed between the strings OPENMP DISPLAY ENVIRONMENT BEGIN and OPENMP DISPLAY ENVIRONMENT END.

  There are three choices for this variable:

  - false - No information is displayed.
  - true - Print the OpenMP version number and the values of all environment variables. These are either the defaults, or the value(s) set by the user prior to program start up.

– `verbose` - In addition to the standard environment variables, vendor-specific extensions may be printed as well. It is up to the implementor to select which environment variables to include.

Below is an example after setting `OMP_DISPLAY_ENV` to `true`. This is printed immediately after program start up:

```
OPENMP DISPLAY ENVIRONMENT BEGIN
  _OPENMP='201307'
  OMP_CANCELLATION='FALSE'
  OMP_DISPLAY_ENV='true'
  OMP_DYNAMIC='TRUE'
  OMP_MAX_ACTIVE_LEVELS='4'
  OMP_NESTED='FALSE'
  OMP_NUM_THREADS='16'
  OMP_PLACES='N/A'
  OMP_PROC_BIND='FALSE'
  OMP_SCHEDULE='static'
  OMP_STACKSIZE='8388608B'
  OMP_THREAD_LIMIT='1024'
  OMP_WAIT_POLICY='PASSIVE'
OPENMP DISPLAY ENVIRONMENT END
```

One of the things to observe in this output is that the settings for `OMP_PLACES` are "N/A," which stands for "Not Applicable." This is because processor binding is apparently disabled (`OMP_PROC_BIND` has been set to `false`). This illustrates how useful this environment variable is to perform a sanity check on the settings and to ensure the values are as expected.

• `OMP_NUM_THREADS` - This is probably the most often used OpenMP environment variable, but before OpenMP 3.1 it was not working well in conjunction with nested parallelism.

This has since then been addressed, and it now supports a set of values, which are set by a list of positive integer values. These values are used to define the number of threads at the corresponding nesting level of parallel regions, starting at level 1.

For example, setting `OMP_NUM_THREADS` to "3,2" implies that a top-level parallel region uses 3 threads. The team size of the next nested parallel region is 2.

If the nesting level is deeper than the number of entries in the list, the last value in the list is used to set the number of threads in subsequent nested parallel regions. In the above example, this means that 2 threads are used in every parallel region at nesting level 3 or more.

- `OMP_SCHEDULE` - As before, this variable is used to set the type of workload scheduling for parallel loops in the event the **runtime** option is used on the **schedule** clause.

  In addition to **static**, **dynamic**, and **guided**, as of OpenMP 3.0, the **auto** schedule type is supported as well. With this, the choice of the schedule is determined by the implementation. This new scheduling type does not support a chunk size.

- `OMP_STACKSIZE` - Each OpenMP thread needs a certain amount of storage space to store information, such as private variables. This part of memory is referred to as "the stack."

  An OpenMP runtime system sets aside a certain default amount of storage space for each thread. This is controlled by the `OMP_STACKSIZE` environment variable. The setting can be checked in the documentation or through environment variable `OMP_DISPLAY_ENV`.

  Unfortunately an application is likely to crash if enough (stack) space is not available. In some cases, this problem can be determined at compile time and the compiler may issue a warning, but more often than not, this is not possible and the problem only shows up at runtime.

  That is when this variable needs to be used to increase the thread stack size.

  The syntax supports a case-insensitive unit qualifier that is appended (possibly with whitespace in between) to the number: B for bytes, K for 1024 bytes, M for 1024 Kbytes and G for 1024 Mbytes.

  For example, **export OMP_STACKSIZE=2M** or **export OMP_STACKSIZE="2 m"** both set the thread stack size to 2 Mbyte using Bash shell syntax.

  There are two more things worth noting:

- In the absence of a unit qualifier (B, K, M or G), the default unit is *Kbytes*, not bytes. This is easily overlooked, resulting in very high memory requirements that may cause the application to fail.

- The application may require its own *main* stack size to be set if the OS does not provide sufficient stack space by default. This has no relation to OpenMP and is *not* affected by the OMP_STACKSIZE variable. Typically this stack is set through an OS-specific command (e.g. limit or ulimit on Unix systems) and is most likely specified in bytes, but one is advised to check the documentation when in doubt.

- OMP_WAIT_POLICY - In the optimal scenario, all threads are busy all the time doing useful work, but in practice there are often shorter or longer periods of inactivity for one or more threads.

  The question is what to do with such threads. Putting them to sleep saves processor cycles and other resources, but waking up such a thread is relatively costly. Simply keeping the processor busy doing nothing wastes cycles.

  Until the OMP_WAIT_POLICY variable was introduced in OpenMP 3.0, there was no portable solution to specify the desired behavior.

  There are currently two settings for OMP_WAIT_POLICY to specify the behavior of such waiting threads, also called *idle threads*:

  - active - Idle threads should mostly be kept active. This is good for the performance of the application, because an idle thread is ready to execute as soon as it is needed again.

    The word *mostly* is important here. It is not good for the system throughput to keep idle threads in a busy loop for an extended period of time. It only wastes cycles.

    This is why, by default, an implementation may decide to put an idle thread to sleep after a certain time out. Obviously this choice, and the length of the time out, is implementation-, or even system-dependent.

    By setting the idle mode to active, this is overruled and threads are ready to go any time they are needed.

  - passive - Idle threads should mostly do nothing and not use any processor cycles. This favors overall system throughput, but activating an idle thread may take longer compared to the active setting.

Remember that the setting is merely a suggestion. The implementation is free to ignore it.

If more explicit control is needed, we recommend checking the documentation of the specific runtime environment used. Several OpenMP implementations support more control than provided by this environment variable.

- `OMP_MAX_ACTIVE_LEVELS` - The `OMP_MAX_ACTIVE_LEVELS` variable is set to a non-negative integer that defines the upper limit on the number of active parallel regions that may be nested.

  If the value is negative, not an integer at all, or exceeds the limit supported by the implementation, the behavior is undefined.

- `OMP_THREAD_LIMIT` - The `OMP_THREAD_LIMIT` variable is set to a non-negative integer that defines the maximum number of threads to be used in a *contention group*, where a contention group consists of an initial thread and its descendant threads.

  Its main use is to prevent an application from generating too many threads. Especially with recursive types of algorithms, this can easily happen. As a result, the system may become unresponsive. This limit can be used to avoid such a situation.

  If the value is negative, not an integer at all, or exceeds the limit supported by the implementation, the behavior is undefined.

- `OMP_MAX_TASK_PRIORITY` - The `OMP_MAX_TASK_PRIORITY` variable is set to a non-negative integer that defines the maximum priority level to be used in the `priority` clause on the `task` construct.

  If this variable is not set explicitly, the default value is zero, and all priority settings in the application are effectively ignored.

- `OMP_PLACES` - The `OMP_PLACES` variable is extensively covered in Chapter 4, starting on page 151. This is why there is only a very brief discussion here.

  The `OMP_PLACES` variable defines the OpenMP place list to be used by the runtime environment.

  A single place is defined through an *unordered* set of comma separated non-negative numbers enclosed in curly braces ({ and }). For example {8,0,4} defines a place with three entries, and the order is irrelevant.

Places are the building blocks of the *place list*, which consists of an *ordered* list with one or more comma-separated places.

In other words, the order within a place definition does not matter, but the order in which the places are specified in the place list does matter.

The integer numbers are system-specific and may need to be adapted in case a different system is used. This is not very convenient and that is why an alternative to such lists is supported.

Three *abstract names* to cover several common scenarios are available. The names are `sockets`, `cores`, and `threads`. They cannot be combined with a list specification.

As with most OpenMP environment variables, if `OMP_PLACES` has not been set, a *system-dependent default place list* is used. It is important to note that this means there is *always* a place list.

- `OMP_PROC_BIND` - The `OMP_PROC_BIND` variable sets the thread affinity policy, or policies, to be used for parallel regions.

  The settings control if and how OpenMP threads are bound to computational resources, such as sockets, cores and/or hardware threads.

  This is achieved through a tight coupling between binding and *OpenMP places*, a new concept introduced in OpenMP 4.0 and briefly covered under the description of the `OMP_PLACES` environment variable.

  The `OMP_PROC_BIND` variable was already introduced in OpenMP 3.1, but could be set to only `true` or `false`. With the introduction of thread affinity support in OpenMP 4.0, the functionality has been greatly enhanced and provides very fine-grained control over thread placement.

  There are three policies regarding how to place the threads: `master`, `close`, and `spread`.

  In the case of nested parallel regions, multiple and potentially different placement types may be defined by using a comma-separated list. For example `OMP_PROC_BIND="spread,close"`.

  If the nesting level exceeds the number of policies in the list, the last policy is applied to the remaining levels.

  If binding is requested, but no place list is defined, a default place list is used.

Note that if `OMP_PROC_BIND` is not set, the default may be `false`. In this case, or if it is explicitly set to `false`, the settings for the place list are *ignored*.

Much more detailed coverage of binding and places can be found in Chapter 4, which is dedicated to thread affinity, binding, and the places concept.

- `OMP_CANCELLATION` - If `OMP_CANCELLATION` variable is set to `true`, cancellation is activated. The effects of the `cancel` construct and of cancellation points are enabled. If set to `false`, cancellation is disabled.

  If this variable is not set explicitly, the default value is `false`.

- `OMP_DEFAULT_DEVICE` - The `OMP_DEFAULT_DEVICE` variable may be used to define the default device number to be used in device constructs. The value must be a non-negative integer.

2.3   New Runtime Functions

Since OpenMP 2.5, quite a number of runtime functions have been added to the functions listed in Figure 1.29 on page 36. Existing functionality has been expanded and newly introduced features have been augmented by a set of functions specific to the feature.

As before, these functions may be used to query settings and also change them, but in the case of heterogeneous systems, they go a step further. The device memory functions may be used to manage memory on the target device(s).

A new element in the specifications is that some functions require an OpenMP-specific data type. They are defined in include file `omp.h` in C/C++. Fortran programs require either file `omp_lib.h` to be included or a module called `omp_lib` to be used.

In Fortran, these new data types are specified using the KIND type selector.

For example, function "`omp_proc_bind_t omp_get_proc_bind()`" in C/C++ is "`integer (kind=omp_proc_bind_kind) function omp_get_proc_bind()`" in Fortran.

In the remainder of this section, functions added since OpenMP 2.5 are listed and discussed. To avoid lengthy tables, the list has been split into three parts, each covered in its own section. The syntax given is for C/C++ only, but the usage in Fortran is very similar. The exception are the device memory functions. There are

Function name	Description
omp_get_thread_limit	Return the maximum number of threads in the contention group.
omp_get_schedule	Return the loop schedule (and chunk size) in case the **runtime** clause is used.
omp_set_schedule	Change the loop schedule (and chunk size) in case the **runtime** clause is used.
omp_get_max_active_levels	Return the maximum number of nested active parallel regions.
omp_set_max_active_levels	Change the maximum number of nested active parallel regions.
omp_get_level	Return the number of nested parallel regions enclosing the current task.
omp_get_active_level	Return the number of nested *active* parallel regions enclosing the current task.
omp_get_ancestor_thread_num	Return the thread number of the ancestor of the current thread.
omp_get_team_size	Return the size of the thread team to which the current thread or ancestor belongs.

Figure 2.17: **Runtime functions for thread management, scheduling, and nested parallelism** – These functions provide support for thread management, workload scheduling and nested parallelism. The names are the same in C/C++ and Fortran, but the usage follows the language syntax.

no native interfaces for Fortran. One may be able to call the C/C++ versions from Fortran, but there is no such guarantee.

2.3.1 Runtime Functions for Thread Management, Thread Scheduling, and Nested Parallelism

The first set of additional runtime functions consists of functions related to thread management, loop iteration scheduling, and nested parallelism. They are listed in Figure 2.17. These functions augment the constructs already supported in OpenMP 2.5. The next two sections cover the functions related to the new features introduced since then.

- `int omp_get_thread_limit()` - This function returns the maximum number of OpenMP threads that the application is allowed to create in the current contention group.

  While the number of hardware scheduling resources is fixed for a given system configuration, this upper limit on the number of threads is controlled by the OpenMP implementation. This function returns the limit. Environment variable `OMP_THREAD_LIMIT` may be used to change this limit.[1]

  The difference between this function and the older `omp_get_num_procs()` function is that the latter returns the number of "processors" available on the system. The notion of what a processor is exactly, can be somewhat ambiguous, so it is up to the OS to decide. It could be a core, or a hardware thread, for example.

- `void omp_get_schedule(omp_sched_t *kind, int *chunk_size)` - The first argument of this function returns a pointer of type `omp_sched_t` to identify the schedule used to assign loop iterations to threads. Where relevant, the second argument returns an additional qualifier, such as the chunk size.

  There are four pre-defined schedule types: `static`, `dynamic`, `guided`, and `auto`. The corresponding codes are 1, 2, 3, and 4, respectively. Note that the first value is 1, not 0. This may require care if used as an index into an array in C/C++.

  An implementation has the freedom to support additional scheduling types. If so, the definition of the second argument for that type is implementation-dependent and the reason we also refer to it as a "qualifier."

- `void omp_set_schedule(omp_sched_t kind, int chunk_size)` - Function to change the scheduling type and (optionally) the chunk size. The first argument is an integer identifier (or a specific reserved variable name) to specify the schedule to be used.

---

[1]There may also be an OS or installation-specific upper limit. Getting this changed depends on the specific environment and local situation.

The currently supported reserved variable names include the name of the schedule:

- omp_sched_static = 1
- omp_sched_dynamic = 2
- omp_sched_guided = 3
- omp_sched_auto = 4

If supported by the scheduling type, the second argument may be used to pass on the chunk size. Any value less than one implies the *default* chunk size is used.

This function may be used to adapt the loop schedule on a per-loop basis. In Figures 2.22 and 2.23 the usage of the functions to get and set the schedule is demonstrated.

Note that this function has an effect only in combination with the runtime clause.

- int omp_get_max_active_levels() - This function returns how deep parallel regions may be nested.

- void omp_set_max_active_levels(int max_levels) - Environment variable OMP_MAX_ACTIVE_LEVELS may be used to initially set the maximum level of parallel regions that are allowed to be nested. This function increases or decreases this limit at runtime to adapt to specific needs.

- int omp_get_level() - This function returns the number of nested parallel regions enclosing the current task, regardless of whether the region is active or not. Recall that *active* in an OpenMP context means that more than one thread executes the region.

This function is used to determine at which level a (nested) parallel region is. The first-level region is assigned a level of 1, the one nested within this region has a level of 2, and so on.

One of the uses of this functionality is to determine a unique thread ID at any level. Figure 2.26 on page 83 shows a source code example of how to do this.

- `int omp_get_active_level()` - This function provides the same functionality as the function `omp_get_level()` described above, but it is restricted to active parallel regions only.

  Both functions may be used to determine at which level a (nested) parallel region is. The first level region is assigned a level of 1, the one nested within this region has a level of 2, and so on.

- `int omp_get_ancestor_thread_num(int level)` - The thread ID of the ancestor thread is returned by this function. The function argument is the nesting level this applies to.

  There is one important thing to point out. This is the level of the *ancestor*, not the level of the thread calling this function. For example, if at level 3, the function argument should be 2, not 3, to get the thread ID of the ancestor.

  If this function is called with the nesting level of the caller, the regular thread ID is returned. This is the same value as returned by function `omp_get_-thread_num()`.

- `int omp_get_team_size(int level)` - This function returns the number of threads in the team executing the parallel region at the nesting level specified by the argument.

  If this function is called with the nesting level of the caller, the number of threads in the caller's current team is returned. This is the same value as returned by function `omp_get_num_threads()`.

2.3.2   Runtime Functions for Tasking, Cancellation, and Thread Affinity

This section presents and discusses the functions related to tasking, thread cancellation, and thread affinity. These functions return a value, or setting, only. There are no functions to change a setting.

The functions are listed in Figure 2.18. Note that for the affinity-related functions, we do not use the word "processor" as the specifications do. Instead, we use "(hardware) resource number" or simply "resource" for short. This terminology is explained in detail in Section 4.5.1 in Chapter 4.

- `int omp_in_final()` - This function returns `true` if called from a task that is final. Otherwise it returns `false`.

Function name	Description
`omp_in_final`	Return **true** if executed in a final task region; otherwise return **false**
`omp_get_max_task_priority`	Return the maximum value that may be specified in the **priority** clause.
`omp_get_cancellation`	Return the status of cancellation.
`omp_get_proc_bind`	Return the thread affinity policy to be used for the *subsequent* parallel region that does not use a **proc_bind** clause.
`omp_get_num_places`	Return the number of places in the place list.
`omp_get_place_num_procs`	Return the number of resources associated with the argument, which must be a place number.
`omp_get_place_proc_ids`	Return the numerical identifiers of each resource associated with the first argument, which must be a place number.
`omp_get_place_num`	Return the place number to which the encountering thread is bound.
`omp_get_partition_num_places`	Return the number of places in the subpartition.
`omp_get_partition_place_nums`	Return the list of place numbers corresponding to the places in the subpartition.

Figure 2.18: **Runtime functions for tasking, cancellation, and thread affinity** – These functions provide support for tasking, cancellation, and thread affinity. The names are the same in C/C++ and Fortran, but the usage follows the language syntax.

- `int omp_get_max_task_priority()` - This function returns the maximum value that may be used on the **priority** clause supported on the **task** construct.

- `int omp_get_cancellation()` - This function returns **true** if cancellation is enabled. Otherwise it returns **false**.

- `omp_proc_bind_t omp_get_proc_bind()` - This function uses the setting for environment variable `OMP_PROC_BIND` to return the policy for the *subsequent* parallel region.

The return value has data type `omp_proc_bind_t` and may take one of the following values:

- `omp_proc_bind_false = 0`
- `omp_proc_bind_true = 1`
- `omp_proc_bind_master = 2`
- `omp_proc_bind_close = 3`
- `omp_proc_bind_spread = 4`

This function does not return a meaningful result if the `proc_bind` clause is used on the subsequent parallel region, because this takes precedence over the policy set through `OMP_PROC_BIND`.

Figure 2.28 on page 85 shows an example of how to use this function.

More on the choices for these thread affinity settings may be found under the description of the `OMP_PROC_BIND` environment variable.

- `int omp_get_num_places()` - This function returns the number of places in the place list.

- `int omp_get_place_num_procs(int place_num)` - This function returns the number of hardware resources, for example, hardware threads or cores, in the place identified by `place_num`.

  A value of zero is returned if `place_num` is either less than zero or is equal to or larger than the value as returned by `omp_get_num_places()`.

- `void omp_get_place_proc_ids(int place_num, int *ids)` - This function returns a list in array `ids`. This list contains the (hardware) resource numbers associated with the place identified by `place_num`. This place identifier, as well as the resource numbers, are implementation-dependent numbers to identify a place and its contents. Refer to Section 4.5.1 on page 161 for the definition of a resource number.

  Be sure to allocate sufficient storage for array `ids`. At least `omp_get_place_num_procs(place_num)` locations must be available.

This function has no effect if `place_num` is less than zero, or is equal to, or larger than the value as returned by `omp_get_num_places()`.

- `int omp_get_place_num()` - If the encountering thread is bound to a place, the place number associated with this thread is returned and the value is in the interval $[0, omp\_get\_num\_places() - 1]$.

  If the thread is not bound to a place, a value of -1 is returned.

- `int omp_get_partition_num_places()` - This function returns the number of places in the subpartition of the encountering thread.

- `void omp_get_partition_place_nums(int *place_nums)` - This function returns the list of place numbers corresponding to the places in the subpartition of the encountering thread.

  Array `place_nums` must be sufficiently large to contain the number of integers returned by `omp_get_partition_num_places()`. Otherwise, the behavior is undefined.

2.3.3   Runtime Functions for Locking

Before diving deeper into this, an important warning first: the ownership of locks has changed. In most cases, this has no impact on the application, but we recommend reading Section 2.4.1 on page 86 for the details.

The set of locking functions has been extended to support a *hint* the user may provide. This hint is used to specify the expected behavior of the lock. This allows the implementation to select a locking mechanism tuned for this specific purpose.

The syntax of the new functions is given in Figure 2.19. The hint does not change the mutual exclusion semantics of the lock, and the implementation is free to ignore it. The application should also not rely on the hint in order to work correctly.

The choices for the hint are listed in Figure 2.20. As usual, such values are defined in header file `omp.h` for C/C++ and the Fortran `omp_lib.h` include file and/or module file `omp_lib`.

At first sight, the support for `omp_lock_hint_none` seems somewhat peculiar. This informs the implementation there is no specific preference.

```
void omp_init_lock_with_hint (omp_lock_t *t, omp_lock_hint_t hint);

void omp_init_nest_lock_with_hint (omp_lock_t *t, omp_lock_hint_t hint);
```
```
subroutine omp_init_lock_with_hint (svar, hint)
 integer (kind=omp_lock_kind) svar
 integer (kind=omp_lock_kind_hint) hint

subroutine omp_init_nest_lock_with_hint (svar, hint)
 integer (kind=omp_lock_kind) svar
 integer (kind=omp_lock_kind_hint) hint
```

Figure 2.19: **Syntax of the new locking functions in C/C++ and Fortran –** These functions support an optional hint. This gives the implementation the opportunity to select the most suitable solution, but it is also free to ignore the hint. Both single-level, as well as, nested locks are available.

```
typedef enum omp_lock_hint_t {
  omp_lock_hint_none = 0,
  omp_lock_hint_uncontended = 1,
  omp_lock_hint_contended = 2,
  omp_lock_hint_nonspeculative = 4,
  omp_lock_hint_speculative = 8
} omp_lock_hint_t;
```
```
integer (kind=omp_lock_hint_kind), &
  parameter::omp_lock_hint_none = 0
integer (kind=omp_lock_hint_kind), &
  parameter::omp_lock_hint_uncontended = 1
integer (kind=omp_lock_hint_kind), &
  parameter::omp_lock_hint_contended = 2
integer (kind=omp_lock_hint_kind), &
  parameter::omp_lock_hint_nonspeculative = 4
integer (kind=omp_lock_hint_kind), &
  parameter::omp_lock_hint_speculative = 8
```

Figure 2.20: **Definition of the hint data type in C/C++ and Fortran –** These are the various choices supported for the hint. An implementation may add to this list. For an explanation of these hints, refer to the main text.

Why would one use a function that supports a hint and then effectively say it doesn't matter? This choice is available to accommodate flexibility in an application. The same locking function may be called for various values of the hint, including the lack of a preference, leaving it up to the system to decide.

The next two choices are about *lock contention*. The lock is said to be "contended," if multiple threads want to access a lock at the same time. If this is the case, a more advanced mechanism to acquire the lock could be beneficial. For example, by using an exponential backoff algorithm in case a lock cannot be acquired right away.

The last two types are included for systems with support for *Transactional Memory*. When using a *speculative lock*, the assumption is that there is no contention and that the code within the locked region can be executed unconditionally. Only afterward is it verified that there was indeed no contention. If there had been contention, a rollback strategy is applied, if necessary, to guarantee the correct results.

This highly improves the efficiency of the locking mechanism if there is little or no contention, but it is not without a potential cost. The rollback part is relatively expensive and if this is executed too often, the performance could be worse than without the speculation.

If the user knows upfront that the lock is only lightly contended, using this hint may improve performance.

There are several restrictions when using hints:

- Hints may be combined through wither the + or | operators in C/C++ or the + operator in Fortran, but the behavior is implementation-defined and may even be ignored.

- Combining `omp_lock_hint_none` with any other hint is equivalent to specifying the other hint only.

- As one might expect, when combining conflicting settings, for example "contended" with "uncontended," the behavior is undefined.

- An implementation is free to support additional choices for the hint, but be aware that these may not be portable to other implementations.

2.3.4 Runtime Functions for Heterogeneous Systems

One of the main additions to OpenMP is the support for heterogeneous systems, typically consisting of a host system, plus one or more accelerators. In OpenMP these are referred to as "devices."

In this section, only the runtime functions are summarized. For extensive coverage of this topic, plus an introduction to the device-specific terminology, refer to Chapter 6 starting on page 253.

The set of runtime functions supporting devices are used to query the settings, as well to set the default device. OpenMP 4.5 adds functions to explicitly manage the memory between the host and the device(s).

The full list can be found in Figure 2.21. Below is a more extensive description of each function.

- `int omp_get_default_device()` - This function returns the value of the *default-device-var* ICV, which is the default device number. If it is called from within a `target` region, the result is undefined.

- `void omp_set_default_device(int device_num)` - This function assigns the value of the integer argument `device_num` to the *default-device-var* ICV. If it is called from within a `target` region, the behavior is undefined.

- `int omp_get_initial_device()` - This function returns the host device number. If the return value is in the range $[0, \texttt{omp\_get\_num\_devices()} - 1]$, then it may be used in a `device` clause and in all device memory functions. If the value is outside that range, then it may be only in device memory functions only. Calling this function from within a `target` region results in undefined behavior.

- `int omp_is_initial_device()` - This function returns `true` if the thread that calls it is executing on the host device. Otherwise, it returns `false`.

- `int omp_get_num_devices()` - This function returns the number of available devices. Calling it from within a `target` region results in undefined behavior. Whether or not the host device is included in the number of available devices is implementation-defined.

- `int omp_get_num_teams()` - This function returns the number of teams in the current teams region. See Section 6.5 starting at page 275 for more details

Function name	Description
omp_get_default_device	Return the default device number.
omp_set_default_device	Set the default device number.
omp_get_initial_device	Return the host device number.
omp_is_initial_device	Return **true** if the current task is executing on the host device; otherwise return **false**.
omp_get_num_devices	Return the number of devices.
omp_get_num_teams	Return the number of teams in the current **teams** region.
omp_get_team_num	Return the team number of the calling thread.
omp_target_alloc	Allocate a block of memory on a device.
omp_target_free	Free memory allocated on a device by the **omp_target_alloc** function.
omp_target_is_present	Check whether a host address is mapped to a device.
omp_target_memcpy	Copy memory between any combination of host and device pointers.
omp_target_memcpy_rect	The same as **omp_target_memcpy**, but for entire sub-volumes of multi-dimensional arrays.
omp_target_associate_ptr	Associate a device address with a host address.
omp_target_disassociate_ptr	Remove the association between a device address and a host address.

Figure 2.21: **Runtime functions for heterogeneous computing** – These functions provide support for heterogeneous computing, including memory management between the host and the device(s). The last seven functions, the "device memory functions," are not supported in Fortran.

on the **teams** construct. A value of 1 is returned if called from outside a teams region.

- **int omp_get_team_num()** - This function returns the calling thread's team number. The return value is an integer number in the interval $[0, \text{omp\_get\_num\_teams}() - 1]$. If it is called from outside a **teams** region, a value of zero is returned.

- `void* omp_target_alloc(size_t size, int device_num)` - This function returns the device address of a memory block of `size` bytes dynamically allocated in the address space of the device number specified by `device_num`. If the allocation fails, then it returns NULL. The device number should be either the value returned by `omp_get_initial_device()` or in the range $[0, \text{omp\_get\_num\_devices}() - 1]$.

  Upon a successful allocation, the device address may be used in an `is_device_ptr` clause on a `target` construct or in other device memory functions. See Section 6.3.3 starting on page 265 for more details on using device addresses.

  There are several restrictions when using this function:

  - The behavior of the function is undefined if it is called from a `target` region.
  - Pointer arithmetic cannot be performed on a device address returned by this function.
  - Memory allocated by this function can be freed using the `omp_target_free()` function only.

- `void omp_target_free(void *device_ptr, int device_num)` - This function frees a memory block that was dynamically allocated in the address space of the device number specified by `device_num`. The value of the `device_ptr` should be a device address returned by an earlier call to the `omp_target_alloc()` function. The device number should be either the value returned by `omp_get_initial_device()` or in the range $[0, \text{omp\_get\_num\_devices}() - 1]$. If `device_ptr` is NULL, the function has no effect. The behavior of the function is undefined if it is called from a `target` region.

- `int omp_target_is_present(void *ptr, int device_num)` - This function is used to test if a variable is present in a device data environment. The device number should be either the value returned by `omp_get_initial_device()` or in the range $[0, \text{omp\_get\_num\_devices}() - 1]$.

  The function returns `true` if the host address stored in `ptr`, has a corresponding address in the device data environment of the device identified by `device_num`. Otherwise, `false` is returned. The effect of this function is undefined if called from within a `target` region.

- `int omp_target_memcpy(`

  ```
  void *dst,
  void *src,
  size_t length,
  size_t dst_offst,
  size_t src_offst,
  int dst_device_num,
  int src_device_num) -
  ```

  This function copies a contiguous memory block of `length` bytes from a source device to a destination device. The `dst_device_num` and `src_device_num` are device numbers that identify the source and destination devices. The device numbers should either be the value returned by `omp_get_initial_device()` or in the range $[0, \text{omp\_get\_num\_devices}() - 1]$. The source device address is determined by adding the `src_offset` to the value of the `src` pointer variable. The destination device address is determined by adding the `dst_offset` to the value of `dst` pointer variable.

  The return value is zero upon successful completion of the copy and non-zero in the event of a failure. The `dst` and `src` pointers must be valid device pointers. The calculated source and destination addresses must be valid on the respective devices. The effect of this function is undefined if called from within a `target` region. This function contains a task scheduling point.

- `int omp_target_memcpy_rect(`

  ```
  void *dst,
  void *src,
  size_t element_size,
  int num_dims,
  const size_t *volume,
  const size_t *dst_offsets,
  const size_t *src_offsets,
  const size_t *dst_dimensions,
  const size_t *src_dimensions,
  int dst_device_num,
  int src_device_num) -
  ```

This function copies a rectangular sub-volume of memory from a multi-dimensional array in the address space of the source device to a multi-dimensional array in the address space of the destination device.

The `dst_device_num` and `src_device_num` are device numbers that identify the source and destination devices. The device numbers should either be the value returned by `omp_get_initial_device()` or in the range $[0, \texttt{omp\_get\_num\_devices}() - 1]$.

The size of an element in the source and destination arrays is `element_size` bytes. The `volume`, `dst_offsets`, `src_offsets`, `src_dimensions`, and `dst_dimensions` are constant arrays of length `num_dims`.

The `volume` array specifies the length of each dimension for the sub-volume. The `src_dimensions` and `dst_dimensions` arrays specify the length of each dimension for the source and destination arrays, respectively. The sub-volume and the source and destination arrays are defined by their dimensions and the size of an element. The `src_offset` and `dst_offset` arrays specify a multi-dimension offset into the source and destination arrays, respectively.

The starting source device address is determined by the `src` device pointer variable and the `src_offset` array. The starting destination device address is determined by the `dst` device pointer variable and the `dst_offset` array.

The value of `num_dims` must be between 1 and an implementation-defined limit, which must be at least three. The `dst` and `src` pointers must be valid device pointers. The effect of this function is undefined if called from within a `target` region. This function returns zero if successful. Otherwise, it returns a non-zero value. If both `src` and `dst` are `NULL` pointers, the number of dimensions supported by the implementation for the specified device numbers is returned. This function contains a task scheduling point.

- ```
  int omp_target_associate_ptr(
      void *host_ptr,
      void *device_ptr,
      size_t size,
      size_t device_offset,
      int device_num) -
  ```

This function associates a host memory block of `size` bytes with a corresponding memory block in the address space of a device. The device number,
  ```

specified in `device_num`, should either be the value returned by `omp_get_-initial_device()`, or in the range $[0, \text{omp\_get\_num\_devices}() - 1]$. The corresponding device address is determined by adding the `dst_offset` to the value of `dst` pointer variable.

Once associated, the host address range is mapped to the corresponding address range in the device data environment of the `device_num` device. The corresponding address range has an infinite reference count. See Section 6.3.1 starting on page 263 for more details on mapped variables. The value of `device_ptr` must be a valid device address. See Section 6.3.3 starting on page 265 for more details on device addresses.

This function returns zero if successful. Otherwise, a non-zero value is returned. Upon return from the function, the value of the memory in the corresponding address range is undefined. Once associated, the behavior when accessing the corresponding address range from the host device via an `is_-device_ptr` clause or another device memory function is undefined until the association is removed by the `omp_target_disassociate()` function. A host address may correspond to only one device address on one device. Attempting to associate a host address to more than one device address results in a non-zero return value. The `omp_target_is_present()` function may be used to check if a host address is already associated with a device address. The effect of this function is undefined if called from within a `target` region.

- `int omp_target_disassociate_ptr(void ptr, int device_num)` - This function removes the association of a host memory block to a corresponding memory block in the address space of a device. The association would have been established by a previous call to the `omp_target_associate()` function. The device number should either be the value returned by `omp_-get_initial_device()` or in the range $[0, \text{omp\_get\_num\_devices}() - 1]$.

The host address is unmapped. The corresponding address range's reference count is set to zero and removed from the device data environment of the `device_num` device. See Section 6.3.1 starting on page 263 for more details on mapped variables. See Section 6.3.3 starting on page 265 for more details on device addresses.

The effect of this function is undefined if called from within a `target` region. If the host address in `ptr` does not have a corresponding device address associated with it by a previous call to `omp_target_associate_ptr()`, then the behavior of this function is undefined. Upon return from the function, the value of the memory in the corresponding address range is undefined.

2.3.5 Usage Examples of the New Runtime Functions

Now that all new runtime functions are covered, it is time to show some examples in what way these functions may be used.

The first example demonstrates how to query and change the loop schedule, as set through the `runtime` clause. In the next example, the nested parallelism code fragment listed in Figure 1.17 on page 25, is revisited. The relevant runtime functions are used to define a global thread ID. The third example illustrates how to get information on the thread affinity policy (or policies) that are in place.

Examples that use the device memory functions can be found in Section 6.12, starting on page 323. Examples using other heterogeneous runtime functions are shown in Section 6.5, starting on page 275.

Change the Loop Schedule Type at Runtime The `runtime` clause provides flexibility to select an appropriate schedule to distribute the work over the threads. There was one main issue with the original design, though. Recall that the schedule, as set by environment variable `OMP_SCHEDULE`, applied to *all* loops with this clause.

The new runtime functions provide greater flexibility and allow the application to customize the schedule to match the requirements on a per-loop basis. This is illustrated in the following example, which is an extended version of the code given in [2].

The function listed in Figure 2.22 uses the runtime function `omp_get_schedule()` to query the settings. At line 9, this function is called and the information is printed at lines 11 − 15. In case a known value for the schedule type is returned, one of the four regular names is printed. Otherwise, "`implementation-defined`" is printed.

The runtime function also returns a value in the second argument, `schedule_-modifier`. If the schedule type is `static`, `dynamic`, or `guided`, this variable contains the chunk size. It is undefined for schedule type `auto`, and implementation-dependent in case an implementation-specific schedule is used.

```
1 void print_schedule_info(char *comment)
2 {
3   char *alt_schedule = "implementation-defined";
4   char *schedules[4] = {"static","dynamic","guided","auto"};
5
6   omp_sched_t schedule_kind;
7   int         schedule_modifier;
8
9   (void) omp_get_schedule(&schedule_kind, &schedule_modifier);
10
11  printf("Schedule details %s:\n", comment);
12  printf(" schedule kind  = %d\n", schedule_kind);
13  printf(" schedule type  = %s\n",
14    schedule_kind <= 4 ? schedules[schedule_kind-1]:alt_schedule);
15  printf(" schedule modifier = %d\n", schedule_modifier);
16 }
```

Figure 2.22: **A function to verify the loop schedule** – This function queries the current loop schedule and prints the information.

In Figure 2.23, this function is called twice. At line 1, the current settings for the schedule and chunk size are printed. These are applied to the parallel loop spanning lines $3 - 9$.

At line 11, the runtime function `omp_set_schedule()` is called. The first argument is the OpenMP variable `omp_sched_static`. This changes the schedule to **static**, regardless of the previous setting. Any value less than 1 for the second argument, enforces the default settings for the chunk size to be used. In this call, a value of zero is used to achieve this. The new settings are printed by the function call at line 13. This is what is used for the parallel loop at lines $15 - 21$.

The example code has been executed using 3 threads and a loop length of 7. The initial schedule is defined through environment variable OMP_SCHEDULE and set to "dynamic,2". The full results are given in Figure 2.24.

The output confirms that the initial schedule type is **dynamic**, with a chunk size of 2. The assignment of iterations to threads for this first loop is just a snapshot. It can be expected that the results vary from run to run.

The results for the second loop demonstrate that the **static** schedule has indeed been used. Thread 0 executes the first 3 iterations. The remaining 4 iterations are

```
1 (void) print_schedule_info("loop 1");
2
3 #pragma omp parallel for default(none) schedule(runtime)\
4                       shared(n)
5   for (int i=0; i<n; i++)
6   { printf("Iteration %d executed by thread %d\n",
7          i, omp_get_thread_num());
8   for (int j=0; j<i; j++) system("sleep 1");
9 } // End of parallel for
10
11 (void) omp_set_schedule(omp_sched_static, 0);
12
13 (void) print_schedule_info("loop 2");
14
15 #pragma omp parallel for default(none) schedule(runtime)\
16                       shared(n)
17   for (int i=0; i<n; i++)
18   { printf("Iteration %d executed by thread %d\n",
19          i, omp_get_thread_num());
20   for (int j=0; j<i; j++) system("sleep 1");
21 } // End of parallel for
```

Figure 2.23: **Example how to change the loop schedule** – This code fragment prints and changes the loop schedule.

distributed equally over the other 2 threads and are in consecutive order. These results are reproducible.

Nested Parallelism Revisited   The new functions for nested parallelism provide a convenient way to query the environment. In this example, they are used to more easily construct a unique *global* thread ID.

Recall the example given in Figure 1.18 on page 26. Because the threads in each team start with thread ID 0 and are numbered consecutively, the value returned by function omp_get_thread_num() cannot be used to distinguish threads between different teams. Usually this is not an issue, but what if one would like to have a thread ID that is unique at a certain nesting level, or even across all nesting levels?

```
Schedule details loop 1:
 schedule type    = 2
 schedule type    = dynamic
 schedule modifier = 2
Iteration 0 executed by thread 2
Iteration 1 executed by thread 2
Iteration 2 executed by thread 0
Iteration 4 executed by thread 1
Iteration 6 executed by thread 2
Iteration 3 executed by thread 0
Iteration 5 executed by thread 1
Schedule details loop 2:
 schedule type    = 1
 schedule type    = static
 schedule modifier = 0
Iteration 5 executed by thread 2
Iteration 3 executed by thread 1
Iteration 0 executed by thread 0
Iteration 1 executed by thread 0
Iteration 2 executed by thread 0
Iteration 4 executed by thread 1
Iteration 6 executed by thread 2
```

Figure 2.24: **Example results from the program to query and set the loop schedule** – The loop length is set to 7, and 3 threads are used. Environment variable OMP_SCHEDULE is initialized to "dynamic,2".

The following formulas may be used to construct a unique thread ID when the team size is *constant* at a specific nesting level. It can be different across nesting levels, though. Without this restriction the formulas do not apply and one must dynamically scan the tree representing the nesting structure in order to compute a unique thread ID. This is far beyond the scope of this example and is left as an exercise for the reader.

In the remainder, the thread ID at a specific nesting level is referred to as the *Level Thread ID*, or L_{TID} for short. This identifier is unique at each nesting level, but not across the levels. The thread ID that is unique across all nesting levels and thread teams is denoted by G_{TID} (*Global Thread ID*).

These are the formulas for L_{TID} and G_{TID}:

$$L_{TID} = T_{TID} + O_L(L) = T_{TID} + \sum_{k=1}^{L-1}\{AT_{L-k}\prod_{j=1}^{k}TS_{L-j+1}\} \qquad (2.1)$$

$$G_{TID} = L_{TID} + O_G(L) = L_{TID} + \sum_{k=1}^{L-1}\prod_{j=1}^{k}TS_j \qquad (2.2)$$

In formulas 2.1 and 2.2:

- L denotes the nesting level of the parallel region.

- T_{TID} is the team-level thread ID as returned by `omp_get_thread_num()`.

- $O_L(L)$ is the offset added to the team thread ID. Note that $O_L(1) = 0$, as one would expect.

- $O_G(L)$ is the global offset added to L_{TID}, the thread ID unique across one nesting level. Because $O_G(1) = 0$, the values for L_{TID} and G_{TID} are the same at level $L = 1$.

- TS_{level} is the value returned by `omp_get_team_size(level)`.

- AT_{level} is the value returned by `omp_get_ancestor_thread_num(level)`.

As an example, these formulas are applied to the nested parallelism example shown in Figure 1.18 on page 26. There, the team size for the second-level parallel region is 2 for each team. Because this is the second level, $L = 2$ and therefore $k = 1$. To compute the L_{TID} and G_{TID} values for the rightmost thread at this second level, these values are substituted in the formulas to get the following result:

$$L_{TID} = T_{TID} + AT_1 * TS_2 = 1 + 2 * 2 = 5$$

$$G_{TID} = 5 + TS_1 = 5 + 3 = 8$$

The C source function listed in Figure 2.25 returns the offset $O_L(L)$ at the current nesting level L as defined in Formula 2.1. This value can be added to the local thread ID T_{TID} to obtain the G_{TID} for the local thread.

```
1 int level_offset(int *G_offset)
2 {
3   int team_size_prod;
4   int global_prod;
5
6   int level_offset  = 0;
7   int global_offset = 0;
8   int cur_level     = omp_get_level();
9
10   for (int k=1; k<cur_level; k++)
11   {
12     team_size_prod = 1;
13     global_prod    = 1;
14     for (int j=1; j<=k; j++)
15     {
16       team_size_prod *= omp_get_team_size(cur_level-j+1);
17       global_prod    *= omp_get_team_size(j);
18     }
19     team_size_prod *= omp_get_ancestor_thread_num(cur_level-k);
20
21     level_offset  += team_size_prod;
22     global_offset += global_prod;
23   } // End of loop over k
24
25   *G_offset = global_offset;
26
27   return(level_offset);
28 }
```

Figure 2.25: **Function to compute the offsets to the level and global thread ID** – This is a very straightforward implementation to compute the offsets that may be used to compute the L_{TID} and G_{TID} values as given in formulas 2.1 and 2.2. It is assumed that the team is constant within one nesting level. It may be different across nesting levels, though.

The function also computes the offset that can be added to the L_{TID} to obtain the unique G_{TID}. This offset is returned through the argument pointer G_offset.

The computations are deliberately implemented in a very straightforward way, which may not be the most efficient way to do this, but hopefully makes things easier to understand.

At line 8, the current nesting level L is obtained. The for-loop spanning lines $10-23$ computes the sum of the various products. The products of the team sizes are computed at lines $12-18$. At line 19, this result is then multiplied with the appropriate thread ID of the ancestor thread. At lines $21-22$, the total sums for the level and global offsets are updated with their respective contributions.

With this function to compute the two offsets to the team thread ID, it is very easy to obtain the L_{TID} and G_{TID} values. The code given in Figure 1.17 on page 26 has been augmented to get these values. The relevant part of the new source code is shown in Figure 2.26.

A five column header is printed at lines $1-2$. The key lines here are $10-11$ and $22-23$. This is where the offsets are computed and added to variable T_tid, the team level thread ID, and L_tid. The three thread ID values, plus the current level and team size for the respective levels, are printed at lines $13-14$ and $25-26$.

Sample output is shown in Figure 2.27. At the first level, the values for the L_{TID} and G_{TID} are indeed the same. At the second level, there are $3x2 = 6$ threads. Although printed in arbitrary order, it is not difficult to see that each thread at the second level has a L_{TID} level ID in the $[0\ldots5]$ range. The $3+6 = 9$ global G_{TID} values are unique across both regions and in the $[0\ldots8]$ range.

Verify Thread Binding With the support for cc-NUMA, first introduced in OpenMP 4.0, one can now optimize data access for memory locality by informing the runtime system where threads should run. This is extensively covered in Chapter 4, starting on page 151. Here it is shown how to use some of the affinity-related runtime functions to verify that the settings are as intended. The same two nested parallel regions from Figure 2.26 are used, but this time the goal is to control and verify in which way the OpenMP threads are distributed across the system. In the example code in Figure 2.28, the runtime setting at each nesting level is verified. This includes the policy in place for the top-level master region.

At line 1, a variable of type omp_proc_bind_t is declared. It is used to store the return value of function omp_get_proc_bind. Character array binding_choices is declared and initialized at lines $2-3$. It is used to map the binding type to a descriptive name.

After printing a header at line 5, the binding information for the first-level parallel region is printed at lines $8-10$. Keep in mind that the value returned for the

```
1 printf("%7s %7s %9s %7s %7s\n",
2         "T_TID", "Level", "Team Size", "L_TID", "G_TID");
3
4 #pragma omp parallel num_threads(3)
5 {
6   int global_offset;
7   int cur_level     = omp_get_level();
8   int cur_team_size = omp_get_team_size(cur_level);
9   int T_tid         = omp_get_thread_num();
10  int L_tid         = T_tid + level_offset(&global_offset);
11  int G_tid         = L_tid + global_offset;
12
13  printf("%7d %7d %9d %7d %7d\n", T_tid, cur_level,
14                                  cur_team_size, L_tid, G_tid);
15
16  #pragma omp parallel num_threads(2)
17  {
18    int global_offset;
19    int cur_level     = omp_get_level();
20    int cur_team_size = omp_get_team_size(cur_level);
21    int T_tid         = omp_get_thread_num();
22    int L_tid         = T_tid + level_offset(&global_offset);
23    int G_tid         = L_tid + global_offset;
24
25    printf("%7d %7d %9d %7d %7d\n", T_tid, cur_level,
26                                    cur_team_size, L_tid, G_tid);
27
28  }   // End of nesting level 2
29 }   // End of nesting level 1
```

Figure 2.26: **Nested parallelism example revisited** – The function shown in Figure 2.25 is used to compute and print the level thread ID L_{TID} and global ID G_{TID} at both parallel nesting levels. The team thread ID, nesting level, and team size are printed as well.

affinity policy is for the *next* nesting level. This means the value returned in array element binding_choices[binding_setting] is the affinity policy for the upcoming parallel region, *not* the current one.

T_TID	Level	Team Size	L_TID	G_TID
2	1	3	2	2
1	1	3	1	1
0	1	3	0	0
0	2	2	0	3
1	2	2	1	4
0	2	2	4	7
1	2	2	5	8
0	2	2	2	5
1	2	2	3	6

Figure 2.27: **Results for the revisited nested parallelism example** – The G_{TID} value at the first nesting level is indeed the same as the local L_{TID} value. At the second level, there are 6 threads and each thread has a unique ID in the $[0 \ldots 5]$ range.

This is repeated for the two parallel regions spanning lines $12 - 31$. In both cases, a `single` region is used to print the binding only once per parallel region. Because it is the same for all threads in the same team, printing this for all threads is not very meaningful.

Thread placement is achieved by setting environment variables OMP_PLACES and OMP_PROC_BIND. In practice, both must be set, but for the purpose of this example, only OMP_PROC_BIND must be defined. It is set to the following list: `"spread,close,master"`.[2]

The output is given in Figure 2.29 and confirms the outer level threads are spread across the system. The first printed line shows that execution is at level 0, and the next parallel region has the **spread** affinity policy. Likewise, the threads at each second-level parallel region are requested to be scheduled close to each other.

The last three lines are from the three innermost parallel regions and confirm that a subsequent parallel region has the **master** affinity policy. In this case, there is no such third-level region, though.

If there are deeper runtime nesting levels than specified through environment variable OMP_PROC_BIND, the remaining levels inherit the settings from the last level specified. For example, if this variable was set to `"spread"` only, the thread teams have affinity type "spread" at all nesting levels.

---

[2]For a definition of these keywords, refer to Section 4.6, starting on page 168.

```
 1 omp_proc_bind_t binding_setting;
 2 char           *binding_choices[5] = \
 3                    {"false", "true", "master", "close", "spread"};
 4
 5 printf("%13s %25s\n\n","Current Level","Binding Type/Level");
 6
 7 binding_setting = omp_get_proc_bind();
 8 printf("%7d %23s/%-3d\n",omp_get_level(),
 9                            binding_choices[binding_setting],
10                            omp_get_level()+1);
11
12 #pragma omp parallel num_threads(3)
13 {
14  #pragma omp single
15  { omp_proc_bind_t binding_setting = omp_get_proc_bind();
16    printf("%7d %23s/%-3d\n",omp_get_level(),
17                               binding_choices[binding_setting],
18                               omp_get_level()+1);
19  } // End of single region
20
21  #pragma omp parallel num_threads(2)
22  {
23     #pragma omp single
24     { omp_proc_bind_t binding_setting = omp_get_proc_bind();
25       printf("%7d %23s/%-3d\n",omp_get_level(),
26                                  binding_choices[binding_setting],
27                                  omp_get_level()+1);
28     } // End of single region
29
30  } // End of nesting level 2
31 } // End of nesting level 1
```

Figure 2.28: **Example to verify the thread affinity settings** – There is one master region with two nested parallel regions. At each level, the upcoming thread affinity setting, as defined by environment variable OMP_PROC_BIND, is verified.

Current Level	Binding Type/Level
0	spread/1
1	close/2
2	master/3
2	master/3
2	master/3

Figure 2.29: **Output from the code shown in Figure 2.28** – Prior to executing the program, environment variable OMP_PROC_BIND is set to "spread,close,master". The output confirms these settings. Note that the "master" policy applies to a possible third-level parallel region, but this example has two levels only.

2.4   New Functionality

Compared to OpenMP 2.5, OpenMP 4.5 has significant new functionality. In this section, those new features that have a relatively small impact on the programming model and are often implemented as an extension to already existing functionality are presented and discussed.

In subsequent chapters, the new concepts and features that introduce entirely new concepts in OpenMP are covered extensively.

2.4.1   Changed Ownership of Locks

The ownership of locks has changed. Although this is not new functionality, it is important enough to mention. Whereas the ownership of a lock was tied to threads in OpenMP 2.5, as of OpenMP 3.0, locks are owned by task regions.

In many cases, this should not have any consequences, but in the example in Figure 2.30, there is a difference.

The lock variable my_lock is declared, initialized and acquired at lines $1-4$. This code is executed by the master thread and because it executes the omp_set_lock() function, it owns the lock.

Within the parallel region spanning lines $6-15$, the release of the lock at line 11 is guaranteed to be performed by the master thread again.

The task region where the lock is released is not same task region where it was acquired. Although this was allowed in OpenMP 2.5, this is no longer OpenMP compliant code as of version 3.0.

```
1   omp_lock_t my_lock;
2
3   (void) omp_init_lock (&my_lock);
4   (void) omp_set_lock  (&my_lock);
5
6   #pragma omp parallel
7   {
8       #pragma omp master
9       {
10              ......
11          (void) omp_unset_lock (&my_lock);
12              ......
13      } // End of master region
14      ......
15  } // End of parallel region
16
17  (void) omp_destroy_lock (&my_lock);
```

Figure 2.30: **Non-conforming use of locks** – The master thread sets the lock and therefore owns it. In OpenMP 2.5 it was permitted to have the master thread release the lock within the parallel region. This is however no longer allowed, because these two actions occur in different task regions.

Although one may, of course, write code like this, a better and cleaner approach is shown in Figure 2.31. There are two different task regions again, and the lock is accessed in both, but this program is OpenMP-compliant. The reason is that the lock is acquired (line 10) and released (line 12) in the same task region.

2.4.2   Cancellation

There are two reasons for a parallel region to terminate prematurely. An error may have occurred, for example a memory allocation that fails, and the thread(s) can no longer continue execution. It doesn't always have to be a fatal situation however. There may be a good reason the threads no longer need to continue. An example is a parallel search. Once the target element has been found, all threads can stop searching.

Prior to OpenMP 4.0, it was impossible to end the execution of an individual parallel region or, in general, any OpenMP construct within a parallel region. This

```
1  omp_lock_t my_lock;
2
3  (void) omp_init_lock (&my_lock);
4
5  #pragma omp parallel
6  {
7     #pragma omp master
8     {
9              ......
10          (void) omp_set_lock (&my_lock);
11             .....
12          (void) omp_unset_lock (&my_lock);
13    } // End of master region
14  } // End of parallel region
15
16  (void) omp_destroy_lock (&my_lock);
```

Figure 2.31: **Conforming use of locks** – This program is OpenMP-compliant, because the lock is initialized and released in the same task region.

implied that every OpenMP region either had to be executed to the very end, or not started at all.

Other than to abort program execution, the only alternative was for the application to detect a certain situation and if needed, take action after the parallel region finished. With the introduction of the *cancellation constructs* in OpenMP 4.0, an elegant way to terminate the execution of an OpenMP region is supported. Aside from gracefully handling certain types of errors, this feature is useful for specific parallel methods with a dynamic behavior, such as divide-and-conquer algorithms.

Cancellation is supported on the **parallel** construct, as well as the **sections** and **for** (do in Fortran) worksharing constructs. When using tasks, the **taskgroup** construct may be used for cancellation.

The syntax of the **cancel** and **cancellation point** constructs in C/C++ and Fortran is shown in Figure 2.32. Both constructs are stand-alone directives. They trigger an action if, or when, encountered at runtime. The idea is similar to exception handling, supported in some programming languages. A thread that wishes to terminate execution, needs to have the **cancel** directive in its execution path. This is most likely under control of an if-statement. The effect of the **cancel** direc-

```
#pragma omp cancel construct-type-clause[[,]if-clause] new-line
!$omp cancel construct-type-clause[[,]if-clause]
```
```
#pragma omp cancellation point construct-type-clause new-line
!$omp cancellation point construct-type-clause
```

Figure 2.32: **Syntax of the cancellation construct in C/C++ and Fortran** – The `cancel` directive requests the termination of the corresponding construct. For the other threads, this takes effect at the next cancellation point.

tive is to raise a flag to signal that cancellation has occurred. The `cancellation point` directive defines a point where the encountering thread checks the status of cancellation.

This is not the only place though. The request for cancellation is checked at the following *cancellation points*:

- A `cancel` region.

- A `cancellation point` region.

- A `barrier` region.

- An implicit barrier region.

Cancellation is controlled through environment variable `OMP_CANCELLATION`, described in Section 2.2. This variable needs to be explicitly set to `true` to enable cancellation. To reduce the runtime overhead, it is *disabled* by default. If a `cancel`, or `cancellation point`, directive is encountered, while this feature is not enabled, the constructs have no effect.

When a thread raises the cancellation flag, the event is not detected by another thread, until it has encountered one of the cancellation points listed above. As a consequence, cancellation may not take effect immediately.

This is illustrated in Figure 2.33, where time flows from top to bottom. A team of five threads executes an "enclosing construct." This is one of the constructs `parallel`, `for` (or `do`), `sections`, or `taskgroup` that supports cancellation. Events 1 to 6 are assumed to happen in the order depicted by their position on the timeline.

At event 1, thread three encounters a `cancellation point` directive. At this point, cancellation has not yet been requested. The `cancellation point` has no effect and this thread continues to execute the enclosing construct.

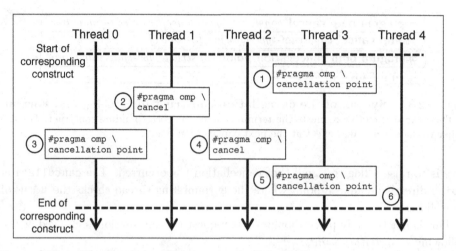

Figure 2.33: **Illustration of the cancellation feature** – In this diagram, time flows from top to bottom. Once cancellation is requested, threads only respond at the next cancellation point encountered at runtime.

Thread one encounters a `cancel` directive at event 2, and execution of the enclosing construct is cancelled. This raises a flag to indicate that cancellation has been requested. At the implied barrier or synchronization point at the end of the enclosing construct, thread one waits for all other threads to either complete execution of the enclosing construct, or be cancelled.

At event 3, thread zero encounters a `cancellation point` directive. Because the cancellation flag has already been set, it immediately cancels the execution of the enclosing construct. Again, the thread waits at the implied barrier, or synchronization point at the end of the enclosing construct, for all other threads, and then continues execution after the enclosing construct.[3]

Thread two encounters a `cancel` directive at event 4. Cancellation has already been requested and this thread immediately cancels execution of the enclosing construct. Thread three encounters a second `cancellation point` directive at event 5. This time (as opposed to event 1), cancellation is already requested and the thread cancels the execution of the enclosing construct.

---

[3]If the flag is set, the OpenMP runtime function `omp_get_cancellation()` returns the value `true`.

Thread four never encounters any cancellation points and completes execution of the construct.

To ensure timely cancellation, the user must insert `cancellation point` directives at suitable locations throughout the code, which is illustrated in the example in Figure 2.34.

Where exactly does a thread continue execution after the enclosing construct has been cancelled? This depends on the type of construct that is specified as a clause on the `cancel` directive. The clause can be any of these types:

- `parallel` - The thread cancels the current execution and the master thread continues after the implicit barrier at the end of the `parallel` construct. All tasks created in the parallel region are cancelled. In the case of a nested parallel region, cancellation only applies to the innermost parallel region.

- `for` (or do in Fortran), or `sections` - The thread cancels the current execution and jumps to the implicit barrier at the end of the worksharing construct. Task cancellation does not occur. If a `reduction` or `lastprivate` clause is specified on a worksharing construct and cancellation has occurred, the value of the corresponding variables are undefined.

  There are two restrictions. The worksharing loop construct (`for`, or do) may not contain an `ordered` construct. The `nowait` clause is not allowed on the worksharing constructs supported with cancellation.

- `taskgroup` - The task encountering the `cancel` directive sets the flag for the entire `taskgroup` region, but it continues execution to its end and then continues execution after the `task` region. The same holds for all tasks of the `taskgroup` that have already started execution. All other tasks belonging to the `taskgroup` are cancelled. If a task belongs to multiple (nested) `taskgroup` regions, and encounters a `cancellation point` construct, it checks if cancellation is requested in any `taskgroup` region it belongs to, and responds accordingly.

The use of the `cancel` and `cancellation point` directives is illustrated in Figure 2.34. This code fragment contains a nested parallel region. The outer parallel region spans lines $1 - 18$, and the inner parallel region spans lines $4 - 17$.

When a thread encounters the `cancel` construct at line 11, cancellation is requested for the innermost parallel region. If and when the condition at line 9

```
1 #pragma omp parallel
2 {
3    // Do some work
4    #pragma omp parallel
5    {
6      for (int i = 0; i < N; i++)
7      {
8        // Do some work
9        if ( <some_condition> )
10       {
11           #pragma omp cancel parallel
12       }
13       // Do some more work
14       #pragma omp cancellation point
15       // Do even more work
16     }
17   } // End of inner parallel region
18 } // End of outer parallel region
```

Figure 2.34: **Cancellation of a parallel region** – Execution of the innermost parallel region is cancelled by the thread executing the cancel construct at line 11. Depending on where they are when this happens, the other threads either also cancel their work, or complete execution.

evaluates to **true**, the thread encountering the **cancel** construct terminates execution. At line 11, it is specified that the parallel region is affected. As a result, all remaining work is skipped and the thread waits in the implied barrier at the end of the inner parallel region (line 17). Those other threads that encounter the **cancellation point** at line 14, cancel the execution of the parallel region, and wait in the barrier. It a thread encounters line 14 before cancellation has been requested, the **cancellation point** has no effect. In case a thread is already past the cancellation point, it continues to execute and also waits in the barrier.

The execution of the outer parallel region is not affected by the cancellation. There is no support in OpenMP to request cancellation for an outer parallel region, or for both regions. If needed, the user needs to implement this manually.

Figure 2.35 illustrates the use of the **cancel** construct in a recursive algorithm employing tasks. Tasks are covered in great detail in Chapter 3, starting on page 103.

In this example, a binary tree, called `t`, is searched for the element `e`. Variable `present` is used to mark the termination of the search. Assuming it is initialized to `false`, it is changed to `true`, once the element has been found.

The search is parallelized using tasks that recursively process the left and right subtree of each element.[4]

The tasks are embedded in a `taskgroup` construct (line 7), because that is the granularity for cancellation with tasks. The `taskgroup` is embedded into a `master` construct to ensure that one thread only initiates the parallel search. Instead of `master`, a `single` construct has the same effect.

When the element is found (line 17), cancellation of the `taskgroup` is requested (line 19). Because the task executes to its end, the assignment to `present` may happen either after the `cancel` construct, or before. In this particular example, there is no need to use explicit `cancellation point` directives, because the generation of new tasks is terminated as soon as cancellation has been requested. All previously created, but not yet started, tasks are also terminated then.

If the element is not found, the initial value of variable `present` does not change. The algorithm terminates, because the recursion of `search` ends at leaf nodes, because then `t->left` and `t->right` are `NULL` and the `if` conditions (lines 22 and 27) evaluate to false.

2.4.3 User-Defined Reduction

Until OpenMP 4.0, there was no support to provide an application-specific reduction operation in case the standard reductions were not sufficient. Although one can always implement a reduction explicitly, this is not desirable. Through a feature called *User-Defined Reduction* (UDR) , a user has the option of defining a customized reduction operation and using it in a `reduction` clause to leverage the ease of use that OpenMP provides for such operations.

Recurrence calculations, such as the one shown in Figure 2.36, are common in scientific and engineering programs, but are also encountered in other disciplines. Recall from [2] that the `reduction` clause is provided to parallelize recurrence operations without the need for code modifications.

---

[4]A detailed example of a recursive algorithm parallelized with tasks can be found in Section 3.3, starting at line 118.

```
 1 void search_parallel(btree *t, element e, bool* present)
 2 {
 3   #pragma omp parallel
 4   {
 5     #pragma omp master
 6     {
 7       #pragma omp taskgroup
 8       {
 9         search(t, e, present);
10       }
11     } // End omp master
12   } // End omp parallel
13 }
14
15 void search(btree* t, element e, bool* present)
16 {
17   if (t->element == e)
18   {
19     #pragma omp cancel taskgroup
20     *present = true;
21   }
22   if (t->left)
23   {
24     #pragma omp task
25       {search(t->left, e, present);}
26   }
27   if (t->right)
28   {
29     #pragma omp task
30       {search(t->right, e, present);}
31   }
32 }
```

Figure 2.35: **Cancellation of a taskgroup in a recursive algorithm** – The binary tree is searched for element e and the parallel descent is cancelled if this element is found.

```
1 int sum = 0;
2 int *a, *b;  // Assume allocation and initialization occurred
3
4 #pragma omp parallel for default(none) firstprivate(n)\
5              shared(a,b) reduction(+:sum)
6 for (int i=0; i<n; i++)
7   sum += a[i] * b[i];
```

Figure 2.36: **Example of a recurrence calculation** – The reduction clause is used to parallelize the loop. Both the operation (+) and result variable (sum) are specified as part of the clause.

The reduction operator(s) and variable(s) are specified in the reduction clause. By definition, the result variable, like sum in this case, is shared in the enclosing OpenMP region.

This operation is implemented as follows: The thread performs the addition operation on a subset of the data. It uses a local, or private, variable to store the partial result. After completion of the operation, a thread updates the global result with its contribution. To avoid a data race, this update is protected through a lock.

The private copy of the reduction variable must be initialized with a value that is mathematically consistent with the reduction operation. The reduction operation must also be mathematically associative and commutative. This is because the order in which threads combine their value to construct the value for the shared result variable is non-deterministic.

A side effect of this is that floating-point results may vary (slightly) from run to run, and/or depend on the number of threads used. This is a numerical effect caused by round-off differences introduced when combining the result. It has nothing to do with the reduction operation as such, but could be a reason for numerical results to be somewhat different.

Figure 2.37 gives an overview of the pre-defined reduction operators supported in OpenMP. In this table, the second column lists the initialization value for the private instance of the reduction variable. This is the neutral element for the specific reduction operation. The third column is labeled "Combiner" and defines the arithmetic operation that needs to be performed to produce the result.

Variables omp_priv, omp_in, and omp_out used in this table are also needed in case of a UDR. This is discussed in more detail below.

Operator	Initializer	Combiner
+	omp_priv = 0	omp_out += omp_in
*	omp_priv = 1	omp_out *= omp_in
-	omp_priv = 0	omp_out += omp_in
&	omp_priv = ~0	omp_out &= omp_in
|	omp_priv = 0	omp_out |= omp_in
^	omp_priv = 0	omp_out ^= omp_in
&&	omp_priv = 1	omp_out = omp_in && omp_out
||	omp_priv = 0	omp_out = omp_in || omp_out
max	omp_priv = $Least(T)$	omp_out = omp_in > omp_out ? omp_in : omp_out
min	omp_priv = $Largest(T)$	omp_out = omp_in < omp_out ? omp_in : omp_out
+	omp_priv = 0	omp_out = omp_in + omp_out
*	omp_priv = 1	omp_out = omp_in * omp_out
-	omp_priv = 0	omp_out = omp_in + omp_out
.and.	omp_priv = .true.	omp_out = omp_in .and. omp_out
.or.	omp_priv = .false.	omp_out = omp_in .or. omp_out
.eqv.	omp_priv = .true.	omp_out = omp_in .eqv. omp_out
.neqv.	omp_priv = .false.	omp_out = omp_in .neqv. omp_out
max	omp_priv = $Least(T)$	omp_out = max(omp_in, omp_out)
min	omp_priv = $Largest(T)$	omp_out = min(omp_in, omp_out)
iand	omp_priv = not(0)	omp_out = iand(omp_in, omp_out)
ior	omp_priv = 0	omp_out = ior(omp_in, omp_out)
ieor	omp_priv = 0	omp_out = ieor(omp_in, omp_out)

Figure 2.37: **The pre-defined reduction operators supported by the reduction clause in C/C++ and Fortran** – The upper half of the table is for C/C++. The lower half of the table is for Fortran. This table lists the pre-defined reduction operators, along with their associated initializer and combiner expressions. Least(T) and Largest(T) are the least and largest representable values of the arithmetic type T.

While the reduction clause provides significant convenience to the user, certain applications have their own reduction operation that is not supported by OpenMP. Examples of that include the merging of lists or sets, the computation of a standard deviation over a set of elements, etc. It is always possible to explicitly code a reduction, but this adds to the complexity of the code, and it may not perform optimally.

```
 1 int *a; // Assume allocation and initialization occurred
 2 int result = INT_MAX;
 3
 4 #pragma omp declare reduction(my_abs_min : int :\
 5   omp_out = abs(omp_in) < omp_out ? abs(omp_in) : abs(omp_out))\
 6   initializer (omp_priv = INT_MAX)
 7
 8 #pragma omp parallel for default(none) firstprivate(n)\
 9             shared(a) reduction(my_abs_min : result)
10 for (int i=0; i<n; i++) {
11    if (abs(a[i]) < result) {
12        result = abs(a[i]);
13    }
14 }
```

Figure 2.38: **Example of a User-Defined Reduction** – The definition of a UDR used in combination with the **reduction** clause to compute the minimum absolute value of the array elements in parallel.

This is why the UDR was introduced in OpenMP 4.0. A UDR is defined through the **declare reduction** directive and consists of the following three components:

- Identifier - A name, or symbol, that identifies the reduction and the type(s) to which it applies.

- Combiner - A recipe to generate a result. It is expressed as an operation involving the two symbolic variables **omp_in** and **omp_out**, thus defining the actual reduction operation as applied on any given two arguments.

- Initializer - This is used to define the initial value for the private instances of a reduction variable.

The **declare reduction** directive must be used to define a UDR. Before introducing the formal syntax, the example in Figure 2.38 is presented and discussed. In this code, a UDR is defined to compute the minimum of the absolute values of an array.

At lines $4 - 6$, the **declare reduction** directive defines the UDR called **my_-abs_min**. It returns a value of type **int**.

#pragma omp declare reduction*(reduction-identifier : typename-list : combiner) [initializer-clause] new-line*
!$omp declare reduction*(reduction-identifier : typename-list : combiner) [initializer-clause]*

Figure 2.39:   **Syntax of the declare reduction directive in C/C++ and Fortran** – This directive defines a user-defined reduction. The various components are explained in the text. Figure 2.40 contains an explanation of the terminology.

Name	Description
reduction-identifier	A C, C++, or Fortran identifier or one of the pre-defined OpenMP reduction operators.
typename-list	The list with data type(s) to be used.
combiner	An expression in C/C++. In Fortran, it is an assignment statement, or subroutine name, followed by an argument list.
initializer-clause	This is of the form `initializer`*(initializer-expr)* with *initializer-expr* being one of the following: omp_priv = *initializer* (C/C++) omp_priv = *function-name(argument-list)* (C/C++) omp_priv = *expression* (Fortran) omp_priv = *subroutine-name(argument-list)* (Fortran)

Figure 2.40:   **Terminology used with the declare reduction directive** – This table explains the various elements used to define a reduction.

The *combiner* is defined at line 5. Symbolic variable `omp_in` represents the variable used to store the partial result. This variable is private to each thread. Likewise, symbolic variable `omp_out` refers to the result of the combiner operation.

The expression at line 5 returns the absolute value of `omp_in` when it is less than the previous value of `omp_out`; otherwise, it returns the absolute value of the latter variable.

At line 6, another special variable, `omp_priv`, is set to the initial value each thread assigns to the local variable `omp_in`. In this case, it is `INT_MAX`, the largest integer value the system provides.

In this initialization expression, only special variables `omp_priv` and `omp_orig` are allowed. Although not used here, `omp_orig` represents the original value of the reduction variable. This variable is not allowed to be modified.

```
1 typedef std::vector< float > TVec;    // Assume some type here
2
3 #pragma omp declare reduction(+ : TVec : \
4        std::transform(omp_in.begin(),  omp_in.end(), \
5                       omp_out.begin(), omp_out.begin(), \
6                       std::plus< T >() ) ) \
7        initializer (omp_priv(omp_orig))
```

Figure 2.41: **Example of a User-Defined Reduction on C++ arrays** – The use of a UDR allows for the parallelization of the loop employing a C++ array type.

Now that the elements of the reduction operation are defined, it may be used in a regular `reduction` clause. This is shown at line 9, where the name `my_abs_min` is used in the clause.

The loop spanning lines $10 - 14$ does not need to be modified. At runtime, the reduction operation is executed the same way a pre-defined reduction is handled.

After this example, it is time to look at the more formal description. The syntax of the `declare reduction` directive is given in Figure 2.39. The terminology used is defined in Figure 2.40.

OpenMP defines the special variables `omp_orig`, `omp_priv`, `omp_in`, and `omp_out`. They are all of the same type and the only variables to be used when defining a UDR operation.

This might raise the question why the description of *typename-list* in Figure 2.40 shows that a list with multiple types is allowed. This is a convenience. It avoids the need to repeat the `declare reduction` directive for the data types to be supported. With a list, it is as if the definition is repeated for all the types in the list.

Neither the number of times the combiner is executed, nor the number of times and the order in which the initializer expression is evaluated, are implementation-defined. The results are undefined if a program makes any assumption about this.

Instead of the initializer expression, it is also possible to provide a function, or subroutine name in Fortran, with an argument list. In this case, one of the arguments must be the special variable `omp_priv`. For C++ programs, the `initializer` clause also accepts an expression that is not an assignment to `omp_priv`. This is demonstrated in Figure 2.41.

The code shown in Figure 2.41 implements a UDR called `+` to perform the reduction on arrays. The C++ data type `std::vector` represents the array, for which a

depend *(dependence-type: iteration-vector)*
depend *(dependence-type)*

Figure 2.42: **Syntax of the depend clause for the doacross loop in C/C++ and Fortran** – In the context of a `doacross` loop, this clause accepts two new keywords for the dependence-type. This can either be `sink`, followed by the iteration vector, or `source`, which does not have any further qualifiers. Refer to the main text for an explanation of these terms.

given type `T` is assumed. The code provides the `+` reduction operation for this data type. For the standard data types, the pre-defined reduction operation is used.

The combiner (lines $4 - 6$) makes use of the `std::transform` function. The initializer at line 7 specifies that every thread's private copy is constructed with the copy constructor, using the original reduction variable as the argument. The advantage is that by using this feature, the thread's private arrays in this example do not need to have a known size at compile time. Instead, the length is derived from the original list item.

2.4.4   The Doacross Loop

As of OpenMP 4.5, an additional type of parallel loop is supported. It is called the "doacross loop" [24].

A `doacross` loop has a loop-carried dependence. Such loops cannot be parallelized in a straightforward way, but through compiler transformations and/or additional synchronization, the code may be partially parallelized. It is important to note that these are *static* dependences. This technique cannot be used to handle runtime dependences.

In contrast with other newly introduced features, there is no specific construct to implement this functionality. Instead, it is supported through extensions on the `ordered` and `depend` clauses. The latter was introduced in OpenMP 4.0 for tasking. In OpenMP 4.5, the `depend` clause has been augmented to add functionality for tasks, but is also used to implement the `doacross` feature.

The two main new elements are called *sink* and *source*. The former takes an additional description, the *iteration vector*, to describe the dependences *relative* to the current loop variable. The syntax of this vector is $x_1 [\pm d_1], x_2 [\pm d_2], \ldots, x_n [\pm d_n]$. In this notation, x_i is the name of the loop variable of the i-th nested loop, d_i is

```
1 #pragma omp parallel default(none) shared(n,a,b,c)
2 {
3   #pragma omp for ordered(1)
4   for (int i=1; i<n; i++)
5   {
6      #pragma omp ordered depend(sink:i-1)
7          a[i] = a[i-1] + b[i];
8      #pragma omp ordered depend(source)
9
10         c[i] = 2*a[i];
11
12   } // End of for-loop
13 } // End of parallel region
```

Figure 2.43: **Code fragment using a doacross loop** – The doacross loop is defined through the combination of the **ordered** and **depend** clauses.

a *constant* non-negative integer, and n is the value as specified in the **ordered(n)** clause on the loop directive.

Before we continue, it is probably best to show an example first. The parallel region shown in Figure 2.43 contains a **doacross** loop to parallelize the update of vector **a**.

The computation of **a[i]** at line 7 has a data dependence, but it can be partially parallelized. Another thing to note is that the computation of **c[i]** at line 10 depends on the recently computed value **a[i]**. Due to this dependence, this loop cannot be fully parallelized, but there is reduced parallelism that may be exploited by using the support for **doacross** loops. The **doacross** loop is within the parallel region and spans line $3 - 12$.

The **ordered** clause at line 3 should look familiar. Until OpenMP 4.5, this enforced serial execution of the ordered code block defined within the loop. The clause has been extended to support a number between parentheses to indicate the loop is a **doacross** loop. The number, which is 1 in this case, indicates the depth of the parallelism. In general, this number specifies the number of perfectly nested loops constituting the **doacross** loop. For example, if there are three loops with dependences, this number must be 3.

The **ordered** directives at line 6 and 8 are mandatory. They define the dependence region. The **depend** clause at line 6 uses the one dimensional iteration vector to specify that there is a dependence of loop iteration **i** on **i-1** ($n = 1$, $x_1 = i$, the sign is negative, and $d_1 = 1$).

In general, *all* dependences in *all* dimensions must be specified on the **ordered** clause that has the **sink** keyword. If, for example, there are two loops and three dependences, there must be three **depend** clauses, and each clause must use an index vector with two components of the type $x_1 [\pm d_1], x_2 [\pm d_2]$, like **i-1,j+1**.

The **depend** clause with the **source** keyword at line 8 is mandatory and forces the runtime system to make the result **a[i]** available. This is to ensure the computation at line 10 uses the correct value for **a[i]**. If this clause is left omitted, the program deadlocks. The same is true if the dependences are not described correctly.

2.5 Concluding Remarks

In this chapter, a broad overview of where OpenMP stands today has been given. Many OpenMP 2.5 constructs have been enhanced, including the introduction of the **collapse** clause to better support nested loops, refinements on the **critical** construct, plus improved support for the **atomic** construct to support various types of updates.

But there is much more. Through the **doacross** construct, certain loops with dependences can now be parallelized. Another new feature is cancellation, to provide a more robust handling of errors during parallel execution. User-defined reductions allow the user to write application specific reductions.

In addition to all of this, major new functionality has been introduced. Tasking, affinity control, vectorization using SIMD instructions, and the support for heterogeneous architectures, all make OpenMP more suitable for a wider range of systems and applications. These four new features are so substantial that they deserve their own chapter. That is what the remainder of this book is about.

3 Tasking

Tasking was introduced in 2008 and provided a major addition to OpenMP 3.0 [1]. Thanks to this feature, algorithms with an irregular and runtime dependent execution flow may now be parallelized. Before tasking, this was not always possible, or was at least tedious and sometimes downright ugly.

A relatively simple example is a while-loop with independent chunks of work in the loop body. Although these chunks could be executed simultaneously, OpenMP did not provide the means to do so without changing the source code. In the best case, the loop could be manually transformed into a for-loop and then parallelized, but few users would like to do so.

Tasking provides an elegant solution to this problem. A queueing system dynamically handles the assignment of threads to the chunks of work that need to be performed. The threads pick up work from the queue until the queue is empty.

By design, the initial version of tasking was rather rudimentary. The idea was to decide on additional features through feedback from the users. That is indeed what has happened in subsequent releases of the specifications, and we are quite sure the current feature set is not final.

In this chapter, the tasking concepts, as well as all the features, are presented and discussed in detail. We start with a series of examples. Collectively they touch upon many of the features supported with tasking. In many cases, the features are only described briefly, but the follow-on sections after the examples go into much more detail.

3.1 Hello Task

Simply stated, an OpenMP *task* is a block of code contained in a parallel region that can be executed simultaneously with other tasks in the same region.[1]

Before we show the first example, more should be said about tasking in OpenMP. As with almost every feature in OpenMP, a task is part of a parallel region. Depending on the specific situation, this could pose a challenge. Without special precautions, the same task(s) may be executed by different threads. This is very different from the worksharing constructs, where it is well-defined how the work is distributed over the threads. As we shall see shortly, tasks are much more dynamic, and the same approach cannot be applied.

---

[1]This is a simplification. Subsequent sections contain the more formal coverage and definitions.

It may be needed that each thread executes all tasks, but it is more likely that different threads must execute different tasks. The problem is that, unlike a work-sharing construct, the work to be performed is not known upfront. This is why something special needs to be done.

The solution chosen by the OpenMP language committee makes sense, but at first glance may not seem intuitive. To guarantee each task is generated only once, the tasks could be embedded in a `single`, or `master` construct. There is a potential problem with the latter though, which is discussed in Section 3.1.3.

This is already a novel use of these constructs, but the thing that tends to confuse users new to tasking in OpenMP most, is that the tasks are not necessarily executed where they are defined in the source code. Tasks are *guaranteed* to be executed only at special and well-defined points in the code. Such points are implied with some constructs, but they are also under explicit control of the user.

The idea behind this approach is that one thread generates the tasks, while the other threads execute them as they become available. Eventually the generating thread may participate in the execution part, after it has completed generating the tasks. How this works is best illustrated with the example that follows next.

3.1.1 Parallelizing a Palindrome

Consider the following problem. We want to write a program that either prints `"race car "`, or `"car race "`, with no preference for either phrase.[2] At runtime, there is an equal chance of seeing either one of these phrases on the screen.

This could easily be solved using parallel sections, but let's assume these are not available. Instead, we like to use the concept of a task, briefly introduced above. The code fragment using tasks is shown in Figure 3.1.

The parallel region spans lines $1 - 10$ and has one single region only. This would not make any sense if it were not for the new task directives shown here. Each `#pragma omp task` directive defines a task. The code enclosed in the curly braces ({ and }) defines the task. The assumption is that tasks can execute independently. It is the responsibility of the user to ensure this produces correct results.

There are two tasks. One prints `"race "` and the other prints `"car "`. The order in which the tasks are executed is non-deterministic and most likely varies from run to run. For a correct parallel program, this should not affect the result. Note the trailing space in both print statements.

---

[2]Yes, the trailing space in the output matters here.

```
 1 #pragma omp parallel
 2 {
 3   #pragma omp single
 4   {
 5     #pragma omp task
 6       {printf("race ");} // Task #1
 7     #pragma omp task
 8       {printf("car ");}  // Task #2
 9   } // End of single region
10 } // End of parallel region
```

Figure 3.1: **Code fragment with two tasks** – There are two tasks. One prints the word "race ". The other one prints "car ". The order in which tasks are executed is runtime dependent and may vary across multiple runs.

How about this single region then? Here is how this code is executed. Assume there are two threads. One thread encounters the **single** construct and starts executing the code block. Both tasks are generated, but not yet executed. Meanwhile, the other thread falls through and waits in the implied barrier at the end of the **single** construct.

In the case of tasks, idle threads do not really wait in the barrier though. Instead, these threads are available to execute the tasks, as they are generated.

In this simple case, that means one thread generates the two tasks consisting of a single print statement. Any available thread executes the tasks, but not until it has reached the barrier. The executing thread(s) print **"race "** and **"car "**, but not necessarily in this order.

The thread generating the tasks also ends up in the barrier, once it has completed the generation phase. Therefore, theoretically both threads could print a word each, but both tasks are so short that it is more likely the second thread prints both. The order is non-deterministic however.

This code works, but it is not a real sentence yet. Let's modify the program to print either **"A race car "**, or **"A car race "**. The relevant program fragment is listed in Figure 3.2.

By inserting a print statement before the two tasks, it is guaranteed that **"A "** is printed first. Next, the tasks are generated and executed in the barrier that is implied with the **single** construct.

```
 1 #pragma omp parallel
 2 {
 3   #pragma omp single
 4   {
 5     printf("A ");
 6     #pragma omp task
 7       {printf("race ");} // Task #1
 8     #pragma omp task
 9       {printf("car ");}  // Task #2
10   } // End of single region
11 } // End of parallel region
```

Figure 3.2: **Augmented code fragment with two tasks** – The print statement at line 5 is executed by one thread only and before the tasks are generated. This ensures the sentence starts with "A ".

3.1.2   Parallelizing a Sentence with a Palindrome

Although longer, this is still not a full sentence. We want to append `"is fun to watch."` to it and also include a new-line symbol. That seems easy, doesn't it? The code fragment in Figure 3.3 adds a print statement before the end of the single region.

Although this seems straightforward, the output is not what we would expect to see. The six possible results are listed in Figure 3.4. Which one of these is printed at runtime depends on the number of threads used, the load on the system, and the implementation details of tasking.

The sentence always starts with `"A "`, but what happens next "depends." Remember that the tasks are executed by threads waiting in the barrier.

To simplify the discussion, the reference numbers in the first column of Figure 3.4 are used. The thread executing the single region is referred to as T_S.

In one scenario, assuming there are at least two threads, the other thread(s) could arrive in the barrier after thread T_S has executed the single region. In this case, either output 1 or 2 is printed.

It may also happen that one or more thread(s) arrive in the barrier before T_S has completed the single region. Then, one of the outputs $3 - 6$ is printed. In the case of 3 or 4, one task was executed after T_S finished. If this thread finishes after the other threads, outputs 5 or 6 are printed.

```
 1 #pragma omp parallel
 2 {
 3   #pragma omp single
 4   {
 5     printf("A ");
 6     #pragma omp task
 7       {printf("race ");} // Task #1
 8     #pragma omp task
 9       {printf("car ");}  // Task #2
10     printf("is fun to watch.\n");
11   } // End of single region
12 } // End of parallel region
```

Figure 3.3: **An incorrect sentence with a palindrome and two tasks** – This
program does not produce the desired result. The print statement at line 10 is executed
by one thread only. Although at the end of the single region, this line may be printed
before the tasks get to print their word.

Reference ID	Text printed
1	A is fun to watch. race car
2	A is fun to watch. car race
3	A race is fun to watch. car
4	A car is fun to watch. race
5	A race car is fun to watch.
6	A car race is fun to watch.

Figure 3.4: **The six possible outputs from the program in Figure 3.3** –
The first column contains a reference number used in the explanation. The second column
lists the possible lines printed from this program.

Any of the above scenario's are possible. It depends on the number of threads
used. With two threads the behavior is different compared to using three threads.
Also the load on the system has an impact. If, for example, one thread gets delayed,
the output may be different.

```
1 #pragma omp parallel
2 {
3   #pragma omp single
4   {
5     printf("A ");
6     #pragma omp task
7       {printf("race ");} // Task #1
8     #pragma omp task
9       {printf("car ");}  // Task #2
10    #pragma omp taskwait
11      printf("is fun to watch.\n");
12  } // End of single region
13 } // End of parallel region
```

Figure 3.5: **A correct sentence with a palindrome and two tasks** – At line 10, the `taskwait` construct forces the pending child tasks to complete before execution resumes. In this way it is guaranteed the words are printed in the right order.

The tasking implementation details matter also. A work queueing system is used to handle the generation and execution of tasks. There are several different ways to assign threads to tasks, and this impacts the order of execution.

In a way, none of this matters though, because this program is not guaranteed to produce the output we want to see. What we need to do is to guarantee the two tasks are completed *before* the print statement at line 10 is executed. In this simple case, we could easily solve this by moving the last print statement out of the parallel region, but what if this is not possible? For such cases, the `taskwait` construct can be used. This feature is used in Figure 3.5 to achieve the desired result.

Execution proceeds as follows. Thread T_S enters the single region and executes the statement at line 5, printing "A ". Next, it generates the two tasks with the print statement. At some point in time, the other threads enter the implied barrier that is part of the `single` construct. Once the tasks become available, they will be executed by those threads.

The `taskwait` construct forces thread T_S to wait, until the two tasks have completed. In this case this means it must wait for "race car " or "car race " to have been printed. After that, it prints "is fun to watch.".

3.1.3   Closing Comments on the Palindrome Example

In this example the `single` construct is used to ensure each task is generated only once. Theoretically, the same could be achieved using the `master` construct, but there is a problem with that. In the barrier, all explicit tasks generated by the team must be executed to completion. The `master` construct has no implied barrier, however.

In this case, no harm is done, because then the tasks are executed in the barrier that is implied with the parallel region. This is, of course, specific to the example. In general, if the `master` construct is used with tasks, care needs to be taken when they are executed.

Generally, this is not the best approach anyhow. The master thread tends to be quite busy with the overall execution already. Why add more burden to it? Instead, we recommend using the `single` construct, possibly with the `nowait` clause. In the case of the latter, the same caveat about task completion holds.

Another option is to use parallel sections, but with only one single section. As with the `single` construct, the `nowait` clause can be used to eliminate the redundant barrier.

Another thing worth mentioning is that in this particular example, there is no data environment to worry about. This is very unlikely to be the case in more realistic applications. What you need to know about the data environment in tasks is extensively covered in the sections to follow, in particular in Section 3.5 on page 136.

3.2   Using Tasks to Parallelize a Linked List

The previous example introduced tasking at a very basic level and was somewhat crafted in the sense that other OpenMP constructs are more suitable and easier to solve the problem. The next example does not have such an easy solution though.

This program uses a linked list. The assumption is that each node in the linked list represents work independent of the other nodes. The independence opens up opportunities for parallelism, but unfortunately a linked list needs to be traversed sequentially, ruining the parallelism.

That is, unless we can generate a list with all the nodes first. The data elements from this list can then be processed simultaneously. This makes it a natural candidate for tasking.

```
1 struct linked_list {
2   int64_t value;
3   struct linked_list *next;
4 };
5
6 typedef struct linked_list my_data;
7
8 static int function_call_count = 0;
9
10 int main(int argc, char *argv[])
11 {
12  my_data *previous, *ptr, *current, *head_of_list;
13
14  int64_t ntasks;
15  int64_t no_of_tasks_failed = 0;
16
17  (void) get_parameters(argc, argv, &ntasks);
18
19 }
```

Figure 3.6: **The first part of the sequential implementation of the linked list program** – The key data structures are defined and the input parameters are read.

3.2.1   The Sequential Version of the Linked List Program

This program is relatively lengthy, but for reasons that become clear soon, most of the code is presented and discussed. The initial part of the code is listed in Figure 3.6.

This first part is fairly straightforward. At lines $1-4$, the key list data structure, called linked_list, is defined. The list has two elements only: an integer value and a pointer to the next node in the list. To make things easier, an alias named my_data to reference the linked list is defined. Line 8 defines and initializes a static (global) variable called function_call_count to be used later on. Lines $12-15$ define other program variables needed. This includes four pointers to my_data. At line 17, a single input parameter is returned by the function call. This variable is called ntasks and defines the length of the list. As we shall see shortly, the number of tasks corresponds to the number of entries in the list, hence the name. Although

```
20  for (int64_t i=0; i<ntasks; i++) {
21      if ( (ptr = (my_data *) malloc(sizeof(my_data))) == NULL ) {
22          perror("ptr"); exit(-1);
23      }
24
25      if (i == 0 ) {
26          head_of_list = ptr;
27      } else {
28          previous->next = ptr;
29      }
30
31      ptr->value = i+1;
32      ptr->next  = NULL;
33      previous   = ptr;
34  }
```

Figure 3.7. **The second part of the sequential implementation of the linked list program** – By design, the linked list has **ntasks** entries. A for-loop with this length is used to construct the list.

seemingly a detail, variables **ntasks** and **no_of_tasks_failed**, are declared to be a 64-bit integer. This is because the number of tasks may easily be very large.

In the next block of code, the linked list is initialized. The code fragment is listed in Figure 3.7. By design, the list has **ntasks** entries and a for-loop is used to initialize these entries. This loop spans lines $20 - 34$. Memory for the next node in the list is allocated at lines $21 - 23$. Variable **ptr** contains the pointer to the new memory block. At line 26, the starting point of the linked list is saved in variable **head_of_list**. Upon subsequent loop iterations, the previous value of the pointer is saved (line 28). Lines $31 - 32$ assign a value to the data part of the list and the **NULL** pointer to the next node. The latter is because the end of the linked list needs to be terminated by the **NULL** pointer. At line 33, the list is updated with the new pointer.

After execution of this for-loop, a **NULL**-terminated linked list, consisting of **ntasks** nodes has been created. Variable **head_of_list** contains the start of the list.

The most interesting and relevant part of this example is shown in Figure 3.8. This is where the linked list is processed. Pointer variable **current** is used to keep track of the most recent node. At line 35, it is initialized to the start of the linked list.

```
35  current = head_of_list;
36  while (current != NULL) {
37    int64_t return_value;
38    return_value = do_work(current->value);
39    if ( return_value < 0 ) {
40      no_of_tasks_failed++;
41    }
42    current = current->next;
43  } // End of while loop
```

Figure 3.8: **The third part of the sequential implementation of the linked list program** – This is where the linked list is processed. At line 35, the most recent node location is set to the start of the list. The while-loop spans lines 36 − 43 and executes a function called do_work() for each data element in the list. The parameter to the function call is the value of the data element. At line 42, the pointer advances to the next node in the list.

The key part of this program is the while-loop spanning lines 36 − 43. This loop terminates in case the pointer to the next node is NULL. At line 38, a function called do_work() is called. It has one input parameter, current->value, that contains the value of the data element in the current node.

In case there was a problem executing do_work(), a negative value is returned. This is checked for at line 39 and if a problem has occurred, status variable no_of_tasks_failed is incremented by one (line 40). Note that it was initialized to zero at line 15 in Figure 3.6. After completion of the while-loop, the main program can use the value of variable no_of_tasks_failed to check for failures.

The details of function do_work() need to be discussed, because it requires some attention in the next section. The source code is listed in Figure 3.9. This function emulates a runtime error and uses a global variable, called function_call_count, to control the value returned to the caller.

At line 3, this variable is updated each time the function is called. By design, the first MAX_ERRORS calls to this function return a negative value, emulating a runtime error. After this, the function returns zero, indicating there were no errors. This is what the code at lines 5 − 9 accomplishes. This block of code could be replaced by a single statement, but as shown in the next section, these lines need special care. This would be equally true for the one-liner. Note that the input parameter is not used, but has been included here to make the code look more realistic. In a

```
1  int64_t do_work(int64_t input_value)
2  {
3    function_call_count++;
4
5    if ( function_call_count <= MAX_ERRORS ) {
6       return(-1);
7    } else {
8       return(0);
9    }
10 }
```

Figure 3.9: **The source code of function do_work()** – This function is a template to emulate an error that may have occurred during execution. For demonstration purposes, a global variable, called `function_call_count`, is updated.

real-world application, this value is most likely needed.

This concludes the description of the sequential version of this program. From now on, the focus is on the core part of the program, as shown in Figure 3.8. The challenge is going to be to parallelize it.

3.2.2 The Parallel Version of the Linked List Program

The NULL terminated while-loop is not straightforward to parallelize, because, unlike a for-loop, it is not known at runtime how often the loop body is going to be executed.

The main thing to realize here is that there is actually no need to know this. What if there was a dynamic queueing system to handle the assignment of threads to the chunks of work that need to be performed? If such a system is available, the threads can pick up work from the queue until the queue is empty. This is somewhat akin to the `dynamic` and `guided` loop iteration scheduling algorithms, available for parallel loops. The big difference is that the tasking concept is much more flexible and dynamic.

This is exactly the idea behind tasking. With tasking, it is up to the implementation to set up an internal (queueing) system that ensures the tasks are generated and executed. This system also decides upon the assignment of threads to the tasks in the queue. Therefore, we need to find a way to define the execution of the

```
1 current = head_of_list;
2 #pragma omp parallel firstprivate(current) \
3                      shared(no_of_tasks_failed)
4 {
5   #pragma omp single nowait
6   {
7     printf("Thread %d executes the single region\n",
8             omp_get_thread_num());
9     while (current != NULL) {
10      #pragma omp task firstprivate(current) \
11                       shared(no_of_tasks_failed)
12      {
13        int64_t return_value;
14        return_value = do_work(current->value);
15        if ( return_value < 0 ) {
16            #pragma omp atomic update
17              no_of_tasks_failed++;
18        }
19      } // End of task
20      current = current->next;
21    } // End of while loop
22  } // End of single region
23 } // End of parallel region
```

Figure 3.10: **The parallel implementation of the linked list program** – The entire while-loop is embedded inside a parallel region, spanning lines $2-23$. This region consists of one single region (lines $5-22$). The thread executing this region creates the tasks defined at lines $10-19$. Tasks are executed in the implicit barrier at the end of the parallel region (line 23). For more details, refer to the main text.

while-loop in terms of tasks. Due to the sequential nature of scanning the nodes of the list, a `single` construct is ideally suited to generate the tasks.

The relevant code fragment is shown in Figure 3.10. As before, the current node in the linked list is stored in variable `current` and initialized to head_of_list (line 1). The entire while-loop is embedded inside a parallel region, spanning lines $2-23$.

The scoping is fairly straightforward. All threads get their private copy of pointer variable `current`. Thanks to the `firstprivate` clause, every thread has a copy, initialized to point to the first node in the list. Variable no_of_tasks_failed needs to be updated by all threads and is therefore a shared variable. The same scoping is used for the tasks (lines $10 - 11$).

The parallel region consists of one relatively gigantic single region starting at line 5 and ending at line 22. Similar to what was seen in the previous example in Section 3.1.1, this approach is used to ensure one thread generates the tasks. For diagnostic purposes, the thread ID of the thread executing this single region is printed (lines $7 - 8$).

The two adjacent implied barriers at lines $22 - 23$ are not needed. We can easily eliminate the one at line 22 by using the `nowait` clause in line 5. As a result, all other threads wait in the implied barrier at the end of the parallel region at line 23.

The tasks are defined at lines $10 - 19$. Ignoring the details of the tasks for a moment, we know that this one thread executes the while-loop and scans through the linked list. This is exactly the same as we saw earlier with the sequential version. When this thread encounters the task region (lines $10 - 19$), it generates the appropriate code, plus data environment, to execute the specific task. At line 20, the pointer advances to the next node and at line 10 the next task can be generated. This is still a sequential operation. Meanwhile, the other threads wait in the barrier at line 23, but they are not really waiting. Instead, they start executing the tasks, generated by the thread executing the single region. Once this thread has finished, and if there is still work left to do, it joins the other threads and starts executing tasks from the queue.

Now that it is covered in what way these tasks are generated and executed, it is time to zoom in on the code that defines a task. At line 13, variable `return_value` is declared. It is private to the task and used to store the value returned by function `do_work()`.[3]

At this point, things get interesting, because we want to detect a possible error that has occurred when executing this function. For good reasons it is not allowed to jump out of a parallel region, because then other threads wait in the next barrier for one or more threads that never arrive there.

In Section 2.4.2 it is shown how the thread cancellation feature can be used for these situations, but in this example the more conventional approach is chosen. After the parallel region has completed, the value of variable `no_of_tasks_failed`

---

[3]This variable can be eliminated, but is used here to show the (simple) use of such a private variable.

```
1 int64_t do_work(int64_t input_value)
2 {
3   int64_t TID, return_value;
4
5   TID = omp_get_thread_num();
6
7   #pragma omp critical
8   {
9     function_call_count++;
10
11    printf("TID = %-61d Input: %-61d function_call_count: %d\n",
12            TID, input_value, function_call_count);
13
14    if ( function_call_count <= MAX_ERRORS ) {
15        return_value = -(TID+1);
16    } else {
17        return_value = 0;
18    }
19  } // End of critical region
20
21  return(return_value);
22 }
```

Figure 3.11: **The thread-safe version of function do_work()** – This is the thread-safe version of the sequential code shown in Figure 3.9. The update at line 9 needs to be guarded against a data race and the read of this variable at line 14 has to be protected as well. This is achieved by using a critical section spanning lines 7 − 19.

may be checked. If it is non-zero, an error has occurred and the program can take appropriate action.

Simply incrementing variable no_of_tasks_failed in case the function returns a negative value, is correct in the sequential version. For the parallel version, it is necessary to prevent that multiple threads simultaneously update this variable. The solution is straightforward. This is a perfect case to use an atomic update (line 16 − 17) to avoid the data race. See also Section 2.1.6 for more details on the atomic construct.

There is one more thing left to do. Function do_work() needs to be made thread-safe. The modified, parallel, source code of this function is listed in Figure 3.11. It is the thread-safe version of the sequential code listed earlier in Figure 3.9.

At line 5, the thread ID is assigned to variable TID. This is used to ensure that each invocation of this function returns a unique negative number in case an error has occurred. As before, a negative value is returned the first MAX_ERRORS times this function is executed. After that, a value of zero is returned. In this way, the number of erroneous function calls is easily controlled and simulated.

In a sequential program, it is easy to keep track of the number of times the function is called. Global variable function_call_count is simply updated each time the function is called. In a multi-threaded environment, the update of a global variable requires care. Without any precaution, a data race occurs at line 9, because multiple threads are allowed to update the same variable at the same time. Typically, an atomic update is used to avoid this, but in this case there is also a potential data race between the write at line 9, and the read at line 14. This is why the entire code block is a critical region. It is assumed that in a real-world application quite some work is performed here. Otherwise, the cost of the critical region offsets, or even outweighs, any performance gain.

Last, but not least, the return value of this function needs to be handled. In the sequential version in Figure 3.9, the return() function was called at lines 6 and 8, using the appropriate argument. Since control cannot be transferred out of a critical region, calling the return() function is not possible. Instead, the desired value is assigned to variable return_value and this is used as the argument in the return() call at line 21.

Note that when setting the return value at line 15, a value of one is added to variable TID. Otherwise the return value for the master thread is zero, and not distinguishable from the return value set upon correct execution.

For demonstration purposes a print statement has been included in lines 11 − 12. The thread ID, the value of the input parameter, and the number of times the function has been called, are printed. This program has been executed using 10 tasks and 20 threads. The results in Figure 3.12 show that the generating thread, 17, also executes two tasks. Not all threads execute the same number of tasks. The other eight tasks are distributed over six threads. Although there are sufficient threads to execute one task each, this is not what happens at runtime. Apparently, only seven threads were put to work. This demonstrates the dynamic behavior that comes with tasking.

```
Thread 17 executes the single region
TID = 13      Input: 1      function_call_count: 1
TID = 11      Input: 4      function_call_count: 2
TID = 17      Input: 10     function_call_count: 3
TID = 12      Input: 5      function_call_count: 4
TID = 11      Input: 8      function_call_count: 5
TID = 13      Input: 6      function_call_count: 6
TID = 14      Input: 2      function_call_count: 7
TID = 15      Input: 7      function_call_count: 8
TID = 17      Input: 9      function_call_count: 9
TID = 8       Input: 3      function_call_count: 10
```

Figure 3.12: **Example output from the parallel linked list program** – The program was executed for `ntasks=10` and using 20 threads. This output demonstrates that the generating thread, 17, also executes two tasks.

3.2.3   Closing Comments on the Linked List Example

This type of algorithm was notoriously hard to parallelize and one of the reasons to introduce the tasking concept in OpenMP.

What confuses users new to tasking, is that the parsing of the linked list is still a sequential process. Due to the pointer-chasing nature of scanning such a list, this cannot be avoided, but there is also no need to do so.

With tasks, as soon as an entry from the list has been created, the processing can start in a natural way.

3.3   Sorting Things Out with Tasks

Through nested parallelism, OpenMP has supported the parallelization of recursive algorithms, but this is a rather heavy and rigid mechanism. The typical cost of a parallel region is non-negligible. To make it even worse, each parallel region has an implied barrier and there is no way to omit it. Both drawbacks make it very difficult to efficiently parallelize, and load balance, fine-grained portions of work in recursive algorithms.

This example shows how a recursive divide-and-conquer algorithm can be parallelized using tasks. As with the other examples, this is a template for how to tackle similar problems in this category.

The popular quicksort algorithm has been selected [22]. It is conceptually simple, but has a structure that allows us to demonstrate various tasking features needed to implement the parallelism.

3.3.1   The Sequential Quicksort Algorithm

The quicksort algorithm uses a divide-and-conquer algorithm. Such an algorithm splits the work in two independent sections. In a recursive manner, each section is then split again. The sequential quicksort algorithm to sort an array is defined as follows:

1. Select an element, called a *pivot*, from the array.

2. In the *partitioning* phase, the array is re-ordered, such that all elements with values less than the pivot are placed before the pivot. All elements with values greater than the pivot are moved after it.[4] After this partitioning step, the pivot is guaranteed to be in its final position.

3. Recursively apply the above two steps to the elements to the left and right of the pivot.

4. The recursion ends when there is only one, or no, element left.

In the example discussed here, a specific implementation of the algorithm outlined above is presented. This is certainly not the only version. Among other choices, the selection of the pivot and partitioning phase are parameters affecting the performance. The partitioning algorithm used in this section is listed in Figure 3.13.

Function `choosePivot` is defined at lines $1 - 3$. It returns $floor(lo + hi)/2$.[5] If $lo + hi$ is an even number, it returns the array value in the center. Otherwise, it returns the integer value rounded down from $(lo + hi)/2$. For example, for $lo = 3$ and $hi = 6$, a value of 4 is returned.

The actual partitioning algorithm is defined at lines $10 - 24$. After the pivot value and corresponding index are defined (lines $10 - 11$), the pivot value is moved to `a[hi]`, the end of the array section. The value that was originally there has been moved by the `swap` function to where the pivot was.

---

[4]Equal values can go either way
[5]The Glossary contains the definition of this function.

```
1 int64_t choosePivot(int64_t *a, int64_t lo, int64_t hi)
2 {
3  return( (lo+hi)/2 );
4 }
5
6 int64_t partitionArray(int64_t *a, int64_t lo, int64_t hi)
7 {
8   int64_t pivotIndex, pivotValue, storeIndex;
9
10   pivotIndex = choosePivot(a, lo, hi);
11   pivotValue = a[pivotIndex];
12
13   (void) swap(&a[hi], &a[pivotIndex]);
14
15   storeIndex = lo;
16
17   for (int64_t i=lo; i <= hi-1; i++)
18   {
19    if ( a[i] < pivotValue ) {
20       (void) swap(&a[i], &a[storeIndex]);
21       storeIndex++;
22    }
23   }
24   (void) swap(&a[storeIndex], &a[hi]);
25
26   return(storeIndex);
27 }
```

Figure 3.13: **Implementation of the partitioning phase** – This code implements the partitioning phase in the quicksort algorithm. In this case, the pivot element is defined to be $floor(lo+hi)/2$, the value in the center, or one element less, of the array. The value returned by the partitioning function is an index. On return, array elements with an index less than the return value are smaller than the pivot value. The array value at this index is the pivot value.

Variable `storeIndex` is initialized at line 15. It is used to point to the next available index in the left part of the array. This is where the values less than the pivot value are stored.

	0	1	2	3	4	5	6	7	8	9	storeIndex
Initial values	8	6	3	4	4	5	3	9	2	2	
Before initial swap	8	6	3	4	**4**	5	3	9	2	**2**	
After initial swap	8	6	3	4	2	5	3	9	2	4	0
Source line 19 (i = 2)	**8**	6	**3**	4	2	5	3	9	2	4	0
Swap and update (i = 2)	3	6	8	4	2	5	3	9	2	4	1
Source line 19 (i = 4)	3	**6**	8	4	**2**	5	3	9	2	4	1
Swap and update (i = 4)	3	2	8	4	6	5	3	9	2	4	2
Source line 19 (i = 6)	3	2	**8**	4	6	5	**3**	9	2	4	2
Swap and update (i = 6)	3	2	3	4	6	5	8	9	2	4	3
Source line 19 (i = 8)	3	2	3	**4**	6	5	8	9	**2**	4	3
Swap and update (i = 8)	3	2	3	2	6	5	8	9	4	4	4
Before final swap	3	2	3	2	**6**	5	8	9	4	**4**	4
After final swap	<u>3</u>	<u>2</u>	<u>3</u>	<u>2</u>	<u>4</u>	5	8	9	4	6	4

Figure 3.14: **An example of the partitioning phase** – This shows how the array elements are moved around during the partitioning phase. The top row has the array index values. In this example, `lo = 0` and `hi = 9`. The pivot element is 4 and the pivot index is 4 as well. Array elements marked in bold are to be swapped next. In the last column the value of variable `storeIndex` is shown. The last row contains the resulting array. The elements that are moved to the left of the pivot are underlined.

The for-loop spanning lines $17 - 23$ moves all values less than the pivot value, if there are any, to the left. They are stored in a linear fashion, starting at `a[lo]`. After this loop has completed, $a[i] < pivotValue$ for $i = lo, \ldots, storeIndex - 1$. These values are not necessarily sorted yet. At line 24, the pivot value is put back and placed at the end of this sequence. Variable `storeIndex` separates the array values: $a[i] \leq pivotValue$ for $i = lo, \ldots, storeIndex$. Array elements for an index value exceeding `storeIndex` are equal or larger.

Figure 3.14 shows an example for an array consisting of 10 elements. As the partitioning algorithm proceeds, elements are swapped until those strictly less than the pivot value are to the left of the pivot.

Step by step, array elements are moved to their new position. Upon completion of this function, the elements are partially sorted. The index value returned partitions

```
 1 void seqQuicksort(int64_t *a, int64_t lo, int64_t hi)
 2 {
 3   if ( lo < hi ) {
 4     int64_t p = partitionArray(a, lo, hi);
 5
 6     (void) seqQuicksort(a, lo, p - 1); // Left branch
 7
 8     (void) seqQuicksort(a, p + 1, hi); // Right branch
 9   }
10 }
```

Figure 3.15: **The sequential quicksort implementation** – This is the core part of the algorithm. After the partitioning phase, array element a[p] is in the correct place. Elements to the left and right of it are each partitioned in a recursive manner.

the array. The corresponding array element is in its final position. All elements to the left are strictly less than the pivot value. The array elements with a higher index value are equal, or larger.

The next step is to repeat this process for the elements to the left and right of the index value returned. These two operations are independent and can be carried out simultaneously. This process is then applied repeatedly until all elements have been sorted. The key part of the sequential quicksort source code implementing this divide and conquer algorithm is listed in Figure 3.15.

The code is executed as follows. If lo is equal to, or exceeds hi, the function immediately returns, terminating the current execution path. Otherwise, at line 4, array a is partitioned within the range defined by parameters lo and hi. After this call, array element a[p] is in its final position and the array sections to the left (line 6) and to the right (line 8) are partitioned.

This pattern repeats recursively. Because the range decreases, at some point, the if-statement at line 3 evaluates to false and the execution terminates. Step by step, the function calls are skipped and when the program terminates, the array values have been sorted.

3.3.2 The OpenMP Quicksort Algorithm

As a first step towards a parallel implementation using tasking, the framework is set up. The still-to-be-written parallel function is called from here. To underline

```
1 #pragma omp parallel default(none) shared(a,nelements)
2 {
3   #pragma omp single nowait
4   {
5     (void) ompQuicksort(a, 0, nelements-1);
6   } // End of single section
7 } // End of parallel region
```

Figure 3.16: **The driver part for the OpenMP quicksort function** – As seen earlier, the function call is embedded in a parallel region. Since function ompQuicksort uses tasks, the **single** directive ensures only one thread generates the tasks. To avoid a redundant barrier, the **nowait** clause is used.

this is the OpenMP version, the function is called ompQuicksort. The relevant part of the calling program is listed in Figure 3.16. This driver part is straightforward. To ensure only one thread generates the tasks, a **single** directive is used to enforce this. The **nowait** clause at line 3 removes a redundant barrier.

Next, tasks need to be used to parallelize the sequential code shown in Figure 3.15. The main decision to be made is to identify which part(s) of the code should be defined as tasks. In this case, these are the calls at lines 6 and 8 of the sequential code. The modified source code using tasks is shown in Figure 3.17.

When comparing the two listings, it is easy to see that, other than changing the function name to distinguish the sequential and parallel versions, and the addition of two directives, the code has not changed.

As always, one must think about the scoping of the variables and it is good practice to specify this explicitly. Although it is the default, the variables that control the section of the array to be sorted are defined to be **firstprivate**.

The same could be done for the pointer to array **a**, but it is more natural to make it shared. This reflects that all tasks are working on the same block of memory. It is our responsibility to avoid data races. In this case, this is not an issue, because there is never a duplicate index value.

The first time function ompQuicksort is called, two tasks are created. They are working on two disjoint parts of the array to the left and right of the pivot element, which is in its final position.

The very first time the function is called, the entire array is scanned and partitioned. This is a sequential phase in the parallel algorithm, but after this initial

```
 1 void ompQuicksort(int64_t *a, int64_t lo, int64_t hi)
 2 {
 3   if ( lo < hi ) {
 4      int64_t p = partitionArray(a, lo, hi);
 5
 6      #pragma omp task default(none) shared(a) firstprivate(lo,p)
 7         { (void) ompQuicksort(a, lo, p - 1); } // Left branch
 8
 9      #pragma omp task default(none) shared(a) firstprivate(hi,p)
10         { (void) ompQuicksort(a, p + 1, hi); } // Right branch
11   }
12 }
```

Figure 3.17: **The OpenMP quicksort implementation** – The two (recursive) calls to `ompQuicksort` are defined to be tasks. The variables defining the array sections to be sorted are declared `firstprivate`. Although not the only choice, making array `a` shared is most straightforward.

split, there are two disjoint branches executing in parallel. Each branch subsequently splits itself into two more parallel function calls, generating two tasks. This splitting continues until there is only one element left in a particular branch. No more tasks are generated in this branch, ending the sorting process for this part of the array.

Unlike the example in Section 3.1.1, there is no `taskwait` construct needed, because each task executes independently. There is no need to wait for other tasks.

3.3.3   Fine-Tuning the OpenMP Quicksort Algorithm

The implementation shown in the previous section works fine. The code executes in parallel and the array is correctly sorted. There is an issue though. For a sufficiently large array, many tasks are generated. This in itself may already impact performance due to resource constraints, but in case of a divide-and-conquer method, the amount of work performed per task decreases, as the algorithm progresses. The cost of task management does not decrease, however and eventually this overhead dominates.

These performance issues are not restricted to this example. In many algorithms that use tasks, these need to be considered, especially if the amount of work

```
1 void ompQuicksort(int64_t *a, int64_t lo, int64_t hi)
2 {
3   if ( lo < hi ) {
4
5     if ( (hi - lo + 1) < cutoff_seq ) {
6       seqQuicksort(a, lo, hi); // Call sequential version
7     } else {
8       int64_t p = partitionArray(a, lo, hi);
9
10      #pragma omp task default(none) shared(a) firstprivate(lo,p)
11        { (void) ompQuicksort(a, lo, p - 1); } // Left branch
12
13      #pragma omp task default(none) shared(a) firstprivate(hi,p)
14        { (void) ompQuicksort(a, p + 1, hi); } // Right branch
15    }
16  }
17 }
```

Figure 3.18: **The OpenMP quicksort implementation with escape hatch**
– The code at lines $5 - 6$ ensures that a different function is executed in case the array length is below a certain threshold. The obvious choice is to call the sequential version of the algorithm then.

performed decreases over time. Let's first look at limiting the number of tasks generated.

In Figure 3.18, a solution is shown, where an escape hatch is introduced. In case the array length drops below a user-defined threshold cutoff_seq, the sequential version of the algorithm is executed.

This approach is simple and effective, but it has two drawbacks. One must write a sequential version of the algorithm. Admittedly, this is very similar to the OpenMP version, but there is also the issue of having to maintain two (nearly identical) sources.

Another problem to deal with is that one must choose the appropriate value for the threshold variable cutoff_seq. This is not trivial, because the optimal value depends on certain system and OpenMP implementation-dependent characteristics. The problem size may also influence the value for the cutoff. It is therefore highly recommended to conduct some experiments to find the optimal value. As a guideline, the cutoff value can be set, such that the OpenMP version using a single thread performs the same as, or similar to, the sequential version.[6]

The above approach was the most common solution chosen at the time tasking was introduced in OpenMP 3.0, but in OpenMP 3.1 two more clauses were added to make it easier to fine-tune the performance of tasking.

The `final(expr)` clause can be used to avoid the runtime system continuing to generate tasks. It targets recursive algorithms and nested tasks, where the number of tasks tends to increase exponentially. This cannot only clog the runtime system, but especially if the amount of work decreases over time, the tasking overhead may offset any performance gains. The `final` clause takes an expression `expr`. If it evaluates to `true`, no more tasks are generated and the code is executed immediately. This is propagated to all of the child tasks.

This clause can be combined with the `mergeable` clause to avoid a separate data environment being created. This topic is covered in more detail in Section 3.7.

Effectively, the combination of these clauses, together with a suitable cutoff value, eliminates the need to have a separate sequential version. This is demonstrated in Figure 3.19.

The if-statement and call to the sequential version of the algorithm have been removed. Instead, the two clauses have been added on lines 7 and 11. They achieve the same functionality, but eliminate the need to have two separate source trees to maintain. As before, some experimentation is needed to determine the optimal value for the threshold variable `cutoff_tasks`.

There is one more thing that may be done to make this algorithm perform more efficiently. There is actually no need to have two tasks. The source for this approach is shown in Figure 3.20. The code is obviously nearly identical to the previous version. Only the tasking pragma and curly braces around the second call to execute the right branch have been removed. In this way, the tasking overhead is reduced, while there is still parallelism to be exploited.

As trivial as this change may seem, the order matters. With the approach shown, each invocation of the function generates a task. All these tasks are put on the runtime queue and executed by the threads. Meanwhile the sequential calls to the right branch are executed as well.

With tasking pragma on the right branch, there is a sequential path first. Only when this has finished, are the tasks generated and executed.

---

[6]Using bisection, this value can often be found relatively quickly.

```
 1 int64_t omp_quicksort(int64_t *a, int64_t lo, int64_t hi)
 2 {
 3  if ( lo < hi ) {
 4
 5    int64_t p = partition(a, lo, hi);
 6
 7    #pragma omp task final( (p - lo) < cutoff_tasks) mergeable \
 8                      default(none) shared(a) firstprivate(lo,p)
 9    { (void) omp_quicksort(a, lo, p - 1); } // Left branch
10
11    #pragma omp task final( (hi - p) < cutoff_tasks) mergeable \
12                      default(none) shared(a) firstprivate(hi,p)
13    { (void) omp_quicksort(a, p + 1, hi); } // Right branch
14
15    return(p);
16  }
17 }
```

Figure 3.19: **The OpenMP quicksort implementation using the final and mergeable clauses** – The test and call to the sequential version have been removed. Instead the `final` and `mergeable` clauses are used to achieve the same result. Just as with the previous version, finding the correct value for the threshold variable `cutoff_tasks` requires some experimentation.

3.3.4 Closing Comments on the OpenMP Quicksort Algorithm

Although this algorithm has been covered in quite some detail, there are some additional comments to be made.

On the algorithmic side, the most straightforward implementation has been selected, because it is already sufficiently complex to demonstrate the use of tasking to parallelize a divide-and-conquer type of algorithm. Without a doubt, there are more efficient sequential versions out there.

For one thing, the choice of the pivot is quite crucial. In our code, the middle element is selected, because that is good for load balancing. It is however not necessarily the optimal choice to get the best sequential performance.[7]

---

[7]This could be something to consider for the sequential version in Figure 3.18, if available.

```
1 int64_t omp_quicksort(int64_t *a, int64_t lo, int64_t hi)
2 {
3  if ( lo < hi ) {
4
5    int64_t p = partition(a, lo, hi);
6
7    #pragma omp task final( (p - lo) < cutoff_tasks) mergeable \
8                    default(none) shared(a) firstprivate(lo,p)
9    { (void) omp_quicksort(a, lo, p - 1); } // Left branch
10
11    (void) omp_quicksort(a, p + 1, hi);      // Right branch
12
13    return(p);
14  }
15 }
```

Figure 3.20: **The OpenMP quicksort implementation with one task per call** – There is only one task per call now. Each time this function is called, a task is generated and put in the queue for the threads to work on. Note that issuing the task first is more efficient than the other way round.

Last, but not least, when trying this, be prepared to conduct several experiments. Not only should this be done to determine the threshold(s), but also to decide on the best thread affinity strategy, which is covered in Chapter 4.

3.4 Overlapping I/O and Computations Using Tasks

In this section, the code shown in Figure 1.11 on page 21 is revisited. The example shows the use of parallel sections to overlap I/O and computations. Under the assumption that the I/O can be processed in chunks, a pipeline is set up, such that the computational part waits for a read operation to be completed. Once completed, the data is processed and passed on to a post-processing function. This pipeline approach is demonstrated in Figure 3.21.

The pipeline works as follows. At the start, the first chunk of data is read. All subsequent activities need to wait for this operation to be completed. Once finished, the processing can start. Meanwhile, the next chunk of data can be read, resulting in potentially two activities executing concurrently. After the computation on the

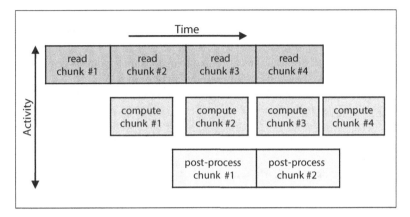

Figure 3.21: **A pipeline to overlap I/O and computations** – There are three activities: read a chunk of data, perform computations on this data and post-process the results. After a start-up phase, these activities can be executed simultaneously, but on different chunks of data.

first chunk of data has finished, the post-processing phase can start, while at the same time, the third chunk of data is read and processing of the second chunk of data starts soon after. At this point, there are three overlapping activities. This continues until the last chunk of data is read and the pipeline starts to wind down.

The code in Figure 1.11 demonstrates how these activities are parallelized using three parallel sections. Through various shared status arrays, the three phases are synchronized.

This approach works, but there is no good way to handle a load-imbalance. Another issue is that the communication of these phases through the status arrays is cumbersome. A polling mechanism is needed to check if the status of a phase has changed, and the OpenMP flush construct is required to ensure changes are made visible to the threads executing the other phases. Although less of a concern, the algorithm also requires either one, or otherwise at least three threads to work correctly.

3.4.1 Using Tasks and Task Dependences

As shown next, tasks provide a much more natural vehicle to implement such a pipeline. The code is listed in Figure 3.22.

```
1 #pragma omp parallel default(none) \
2                  shared(fp_read, n_io_chunks, n_work_chunks) \
3                  shared(a, b, c) \
4                  shared(status_read, status_processing) \
5                  shared(status_postprocessing)
6 {
7   #pragma omp single nowait
8   {
9     for (int64_t i=0; i<n_io_chunks; i++) {
10
11       #pragma omp task depend(out: status_read[i]) \
12                    priority(20)
13       {
14          (void) read_input(fp_read, i, a, b, &status_read[i]);
15       } // End of task reading in a chunk of data
16
17       #pragma omp task depend(in: status_read[i]) \
18                    depend(out: status_processing[i]) \
19                    priority(10)
20       {
21          (void) compute_results(i, n_work_chunks, a, b, c,
22                                     &status_processing[i]);
23       } // End of task performing the computations
24
25       #pragma omp task depend(in: status_processing[i]) \
26                    priority(5)
27       {
28          (void) postprocess_results(i, n_work_chunks, c,
29                                     &status_postprocessing[i]);
30       } // End of task postprocessing the results
31
32     } // End of for-loop
33   } // End of single region
34 } // End of parallel region
```

Figure 3.22: **Overlapping I/O and computations using tasks** – Each phase has been turned into a task. By using task dependences, the correct order of execution is guaranteed. In addition to this, priorities are used to give hints to the runtime system.

As we've seen several times before, the entire parallel region consists of a gigantic single region, but that does not mean this code executes sequentially. On the contrary, this is how parallelism is created. To understand why that is, let's go through the core part of this code fragment line by line.

The for-loop spans lines 9 − 32. The assumption is that `n_io_chunks` of data can be read independently. Since the loop is within a single region, one thread executes all the loop iterations. This thread encounters the tasks, generates the corresponding code, and puts them in the queue.

The queued tasks are made available for execution in, what is called a *task synchronization construct*, which in this case is the barrier implied at the end of the parallel region at line 34. In a task synchronization construct, any thread that is available, may be put to work. More on this can be found in Section 3.7, starting on page 141.

The first task spans lines 11 through 15. This is the task reading the chunk of data corresponding to iteration `i` of the loop. The data is read from the file associated with file pointer `fp_read` and stored in array elements `a[i]` and `b[i]`. Upon successful completion, a status value is written into array element `status_-read[i]`. This value is meant to be checked later on to ensure correct execution.

The new element here is the use of the `depend` clause at line 11. It is used to define *task dependences*.[8] There is also another new clause, the `priority` clause at line 12. We'll get to that soon, but first look at task dependences in more detail.

The `depend` clause takes a dependence type, which can be `in`, `out`, or `inout`, with a variable. The variable is used to set up a dependence between two tasks, while the type defines the direction of the dependence.

In this case, the second task, `compute_results`, needs to be made dependent upon the first task, `read_input`. This is controlled through variable `status_read[i]`. By using the `in` type for the second task, and type `out` on the first task, it is guaranteed that the second task does not start before the first task. In a similar manner, a dependence between the second and third task is set up. Variable `status_processing[i]` is used to define the dependence. By using type `out` on the second task, and type `in` on the third task, the third task starts only upon completion of the second task. The loop variable `i` is included in the dependence variables to allow the runtime system to schedule multiple similar tasks at the same time.

---

[8]This is another use of the `depend` clause. In Section 2.4.4, it is shown how this clause is used to parallelize a `doacross` loop.

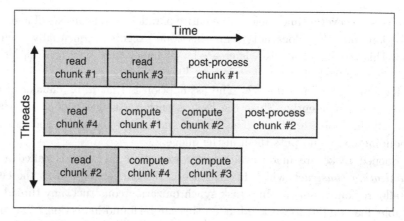

Figure 3.23: **The dynamic behavior of the pipeline** – It is assumed that three threads are used. As long as the dependences are obeyed, the loop iterations can be executed in an arbitrary order, as demonstrated here.

It is however worth noting that these three status arrays are not strictly necessary. Here they are used to verify correct execution afterwards, but as far as the dependences go, simply using the loop variable i instead is sufficient.[9]

The a-synchronous execution of the pipeline is illustrated in Figure 3.23. In the diagram, three threads are used, but this is only for the sake of the example. This code runs fine using any number of threads. The key thing is that for any given iteration, the three different phases must be executed in the correct order. This is achieved using the dependences. Aside from this, there are no restrictions on the order of execution and due to the more flexible scheduling, load balancing is less of an issue.

As mentioned above, in this code, *task priorities* are used as well. These are specified through the `priority` clause. This clause takes a non-negative scalar integer expression, specifying the priority. For example, at line 12, the priority of this task is set to 20. The second task has a priority of 10, and the third task has a priority of 5.

These priorities are hints to the runtime system to assist the scheduler to determine which tasks to choose to execute. The priority values are relative numbers only. In this example we want to emphasize that reading the data is most impor-

---

[9]Error handling can also be handled through cancellation, covered in Section 2.4.2.

tant (because everything else depends on it) and the post-processing part is least important. The priorities are suggestions only and correct execution of the program may not depend on them. In case there is a certain execution order, dependences must be used to enforce this.

Prior to program start up, environment variable `OMP_MAX_TASK_PRIORITY` must be set to the maximum value used. By default this variable is set to zero, that is, there are no higher priority tasks. Runtime function `omp_get_max_task_-priority()` can be used to return the maximum value set through this environment variable.[10]

The solution shown in Figure 3.22 works fine. A major advantage over the original approach using parallel sections is that the explicit flush construct is no longer needed. Load balancing is also less of a concern and this code executes correctly using any number of threads.

The one possible drawback is that there are three tasks for each chunk of data read, and task scheduling overhead could become an issue. Especially if each task does not perform a sufficient amount of work. Features like the `final` and `if` clauses may be used to control this, but there is an alternative solution worth considering and discussed in the next section.

3.4.2   Using the Taskloop Construct

To reduce the tasking overhead, a solution may be to place all three function calls within a single task and apply similar constructs as before. There is, however, a more elegant and powerful construct, available since OpenMP 4.5. It is called the *taskloop construct* and is meant to simplify using tasks in a loop context. It is definitely much more than syntactic sugar and relieves the user from relatively low level coding details when using tasks.

The `taskloop` construct applies to a (nested) loop. The loop iterations are partitioned into tasks and executed as tasks by the runtime system. Many clauses from the tasking construct are inherited, but there are two new clauses worth mentioning.

Figure 3.24 shows the relevant code fragment using the taskloop construct. With one exception, the first few lines are the same as in the previous example. The status arrays, used to express the dependences, are gone. As mentioned earlier,

---

[10]There is no equivalent to set the priorities at runtime. This was considered to be too complex to implement.

```
1 #pragma omp parallel default(none) \
2                      shared(fp_read, n_io_chunks, n_work_chunks) \
3                      shared(a, b, c)
4 {
5   #pragma omp single nowait
6   {
7     #pragma omp taskloop num_tasks(n_io_chunks/10) grainsize(50)
8     for (int64_t i=0; i<n_io_chunks; i++) {
9         (void) read_input(fp_read, i, a, b);
10        (void) compute_results(i, n_work_chunks, a, b, c);
11        (void) postprocess_results(i, n_work_chunks, c);
12    } // End of for-loop
13  } // End of single region
14 } // End of parallel region
```

Figure 3.24: **Overlapping I/O and computations using the taskloop construct** – Each triplet, with the functions called in sequence, is a task. This construct supports many clauses. To reduce the overhead and improve efficiency, the **num_tasks** and **grainsize** clauses can be used to fine-tune the performance. Note the absence of the dependence arrays.

this may be handled in a more simple way, but in any case, a variable to specify the dependences is no longer needed.

The new element is the use of the **taskloop** construct at line 7. Without the additional clauses, this creates a task for each triplet of the function calls inside the loop body. As illustrated in Figure 3.25, this ensures each sequence with the three calls occurs in the right order.

With the new approach, larger units of work are scheduled, and the overhead is reduced. As is typical with tasking, there is the risk that too many tasks are generated (n_io_chunks in this case) and the overhead of managing these tasks could slow down the execution. This is why the **num_tasks** and **grainsize** clauses are so convenient.

The **num_tasks** clause takes an integer expression. The runtime system generates as many tasks as this expression evaluates to, or fewer if there are less loop iterations. The **grainsize** clause takes an integer expression, the *grain-size*. The number of iterations assigned to a task is the minimum of *grain-size* and the number of loop iterations, but does not exceed twice the value of *grain-size*. These two

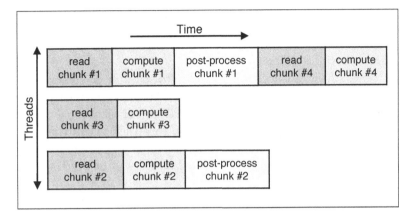

Figure 3.25: **The dynamic behavior of the pipeline using the taskloop construct** – Three threads are used. The loop iterations can be executed in any order, but for each iteration value, the triplet of functions is executed in order.

clauses provide powerful ways to fine-tune the efficiency when using the `taskloop` construct. They are discussed in more detail in Section 3.8, starting on page 146.

Their usage is shown at line 7. The number of tasks is restricted to be 1/10 of the maximum number of `n_io_chunks`. This number of 10% is not based upon actual measurements, or a recommendation. We merely want to demonstrate that this value may be an expression that depends on the runtime value(s) of other variables. The grain-size is set to 50, another arbitrary choice. Possibly, one would like to make this value dependent upon the value of certain program variables and that is supported too.

The effect of the `grainsize` clause is to increase the amount of work performed per task. In general this is a good thing to do, but if the workload is not equally balanced across the loop iterations, a too high value for the `grainsize`, may result in a load-balancing issue. That is ironic, because one of the strengths of tasking is that load-balancing tends to be less of an issue.

In any case, it is strongly recommend to conduct performance experiments to find the optimal values for these parameters. Don't be surprised if they turn out to be dependent upon several factors, and some differentiation depending upon the details of the computer system and OpenMP runtime implementation, may be needed.

3.4.3   Closing Comments on the Pipeline Example

Both versions that implement a pipeline to overlap I/O and computations, use tasks, but the behavior is different.

The first version has the maximum flexibility to schedule the tasks and is most robust in handling load-balancing issues. A downside is that it is easy to generate too many tasks and fine-tuning through the `final` and `if` clauses may be required. The second version uses the powerful `taskloop` construct. This relieves the user of several details to worry about, but load-balancing may be more of an issue. Through the use of the `num_tasks` and `grainsize` clauses, the overhead of tasking can be kept low.

Given the difference in the pros and cons it is difficult to give a recommendation. If the user has more insight into the application characteristics, this may help to select the optimal version.

3.5   The Data Environment with Tasks

So far, we have glossed over the data environment, or *scoping*, with tasking. It is important enough to elaborate upon, though.

Although some of the default scoping rules are intuitively clear, in general it is *strongly* recommended to use the `default(none)` clause and explicitly specify the data sharing attributes of the variable(s). Having said that, let's dig a little deeper into the default rules.

Some rules that apply to the parallel region carry over. For example, global and static variables are automatically shared. Local variables are private by default, by their very nature, as defined in C/C++ within the scope of curly braces (and unlike Fortran). If shared scoping is not inherited, orphaned task variables are `firstprivate` by default, while non-orphaned variables inherit the shared attribute. Variables are `firstprivate`, unless they are shared in the enclosing context.

This is illustrated in the example shown in Figure 3.26, where the scoping and values of the variables are as follows:

- Variable `a` is a global variable and shared. Because the initial value is not changed, it has a value of 1 in all tasks.

- Variable `b` is more challenging. It starts as a shared variable, but is made `private` at line 10. This makes the value undefined within the inner parallel

```
1 int a = 1;
2
3 int main(int argc, char **argv)
4 {
5   int b = 2;
6   int c = 3;
7
8   #pragma omp parallel shared(b)
9   {
10    #pragma omp parallel private(b)
11    {
12      int d = 4;
13      #pragma omp task
14      {
15        int e = 5;
16
17        // Scope of a: shared,      value of a: 1
18        // Scope of b: firstprivate, value of b: undefined
19        // Scope of c: shared,      value of c: 3
20        // Scope of d: firstprivate, value of d: 4
21        // Scope of e: private,     value of e: 5
22
23      } // End of task
24    } // End of inner parallel region
25  } // End of outer parallel region
26 }
```

Figure 3.26: **An example of the default scoping rules for tasking** – This code demonstrates the automatic scoping for several variables. Although the rules are fairly straightforward, it is still recommended to explicitly scope variables.

region spanning lines $10 - 24$. Although by default it is made `firstprivate` within the task, the damage has been done and the value is undefined.

To make the value of b defined within the task, the solution is to scope it as `firstprivate(b)` at line 10.

- By virtue of the default scoping rules for parallel regions, variable c has the **shared** attribute within the outer and inner parallel regions. This is inherited within the task and the value is 3.

- Variable d is a `private` variable inside the inner parallel region and therefore scoped as `firstprivate` within the task. Since the value is set to 4 at line 12, this is also the value inside the task.

- Variable e is declared within the task and therefore a local variable. This makes it a `private` variable with a value of 5.

The above example assumes a fairly deep understanding of the default scoping rules. A possible pitfall is that misinterpretation of a rule can lead to unexpected behavior and in general one should not count on a compiler to detect this.

Variable b is a good example how risky this is. By omitting the scoping on the task definition, an undefined value is used. In this simple case, a compiler might warn against this, but in a more complex code structure, this can easily be much more difficult, or even impossible, to detect.[11]

In summary, one can rely on the default rules, but using the `default(none)` clause can save a significant debugging effort at the expense of some more work in the development phase.

3.6   What is a Task?

Many aspects of tasking were discussed already and several examples of how to use tasks have been shown already. Hopefully these are sufficient to get started, but because several related topics were either skipped, or covered very briefly, a somewhat more formal description of the main constructs and features is given in this section.

To start with, what is a task exactly and how is it defined in an application? In Figure 3.27, the syntax of the task construct is shown. A task consists of the source code in the associated structured block, the data environment as defined through the implicit and explicit data scoping rules, plus the relevant ICVs. When a thread encounters a task, it packages the code and the data environment, such that the task is ready for execution. How and when the task is then executed, is discussed in more detail in Section 3.7.

---

[11]We know of at least one compiler that indeed detects this bug.

```
#pragma omp task [clause[[,] clause]...]
     structured block
!$omp task [clause[[,] clause]...]
     structured block
!$omp end task
```

Figure 3.27: **Syntax of the task construct in C/C++ and Fortran** – This defines the structured block of code to be a task. A task consists of the code to execute, the data environment, plus the relevant ICVs.

```
private (list)
firstprivate (list)
shared (list)
default(shared | none)                              (C/C++)
default(shared | firstprivate | private | none)     (Fortran)
if ([ task :] scalar-logical-expression)
final (scalar-logical-expression)
mergeable
depend (dependence-type : list)
priority (priority-value)
untied
```

Figure 3.28: **The clauses supported by the task construct** – With the exception of the untied clause, the clauses specific to tasking have been introduced in the previous examples, but additional information is given in the text.

Tasks can be dynamically nested, for example in a recursive algorithm, but they may also be lexically nested within other tasks, parallel regions, and worksharing constructs.

The task construct supports various clauses. They are listed in Figure 3.28. The data scoping clauses default, private, firstprivate and shared are the same as used on other constructs, but there are several clauses specific to tasks. With the exception of the untied clause, all of these have been used and discussed in the examples in the previous section. Below they are described in a somewhat more formal way:

- The if clause takes the optional task keyword. Support for a keyword is a general feature of this clause and may be needed in case composite, or combined, constructs are used.

The scalar expression on this clause must evaluate to `true` or `false`. In the case of the latter, the encountering task is suspended and the new task is executed immediately. The parent task resumes, once the new task has completed.

This feature can be used by an implementation to improve the performance by avoiding queueing tasks that are too small.

The difference with the `final` clause below, is that, with the `if` clause, the child tasks are not affected. This is why it was *not* used in the example shown in Figure 3.19. Due to the nature of the quicksort algorithm, once the length of the array drops below the threshold, the length for child tasks is also below this value.

- The `final` clause is a feature to fine-tune the performance of tasks. The clause takes a scalar expression evaluating to `true` or `false`. If this evaluates to `true`[12], the task is considered to be final and no additional tasks are generated.

  This is like a deeper version of the `if` clause, where nested tasks are not affected. With the `final` clause, all child tasks are final tasks too.

- The `mergeable` clause was introduced to reduce the data requirements. Since each task comes with its own data environment, the program may require a significant amount of memory. The `mergeable` clause informs the compiler the data environments can be merged.

- The `depend` clause in the context of tasking is used to specify dependences between tasks.[13] The clause takes a keyword to describe the type of dependence, and a list of variables it applies to.

  The dependence type can be `in`, `out`, or `inout`. The latter is actually a leftover from the initial support for this feature. It is identical to type `out`.

  The two types `in` and `out` are strongly related. They define the direction of the dependence. Through the `out` type, it is specified that the variable(s) in the list are output variables from that task. Any task with dependency type

---

[12]Note the difference between the condition `false` and `true` for the `if` and `final` clause to be triggered.

[13]The `depend` clause is used on other constructs too.

in and the same variable, depends on this task and will not be executed until the task with the corresponding out type has completed.

The list item(s) may include array sections. See also Section 6.3.4 for more information on array sections.

- To indicate which task(s) are relatively important, the priority clause can be used. This is a hint to the OpenMP runtime system to help scheduling the execution of the various tasks.

  The clause takes a scalar expression as an argument. This must evaluate to a non-negative integer value and sets the priority for that task.

  The priorities are relative values. A task with a higher priority is considered to be more important than a task with a lower priority.

  Be aware that the value for the priority may not exceed the value set through environment variable OMP_MAX_TASK_PRIORITY, which is set to zero by default. The consequence is that this variable *must* be set when using priorities.

  The function omp_get_max_task_priority() returns this upper limit. There is no "set" counterpart to change the maximum priority during the execution of the program.

- By default, tasks are tied, but the untied clause changes this to untied. More details on tied and untied tasks can be found in Section 3.7.

The if, final, mergeable, and priority clauses are provided to optimize the performance of the tasking mechanism. These clauses are used to reduce the number of tasks generated, task scheduling overhead, memory requirements, and to express runtime scheduling preferences. An implementation is however free to ignore them.

3.7 Task Creation, Synchronization, and Scheduling

By design, task creation, scheduling, and execution details are meant to be a black box. This not only simplifies the life of the user, but also gives the implementation the freedom to adapt to the underlying architecture and evolve over time, without any impact on the portability of the code.

When a thread encounters a task construct, a new task is created and queued for execution by any thread in the team. Execution of the task could be immediate, or deferred until later, depending on the task scheduling details and thread availability.

Task synchronization construct	Description
barrier	either an implicit, or explicit barrier.
taskwait	wait on the completion of child tasks of the current task.
taskgroup	wait on the completion of child tasks of the current task, *and* their descendants.

Figure 3.29: **The three task synchronization constructs** – Completion of a task is guaranteed at a task synchronization point, but whether descendant tasks are affected also depends on the construct.

The thing that surprises users most the first time they consider using tasking, is that, although tasks are generated when the `task` construct is encountered, they are not necessarily executed then. More often than not, execution occurs "later," or in tasking terminology, the execution is *deferred*.

To be more precise, tasks are only guaranteed to be completed at program exit and at one of the three constructs listed in Figure 3.29. They are called *task synchronization constructs*.

The `barrier` construct can either be implied, at the end of the parallel region for example, or inserted explicitly. In both cases, the tasks are guaranteed to be completed then. The immediate consequence of this is that all tasks are completed at the end of a parallel region, since it has an implied barrier that may not be omitted.

The (lack of) implied barrier is why there is a difference between using the `single` construct versus the `master` construct. The latter has no implied barrier and tasks are not guaranteed to be completed upon exiting the master region.

There are also cases where the tasks need to completed, before the next barrier is encountered. For example, in the code shown in Figure 3.5 on page 108, the two tasks must be completed before the next (print) statement. This is where the `taskwait` construct comes to the rescue. If completion of the tasks needs to be enforced, this construct can be used. It is a stand-alone directive and ensures all child tasks of the current task are completed.

Another situation where the `taskwait` construct could be needed is when the `nowait` clause has been used. Since there is no longer an implied barrier, this clause has the side effect that there is no guarantee that all tasks have completed at the end of the construct to which the clause applies. Should this still be needed,

```
#pragma omp taskgroup  new-line
    structured block
!$omp taskgroup
    structured block
!$omp end taskgroup
```

Figure 3.30: Syntax of the taskgroup construct in C/C++ and Fortran
– This defines the structured block of code to be a taskgroup and provides deep synchronization by ensuring the completion of all child tasks, as well as their descendants.

the `taskwait` construct can be used to enforce completion of all child tasks.

The `taskwait` construct works well, unless there are descendant tasks. Those are not affected and if deeper synchronization of tasks is needed, the `taskgroup` construct should be used. This guarantees that also all descendant tasks are completed. The syntax is given in Figure 3.30.

Now that we have seen how tasks are scheduled and what mechanisms are available to enforce the completion of tasks, it is time to look at *task scheduling*.

Although not required by the specifications, all current tasking implementations use a queueing system. With this, generated tasks are put in a queue and at some point, executed.[14] For the runtime system, managing this queueing system takes time, especially since it is common to have many tasks, and threads need to be assigned to tasks. All of this adds to the parallel overhead.

This is why several features to reduce this overhead are available, such as the `if` and `final` constructs. Both can be used to prevent the queueing system from being flooded with either too small tasks, too many tasks, or both.

To formalize this and support several performance-related features, there are four tasking related concepts in the specifications:

- *A task region* - A region consisting of all code encountered during the execution of a task.

- *An undeferred task* - This is a task for which execution is not delayed, or "deferred," with respect to its generating task region. The generating task region is suspended until execution of the undeferred task has completed.

---

[14]The details of such queueing systems are complex and beyond the scope of this book.

In case the `if` clause on the `task` construct evaluates to `false`, an *undeferred* task is generated and the encountering thread suspends the current task region. Execution resumes only after the generated task has completed.

- *An included task* - This is an undeferred task, executed immediately by the encountering thread.

  If the `final` clause evaluates to `true`, the generated task is a final task. All tasks encountered during the execution of a final task are also final and included.

- *A tied/untied task* - Upon resuming a suspended task region, a tied task *must* be executed by the same thread again. With an untied task, there is no such restriction and any thread in the team can resume execution of the suspended task.

The above means that, while the `if` clause is "shallow" and only affects the encountering task, the `final` clause is a "deep" feature. Once a task is final, all child tasks are final too.

When using tasks, *task scheduling points* are places in the application where a thread executing a task, may temporarily suspend the current task, and switch to execute a different task. It can either begin, or resume this other task. A task scheduling point is included at the following locations:

- The point immediately following the generation of an explicit task.

- After the point of completion of a `task` region.

- In a `taskyield` region.

- In a `taskwait` region.

- At the end of a `taskgroup` region.

- In an implicit and explicit `barrier` region.

- When using the support for accelerators:

    - The point immediately following the generation of a `target` region.

    - At the beginning and end of a `target data` region.

```
#pragma omp taskyield new-line
!$omp taskyield
```

Figure 3.31: Syntax of the taskyield construct in C/C++ and Fortran –
This defines an explicit task scheduling point in the application.

- In a **target update** region.

- In a **target enter data** region.

- In a **target exit data** region.

- In the omp_target_memcpy() runtime function.

- In the omp_target_memcpy_rect() runtime function.

With the exception of the **taskyield** construct, all of these scheduling points are implied. They are there, but not visible. This is actually the reason the stand-alone **taskyield** construct was added. With this construct, the user can add an explicit task scheduling point, allowing the thread to suspend the current task and switch to another task. The syntax is given in Figure 3.31.

One of the clauses listed in Figure 3.28 on page 139 is the **untied** clause. By default, a task is "tied," which means that the *same* thread that executed the task must resume execution after the task has been suspended in a task scheduling point.[15] This could restrict the runtime scheduler and negatively impact performance.

Through the **untied** clause, this limitation is lifted and any thread may resume the execution of the suspended task. Clearly there are performance advantages to allow this kind of scheduling freedom, but there are some important caveats too.

First of all, **threadprivate** variables may not be used. Secondly, explicitly using the thread ID, for example through function omp_get_thread_num(), is not allowed and third, one must be careful using locks, including critical regions.

Last, but not least, untied tasks are an optional feature. An implementation is free to ignore the clause and make all tasks tied.

---

[15]This thread need not be the same thread that created the task.

```
#pragma omp taskloop [clause[[,] clause]...]    new-line
    for-loops
!$omp taskloop [clause[[,] clause]...]
    do-loops
[ !$omp end taskloop ]
```

Figure 3.32: **Syntax of the taskloop construct in C/C++ and Fortran –** The loop iterations are executed in parallel using tasks. At runtime, the iterations are distributed over the tasks.

```
private (list)
firstprivate (list)
lastprivate (list)
shared (list)
default(shared | none)                           (C/C++)
default(shared | firstprivate | private | none)  (Fortran)
if ([ taskloop :] scalar-logical-expression)
grainsize (grain-size)
num_tasks (num-tasks)
collapse (n)
final (scalar-logical-expression)
priority (priority-value)
untied
mergeable
nogroup
```

Figure 3.33: **The clauses supported by the taskloop construct –** The nogroup, grainsize, and num_tasks clauses are specific to this construct. All other clauses are supported on at least one other construct.

3.8   The Taskloop Construct

The taskloop construct has been added in OpenMP 4.5 and combines the ease of use of the parallel loop with the flexibility of tasking. In the example in Section 3.4, it was used to parallelize the loop in this code.

This construct simplifies using tasks in a (perfectly nested) loop. The syntax of the taskloop construct is given in Figure 3.32. The compiler and runtime system create and manage the tasks, while the user does not need to worry about the tasking details.

The `taskloop` construct supports the clauses listed in Figure 3.33. The data-sharing clauses are similar as on other constructs, and as with other constructs, the `if` clause supports the optional `taskloop` keyword. The `collapse`, `final`, `priority`, `untied`, and `mergeable` clauses are the same as on the `task` construct. There are, however, also three clauses that are unique to this construct:

- The `grainsize` clause takes a positive integer expression, the *grain-size*. The number of loop iterations assigned to a task is the minimum of this *grain-size* and the number of loop iterations, but does not exceed twice the value of *grain-size*.

  This clause can be used to adjust the granularity of the work performed by the tasks. It provides an easy way to avoid that the work performed per task is too small

  In absence of this clause, an implementation-dependent default is used.

- The `num_tasks` clause takes a positive integer expression. At runtime, as many tasks as this expression evaluates to, are generated, or fewer, if there are less loop iterations. This clause can be used to limit the number of tasks generated.

  In absence of this clause, an implementation-dependent default is used.

- With the `nogroup` clause, the `taskloop` construct is not embedded in an implied `taskgroup` construct.

The `nogroup` clause is needed in the following scenario. Since by default, the `taskloop` construct is embedded in an implicit `taskgroup` construct, there is a task synchronization point at the end. In case other tasks need to execute concurrently with the tasks executing the `taskloop` construct, this creates a problem. The `taskloop` loop could be executed first, followed by the other task(s). To make matters worse, task priorities are not handled properly either.

With the `nogroup` clause, there is no implied `taskgroup` construct and all tasks can run simultaneously, plus the priorities will be honored, if the implementation supports it.

```
1 #pragma omp parallel firstprivate(n)
2 {
3   #pragma omp single
4   {
5
6     #pragma omp taskloop firstprivate(n) nogroup priority(10)
7     for (int i=0; i<n; i++)
8     {
9        <body of loop>
10    } // End of taskloop
11
12    #pragma omp task priority(50)
13    {
14       <body of task>
15    } // End of task
16
17  } // End of single region
18 } // End of parallel region
```

Figure 3.34: **An example of the nogroup clause on the taskloop construct**
– This code demonstrates the use of the nogroup clause. Thanks to this clause, the task below the taskloop construct is executed simultaneously and if task priorities are implemented, even starts first.

The use of the nogroup clause is illustrated in Figure 3.34. Assuming task priorities are supported, and environment variable OMP_MAX_TASK_PRIORITY has been set to at least 50, the task defined at lines 12 − 15 is executed first. Without the nogroup clause on the taskloop construct at line 6, this is not be the case and the isolated task at line 12 is executed last.

There is a second variant of the taskloop construct, called taskloop simd. The syntax of this construct is given in Figure 3.35. SIMD is explained in great detail in Chapter 5. On those processors supporting SIMD instructions, this construct allows the compiler to exploit them within the generated tasks. This construct supports both the clauses from the taskloop construct, as well as the clauses for the simd directives. The collapse clause is applied only once.

#pragma omp taskloop simd *[clause[[,] clause]...]*   *new-line*
for-loops
!$omp taskloop simd *[clause[[,] clause]...]*
do-loops
[!$omp end taskloop simd]

Figure 3.35: **Syntax of the taskloop simd construct in C/C++ and Fortran** – The loop iterations are executed in parallel using tasks. At runtime, the loop iterations are distributed over the tasks and the resulting loop uses SIMD instructions.

3.9   Concluding Remarks

This chapter has covered all aspects of tasking. Hopefully the examples, plus the additional information presented here, are sufficient to get started.

Tasks work through a queueing system, invisible to the user. A thread that encounters a tasks, generates the code to execute it, including the data environment plus ICVs, and puts it in a queue.

At task synchronization points, threads execute tasks that are waiting in the queue. These points are implied on several constructs, but through the `taskwait` and `taskgroup` constructs, the user can enforce completion of the tasks.

The runtime system is in charge of managing the queue(s), but the user has indirect, yet powerful, controls. The `if`, `final`, `mergeable`, and `priority` clauses allow the user to reduce the pressure on the queueing system, avoid tasks get too small, and help the runtime scheduler to decide which task(s) to execute. Especially if the performance is disappointing, these clauses may make quite a difference and some experimentation is highly recommended.

Task dependences provide a very powerful mechanism to create a chain of tasks, where execution happens in the right order, while leveraging the parallelism in the algorithm.

The taskloop construct makes it easier to leverage tasks in a loop and more efficiently handle a load-imbalance.

An often asked question is whether tasks replace other constructs. The answer is no. Tasks are extremely flexible and powerful, but sometimes other constructs are easier to use and get the job done as well.

4 Thread Affinity

The topic of this chapter is how to leverage the hardware characteristics of the system by controlling the placement of OpenMP threads. This allows the user to optimize for memory bandwidth, memory latency, or cache utilization and is referred to as optimizing for *thread affinity*, or just *affinity*, for short.

OpenMP 4.0 introduced a portable, small, powerful set of features and constructs to support this [8]. In OpenMP 4.5, this was extended with additional runtime support. In this chapter a complete overview of the support for thread affinity is given.

4.1   The Characteristics of a cc-NUMA Architecture

Until relatively recently, only very large shared memory systems had a cc-NUMA architecture, but nowadays, even many small two socket, general purpose systems have this kind of memory system.

The reason this architecture became so dominant is because the number of cores in a processor, as well as the number of sockets, continues to increase. A monolithic memory interconnect, with a fixed memory bandwidth, quickly becomes the bottleneck.

This may be avoided by physically distributing the memory. In a cc-NUMA design, each socket connects to a subset of the total memory in the system. A cache coherent interconnect glues all the sockets together and provides a single system image to the user. Such a memory subsystem is much more scalable, because the aggregate memory bandwidth scales with the number of sockets in the system.

The benefit of the special interconnect is that an application has transparent access to all of the memory in the system, regardless of where the data resides. There is a price to pay though. The time to access data (and instructions for that matter) is no longer uniform: it depends where that data is located in the system.

In Figure 4.1, a generic cc-NUMA architecture is shown. This is a template system with all the processor and memory components found in a contemporary, general purpose, multi-socket system. Throughout the remainder of this chapter it is used to illustrate various features and examples.

This system has two sockets. Each socket has two cores with four hardware threads per core. Each core has its own set of L1 caches. The L1 caches are connected to a shared L2 cache, which is connected to the memory on the socket. The memory access time within a socket is uniform.

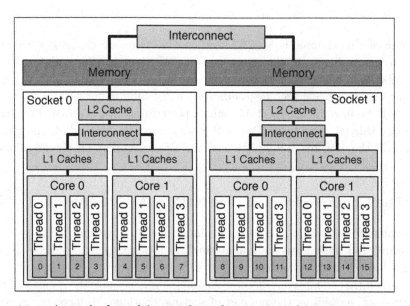

Figure 4.1: **A typical multi-core based server architecture** – This system
consists of two sockets. There are two cores per socket and each core has four hardware
threads. The memory is distributed across the system, but all of the memory may be
accessed from anywhere in the system. The access time is non-uniform however. In the
diagram, each hardware thread has a reference number, ranging from 0 to 15.

The two sockets are connected through a cache coherent interconnect. Memory
access is transparent across the entire system, but it takes longer to access data on
a remote socket.

The hardware threads are the execution vehicles. These are the units that execute
an OpenMP thread. For reference purposes, they are numbered consecutively from
0 to 15. This is the number shown in the diagram for each hardware thread.

Unless otherwise noted, in the remainder of this chapter, reference to a computer
system is implied to be a cc-NUMA system. On a system with a uniform, or
"flat," memory access time, most of the topics covered in this chapter need not be
considered. Such systems are however very rare these days.

4.2   First Touch Data Placement

Before thread affinity in OpenMP is discussed, it is important to know how the Operating System (OS) decides where to place the data.

Regardless where a thread executes, in the good case, data comes from the memory directly connected to the socket where the thread executes. In the worse case, data has to come from a memory connected to a socket far away in the system. This results in a longer, and possibly, non-uniform memory access time.

A non-uniform memory access time adds another dimension to application tuning. The goal is to service most, if not all, data accesses from the local memory connected to the socket where the thread is running. This maximizes bandwidth, and reduces the latency by avoiding relatively expensive accesses to a remote memory.

The OS decides where to run the application threads, but it has no knowledge of the application characteristics. This makes it hard to decide what the best placement is and a default thread placement strategy is used, which may, or may not, be optimal.

The OS manages data at the page level. A page consists of a relatively large chunk of data, for example 4 or 8 Kbyte.[1] The decision where to place data, or better said, the pages containing the data, is made by the OS. The question is when and how it decides to do so. This is controlled by the page placement policy.

4.2.1   The Pros and Cons of First Touch Data Placement

With the *First Touch* placement policy, the thread (or process) that "touches" the data for the first time, has ownership of the corresponding page. This defines the *home* node for that page. More specifically, the first thread that accesses a page, memory capacity issues aside, has the data allocated in the memory closest to this thread.

There is no right or wrong when it comes to the placement policy, but the First Touch policy is a very reasonable default. It ensures that serial applications get the data in their local memory, guaranteeing the minimal data access time for a serial application.

First Touch not only delivers the best performance from the memory system, but also preserves the performance, relative to a comparable system with a flat memory

---

[1] It is often possible to increase the size of a page. There may be valid performance reasons to do so, but this discussion is outside the scope of this book.

architecture. This is the reason general purpose Operating Systems use this policy as a default.

For exactly the same reason it works so well for serial programs, this policy can be a performance bottleneck for a shared memory parallel application. The only thing that matters for the page placement is which thread accessed the data for the first time. First Touch, for example, works well if each thread in a parallel region initializes a new block of memory it just allocated.

Things may not always be so easy though. If, for example, the master thread initializes shared data, all other threads need to access it from its memory. As long as this data is read-only, data caches may help to reduce the cost of a memory access, but in case the data is modified, the cache lines move around. This degrades performance.

I/O is another possible problem. If data is read into data structures that have not been used before, the pages are initialized upon reading the data. Because in most cases only one thread performs the read operation, the same placement problem occurs.

These types of placement issues create a load imbalance, because a certain percentage of the threads run slower due to a longer memory access time. On top of that, a single memory controller receives most, or even all, of the requests. Altogether it means the available total bandwidth in the system is not fully utilized.

Luckily, there is a simple technique to turn First Touch placement into an advantage. If applicable, it provides for an easy and elegant solution.

4.2.2   How to Exploit the First Touch Policy

Knowing how the First Touch policy works, the solution is rather straightforward. Depending on the data access pattern in the application, the data initialization phase may need to be adapted. It has to be parallelized in such a way that each thread touches those portions of data it needs most. This is somewhat of a reversed engineering approach and works best if data access patterns are static. That is, if a thread mostly accesses the same part of the data.

In case the data access pattern is irregular, First Touch does not work well, because there is no data locality. One approach to improve the situation, is to randomly place the pages using a system call, if supported by the OS.[2]

---

[2]The `madvise()` system call supported on most Operating Systems is an example.

```
 1 int *a;
 2    .....
 3 // Redundant parallel initialization to place the data upfront
 4 #pragma omp parallel for default(none) shared(n,a,b)
 5 for (int i=0; i<n; i++)
 6     a[i] = 0;
 7    .....
 8 // At this point, the placement has been decided upon already
 9 fread(a, sizeof(int), n, fp);
10    .....
11 // Reading the data takes advantage of the architecture
12 #pragma omp parallel for default(none) shared(n,a,b)
13 for (int i=0; i<n; i++)
14     b[i] = my_func(a[i]);
```

Figure 4.2: **An example to exploit First Touch** – The redundant parallel loop at lines $4-6$ ensures the pages are placed in the memories of the threads executing this loop. When reading from file at line 9, the elements of array **a** are placed in those memories. This ensures that the parallel bandwidth is maximized in the parallel loop at lines $12-14$.

This is also why the popular `calloc()` memory allocation function may not be the best choice. It is very convenient that this function allocates the memory, as well as initializes the data to zero. The potential drawback is that the latter may mean the pages end up in the wrong place.

A more cc-NUMA friendly solution is to use the regular `malloc()` function, followed by a parallelized data initialization phase.

In some cases, less intuitive approaches are required. For example, if it is not necessary to initialize the data, or in case it is not possible to parallelize the data initialization, the data placement may be non-optimal.

A solution is to insert an extra and *redundant* parallel data initialization, setting all data to zero, say. If this is performed prior to the first use of the data, the First Touch placement policy distributes the pages over the memories in the system.

An example is reading data from disk. This is often performed by a single thread, but this means that all this data ends up in the memory of the socket where the thread is executing. An extra parallel initialization is really beneficial here and illustrated in Figure 4.2.

Name	Set Definition
P_{00}	$\{0, 1, 2, 3\}$
P_{01}	$\{4, 5, 6, 7\}$
P_{10}	$\{8, 8, 10, 11\}$
P_{11}	$\{12, 13, 14, 15\}$

Figure 4.3: **Four set definitions based upon the hardware thread numbers** – Each set contains the hardware thread numbers of one of the cores from Figure 4.1.

In this example, the parallel redundant initialization at lines $4 - 6$ ensures the data is allocated in the memories of those threads executing the loop. In this way, the read operation at line 9 has no impact on the placement and the data is distributed automatically. The read operations in the parallel loop at lines $12 - 14$, utilizes the parallel memory architecture.

Another case where this kind of extra initialization works well, is if the data structure is initialized in a complex way, and/or the initialization is not performed in an isolated location in the application.

In summary, the First Touch placement policy controls where data is located. In the ideal scenario, the threads are close to the data they access most frequently.

4.3 The Need for Thread Affinity Support

A characteristic of a cc-NUMA system is the aggregated bandwidth. If an application is bandwidth hungry, it may be beneficial to spread the threads over the sockets and leverage the bandwidth each memory controller is able to deliver. In the opposite placement scenario, threads are kept close to each other to improve the cache utilization. In case threads exchange data frequently, sharing data via a cache is very efficient.

While the OS is unaware of such characteristics, the user usually knows more about the application. This knowledge may be leveraged to control where the OpenMP threads should run and improve the performance.

This can be achieved as follows. In the generic architecture in Figure 4.1, there are 16 hardware threads. Each one of these is a target location where an OpenMP thread may run. In Figure 4.3, these threads are organized into four disjoint sets. Within each set, the memory access time is uniform. This is also true for the two sets with the same first index, for example P_{00} and P_{01}, but not between sets with a different first index.

With the set definitions, it is easy to define where the threads should run. Suppose we want to use eight threads. In case the threads must stay close to each other, either the combination of sets P_{00} and P_{01}, or sets P_{10} and P_{11}, achieve this. If total bandwidth is important, two sets with a different first index should be selected.

Thread affinity in OpenMP is built upon such sets. These sets, or *places* as they are called in OpenMP, are defined by the user. Through additional user-level controls, they are mapped onto the computational hardware resources in the system. The remainder of this chapter introduces and discusses this in great detail.

4.4 The OpenMP Thread Affinity Philosophy

On a cc-NUMA architecture, performance and scalability critically rely on where the threads get their data from. Ideally, this is from the memory closest to where the threads execute. It is tempting to expose the memory hierarchy to the application and provide controls to migrate the data, but there are significant drawbacks:

- The memory hierarchy is complex today, and even more so in the future.

- The characteristics are detailed and vary substantially across different computer systems.

- Moving data is very costly and the cost increases with the number of hops in the interconnect.

Instead of migrating data to the threads, the alternative is much more attractive. The data is located in a memory connected to a socket in the system. The goal is to provide a mechanism to get the threads to execute close to the data they access most frequently. Even if the threads are initially in the "wrong" place, they can be moved to the data. Although not without a performance penalty either, moving a thread is much cheaper than moving the data to the thread(s).

The thread affinity support in OpenMP is based upon sets, similar as introduced in the previous section. In OpenMP, such sets are called *places*. Through thread affinity it is also guaranteed that, for the duration of the parallel region, a thread stays in the place it has been assigned to, once it has migrated to its destination place. Depending on the affinity policy selected on a subsequent parallel region, the threads may, or may not, migrate again.

This provides for a high level control mechanism to maximize thread affinity. All that needs to be done is to specify where in the system the OpenMP threads are allowed to execute and define their relative position. For example, to keep threads close to each other, or spread them over the system.

In OpenMP, the two key concepts that must be used to specify thread affinity, are the *places* and the *affinity policy*. In absence of either one of these, or both, implementation-defined default settings are used.

- **OpenMP Places** - A place is a hardware resource that can execute an OpenMP thread.

  There are different ways to specify places, but ultimately a list with such execution vehicles for an OpenMP thread to run on, is used by the OpenMP runtime scheduler to decide where to run the threads.

  Environment variable `OMP_PLACES` is used to describe the system in terms of such system resources.

  The easiest way to specify places is to use one of the symbolic names "sockets," "cores," or "threads." Although the interpretation of these words is implementation-defined, it is safe to assume they match the hardware characteristics suggested by the name.

  In addition to this, it is allowed for an implementation to support additional names to provide tailored support for architectural features not easily captured through these standard keywords.

  These symbolic names have several advantages and are recommended to use, but in some cases more explicit control over thread placement may be desired.

  This level of control is supported through an explicit *place list*. Such a list consists of one or more sets with integer numbers. The place list is defined at program start-up and used throughout the execution of the program. In other words, it is fixed.

These numbers are the scheduling units the OS uses to schedule OpenMP threads on. In the most common case, the numbers represent hardware threads, but they could also be related to GPU channels for example.[3]

The selection of the numbers, plus the definition of the places within a place list, provides sufficient flexibility to fully control thread placement.

Because there may be many numbers, resulting in a long list, the interval notation is very convenient. Through a compact notation, it simplifies the list, if a range of numbers is used. For example, the set defined by $\{0 : 4 : 8\}$ is equivalent to $\{0, 8, 16, 24\}$, but the notation is much shorter and less error-prone.

This, and much more about OpenMP places, is explained in detail in Section 4.5.1, starting on page 161.

- **Affinity Policy** - While the place list defines all the resources available to the OpenMP runtime scheduler, the affinity policy may be adjusted on each (nested) parallel region, and controls *how* the threads should be scheduled, relative to each other.

  Environment variable `OMP_PROC_BIND` is set to the appropriate policy, or policies, in case of nested parallel regions. If not set explicitly by the user, an implementation-defined setting is used.

  Within the application, the `proc_bind` clause may be used to specify the policy at any level in the (nested) parallel region. The policy set through the clause is not persistent. It is only valid for the parallel region the clause applies to. In the absence of this clause, the policies set through `OMP_PROC_BIND`, or the default settings if this variable is not defined, are applied. This is regardless of any explicit policy settings on previous parallel regions.

  The following policies are supported: `master`, `close` and `spread`.

  The names are descriptive of the behavior and can be used to schedule the threads on the same place where the master thread runs, keep them close to each other, or spread them out. This is all defined in terms of the places in the place list. The precise definitions of these three policies are covered in detail in Section 4.6, starting on page 168.

---

[3]In the remainder these numbers are assumed to represent hardware threads, but they can easily represent a different scheduling unit.

	Thread Affinity (OMP_PROC_BIND)		
	not set	explicitly set	
Definition of places (OMP_PLACES)		false	true, master, close, or spread
not set	system defaults	*affinity disabled*	default place list used
explicitly set	depends on default	*affinity disabled*	explicit settings used

Figure 4.4: **Interaction between OMP_PLACES and OMP_PROC_BIND** – This table summarizes the interaction between these two environment variables. As usual, the default values are system-dependent.

Implied with an affinity policy is *thread binding*. Threads are not allowed to execute outside of the place they are assigned to.

It is allowed to only request binding, without further specifying where threads should be scheduled to execute. This is achieved by setting environment variable OMP_PROC_BIND to true. If set to false, the place list is ignored and all thread affinity is disabled.

Both these environment variables have a system dependent default value. There is also an interaction between their settings. This is summarized in Figure 4.4.

In case neither of these two variables has been set, thread affinity depends on the system dependent defaults. Affinity may, or may not, be enabled. Given the possible performance impact, we strongly recommend to check the documentation for the defaults, or even better, set them explicitly.

In Figure 4.4, it is seen that if OMP_PROC_BIND is set to false (and remember this could be the default), thread affinity is *always* disabled. If it is set to true, or to one of the supported policies, affinity is enabled and the place list is either the default (again, check the documentation what it is set to), or the list explicitly set through OMP_PLACES. If OMP_PROC_BIND is not set, but OMP_PLACES is explicitly defined, the default setting for OMP_PROC_BIND determines whether thread affinity is enabled, or not. This is something to watch out for.

4.5 The OpenMP Places Concept

OpenMP places define where threads are allowed to run. Places are set through environment variable OMP_PLACES and fixed throughout the execution of the application.

There are two disjoint ways to define OpenMP places. This section starts with the low level approach, using integer numbers to define where threads can run. Although very powerful, most users do not need this. The second way to specify the places is through the more flexible and elegant abstract names, like "cores," or "threads." This is the preferred method and covered in Sections 4.5.3 and 4.7, starting on page 166 and 188 respectively. The motivation to start with the integer numbers is that they make it easier to introduce and explain some of the features.

4.5.1   Defining OpenMP Places Using Sets with Numbers

An OpenMP *place* consists of an *unordered* set of comma-separated non-negative numbers enclosed by braces ({ and }). An example is the set $\{0, 4, 8, 12\}$ that defines four target resources where a thread could run. Because the order within a place does not matter, the set $\{12, 4, 0, 8\}$ defines the same place.

The specifications use the word "processor" in the context of thread affinity. We prefer to use different terminology, because a processor is too coarse. A contemporary system often has sockets, cores and hardware threads. All of these can be a scheduling unit target for thread affinity.

This is why we take the liberty to introduce our own terminology and refer to the numbers that define a place as *(hardware) resource numbers*, or "resources" for short.

The resource numbers are system and configuration dependent. They are intended to represent an entity the OS can assign work to. Examples are a hardware thread, or a GPU lane.[4]

The way to obtain these numbers for a specific configuration depends on the OS. It is very likely to be obtained by checking a configuration file (for example, file /proc/cpuinfo on Linux), through an appropriate OS command (for instance, numactl and lscpu on Linux, or psrinfo on Oracle Solaris), or a specific tool. It is best to check the documentation of the target system and OpenMP compiler for the details.

As an example, Figure 4.5 shows the output of the Linux lscpu command on a two socket system using Intel processors. The output shows that this system has two NUMA nodes (these are the two sockets), where each socket has 18 cores with 2 hardware threads per core. This gives a total of $2x18x2 = 72$ hardware threads.

---

[4]In this chapter we mostly interpret these numbers as hardware thread numbers, but the concept is more general than our usage might suggest.

```
$ lscpu
Architecture:          x86_64
CPU op-mode(s):        32-bit, 64-bit
Byte Order:            Little Endian
CPU(s):                72
On-line CPU(s) list:   0-71
Thread(s) per core:    2
Core(s) per socket:    18
Socket(s):             2
NUMA node(s):          2
Vendor ID:             GenuineIntel
CPU family:            6
Model:                 79
Model name:            Intel(R) Xeon(R) CPU E5-2695 v4 @ 2.10GHz
Stepping:              1
CPU MHz:               2995.781
BogoMIPS:              4205.85
Virtualization:        VT-x
L1d cache:             32K
L1i cache:             32K
L2 cache:              256K
L3 cache:              46080K
NUMA node0 CPU(s):     0-17,36-53
NUMA node1 CPU(s):     18-35,54-71
```

Figure 4.5: **An example of hardware thread numbers** – This is the output from the Linux `lscpu` command on a two socket system. It shows there are two NUMA nodes, the two sockets. This system has a total of $2x18x2 = 72$ hardware threads. The last two lines show the hardware thread numbers and how they map onto the NUMA nodes.

What is most relevant in this output is shown in the last two lines. This shows the hardware thread numbers and how they map onto the two NUMA nodes.

These threads are numbered $0 - 17$ and $36 - 53$ on the first NUMA node. The threads on the second NUMA node are numbered $18 - 35$ and $54 - 71$. The interpretation requires a basic understanding of the architecture of the system. Numbers $0 - 17$ represent the first hardware thread on each of the 18 cores on the first socket. The numbers in the $36 - 53$ range are for the second hardware thread on these cores.

```
$ psrinfo -vp
The physical processor has 16 cores and 128 virtual
processors (0-127)
    The core has 8 virtual processors (0-7)
    The core has 8 virtual processors (8-15)
    The core has 8 virtual processors (16-23)
         ..... output lines omitted .....
    The core has 8 virtual processors (104-111)
    The core has 8 virtual processors (112-119)
    The core has 8 virtual processors (120-127)
      SPARC-T5 (chipid 0, clock 3600 MHz)

The physical processor has 16 cores and 128 virtual
processors (128-255)
    The core has 8 virtual processors (128-135)
    The core has 8 virtual processors (136-143)
    The core has 8 virtual processors (144-151)
         ..... output lines omitted .....
    The core has 8 virtual processors (232-239)
    The core has 8 virtual processors (240-247)
    The core has 8 virtual processors (248-255)
      SPARC-T5 (chipid 1, clock 3600 MHz)
```

Figure 4.6: **Another example of hardware thread numbers** – This is an output fragment of the Solaris `psrinfo -vp` command on a SPARC system. A virtual processor refers to what is called a hardware thread in this book. The output shows there are two sockets with 16 cores each. Each core has 8 hardware threads. This gives a total of 256 hardware threads for this system.

As an example, the first core on the first NUMA node has hardware threads 0 and 36. These numbers are 18 and 54 for the second NUMA node.

When using the integer numbers, this type of output is indispensable to define the places. For example, the place set $\{0, 1, 2, 18, 19, 20\}$ defines the first three hardware threads on the first three cores of both NUMA nodes.

To demonstrate that the numbering scheme depends on the hardware and OS, the output from the `psrinfo -vp` Solaris command on a two socket system using SPARC processors is given in Figure 4.6. For formatting reasons, several lines have been omitted and the layout has been somewhat adapted.

```
<lower-bound> : <count> [:  <stride> ]
```

Figure 4.7: **Syntax of the interval notation to define an OpenMP place** – The `lower-bound` and `count` numbers are positive integers, including zero. The optional `stride` can be any number, including zero, or a negative value. The default is 1.

The output shows this system has two sockets. Each socket has 16 cores with 8 hardware threads ("virtual processor") per core. This means there are $16x8 = 128$ hardware threads per socket. The threads are numbered $0 - 127$ on the first socket. The threads on the second socket are numbered $128 - 255$. On this system, place set $\{0, 1, 2, 8, 9, 10\}$ also defines the first three hardware threads on the first two cores of the first socket, but it is a different set than the one used on the other system.

There is an important thing to remember. The numbers within a single place are *unordered*. From a scheduling point of view, there is no preference for entries within the set. This allows the user to provide flexibility to the OpenMP runtime scheduler. An example may be the hardware threads that are part of a core. There shouldn't be any difference on which hardware thread the OpenMP thread is running.

This also allows to optimize for the situation that the memory access time is uniform for a certain subset of the hardware threads. If an OpenMP place is created that includes all these threads, the scheduler has the freedom to select an arbitrary thread from this set, without an impact on the performance.

Although OpenMP places are designed to express uniformity in the architecture, this is not required and obviously not verified by the runtime system. It is the responsibility of the user to define places in a meaningful way. If for example the memory access time is not uniform for all hardware threads within a single place, performance variations across identical runs may, and probably will, be observed.

The output in Figures 4.5 and 4.6 points to a potential issue: the list with numbers could get rather long. This is not only tedious to type in, but also error-prone. This is the reason that a convenient interval notation is supported. An interval is specified through a lower bound, a count[5], and a stride. The syntax of the interval notation is given in Figure 4.7.

As an example, the following list defines all 36 hardware threads spanning the first socket of the Intel system: $\{0 : 18 : 1, 36 : 18 : 1\}$. This compact notation expands to $\{0, 1, \ldots, 17, 36, 37, \ldots, 53\}$. On the SPARC system, to include the 64

---

[5]Note this is a count, not the maximum.

hardware threads on the first 8 cores of the second socket, the list must be set to $\{128 : 64 : 1\}$.

There are three things worth mentioning in relation to the interval notation:

- The stride can be negative, and although not very meaningful, even be zero.

- The interval notation can be used in combination with comma separated lists.

- The exclusion operator "!" can be used to exclude the number or places immediately following the operator.

4.5.2 The OpenMP Place List

In most cases, a single place is not sufficient and an *OpenMP place list* must be constructed. A place list is an *ordered* list of places.

It is important to note that, while the order of the resource numbers within an individual place is irrelevant, the order of the places in the place list matters, As an example, consider the place list defined by "$\{0, 8\}, \{128, 136\}$." The place list "$\{8, 0\}, \{136, 128\}$" is equivalent, but list "$\{128, 136\}, \{0, 8\}$" is different. Both choices regarding the ordering (or lack thereof) make sense.

Multiple resource numbers within a single place give the scheduler more freedom to select a target location where to run the thread. As all resource numbers within one place are considered to be equivalent, the order does not matter.[6]

This is different for the place list. The order of the places within the place list affects the selection of places for a specific affinity policy. The same policy with a permuted place list may result in a different mapping of threads onto the hardware. The interpretation of the place list under a given affinity policy is extensively covered in Section 4.6, starting on page 168.

The interval notation may also be applied to an entire place. This provides a convenient way to define long place lists through a compact notation. The entire place definition is used as the lower bound. The stride is added to each of the resource numbers in this place.

As an example, consider this place list: $\{0, 1, 2, 3\} : 3 : 5$. By definition of an interval, this means there are 3 copies, each separated by a stride of 5. The resulting expanded list consist of the following places: $\{0, 1, 2, 3\}, \{0 + 1 * 5, 1 + 1 * 5, 2 + 1 *$

---

[6]In case this kind of freedom for the runtime scheduler is not desirable, the solution is to create places consisting of one element only.

$5, 3 + 1 * 5\}, \{0 + 2 * 5, 1 + 2 * 5, 2 + 2 * 5, 3 + 2 * 5\}$. In other words, the resulting place list is the following: $\{0, 1, 2, 3\}, \{5, 6, 7, 8\}, \{10, 11, 12, 13\}$. This may even be written in a more compact way, because the base place may also be defined as $\{0 : 4 : 1\}$. Using this notation, the same place list is defined by $\{0 : 4 : 1\} : 3 : 5$.

4.5.3 Defining OpenMP Places Using Abstract Names

Specific resource numbers in places, and the place list, provide full control where threads should run, but portability of the definitions is not guaranteed. On a different system, or even a different configuration of the same system, the numbers most likely need to be adjusted. This is why the following three *abstract names* are supported as an alternative:

- sockets - Each place corresponds to a single socket. A socket can have multiple cores.

- cores - Each place corresponds to a core. A core can support multiple hardware threads.

- threads - Each place corresponds to a single hardware thread.

Although the definition of these abstract names is system dependent, they can be expected to be meaningful and reflective of the underlying architecture. This is why they are recommended over the resource numbers. The abstract names and resource numbers are mutually exclusive. In other words, an abstract name can *not* be combined with a list specification.

An implementation can add abstract names to the above list. The usual pros and cons apply. Most likely, these names better support the target architecture, but portability is lost.

The abstract names are hierarchical. A socket typically has multiple cores and each core can have multiple hardware threads. As an example, the OMP_-PLACES=sockets place list definition implies that the OpenMP threads may run on any of the hardware threads associated with a socket. There is no distinction as to which cores are used for example.

Transparent to the user, an abstract name defines a place list. The places in this list span the resource specified. Each place can have more than one resource number in case the name used has multiple hardware scheduling units associated with it. For example, the OMP_PLACES=cores definition internally uses a place list that consists of a set of places. Each place contains the resource number(s) corresponding to a core. If a core supports eight hardware threads, say, each place consists of a set with eight unique numbers.

The abstract name can be appended with an optional number between parentheses. This specifies the length of the place list that is created. For example a place list defined by `OMP_PLACES=cores(4)`, restricts the list to only four cores. It is not possible to specify which cores. They may be on the same socket, or not. If this level of detail is needed, resource numbers must be used.

In case the length of the list exceeds the number of resources (of the named type) available, the length of the generated place list is also implementation dependent.

The place list is only half of the solution. The affinity policy dictates in what way the places are mapped onto the hardware. A much more extensive coverage of the abstract names, in combination with the affinity policy, may be found in Section 4.7, on page 188.

4.5.4 How to Define the OpenMP Place List

The place list is defined through the `OMP_PLACES` environment variable. If the user does not set this variable to define the place list explicitly, the system uses an implementation-dependent list.

An example how to set the place list is given below. For demonstration purposes, the list based notation is combined with the interval notation:

`OMP_PLACES="{0,8},{128,136},{112:8},{240:8}"`. This list consists of four places. The first two places contain two resource numbers each, while the remaining two places each consist of eight resource numbers. The abstract names are set through the same environment variable. For example: `OMP_PLACES="cores(4)"`.

The places and the place list definitions are *static*. There are no runtime functions to change the place list while the program is executing. In case the place list contains resources that are not available, for example a non-existing hardware thread number, the behavior is implementation-dependent. The runtime system may ignore it and use a default place list, or chose to abort with an appropriate error message. More information on this environment variable can be found on page 58 in Section 2.2.

4.6   Mapping Threads onto OpenMP Places

The next question to answer is how the places are used to map the OpenMP threads onto the hardware. This is controlled through an interaction between the place list and the thread affinity policy. More specifically, the selected affinity policy is applied at the level of the places in the place list.

Implied with thread affinity is "thread binding" at the level of an OpenMP place. This means that the threads within the same team are not allowed to move out of the place they were originally assigned to.

Once the destination place to run on has been determined, the OpenMP thread is not allowed to execute elsewhere. The thread may be temporarily de-scheduled to make room for another activity, but once it is scheduled to run again, it must be put back onto the same place. If the place has multiple resource numbers (e.g. {0,1,2}), the thread is allowed to be scheduled to run on a different resource number, as long as it is within the same place.

Affinity and binding are controlled through environment variable `OMP_PROC_-BIND`. This variable defines the policy, or policies in case of nested parallelism, applied to parallel regions.

- `OMP_PROC_BIND=false` - All thread affinity and binding is disabled. Any place list, set through environment variable `OMP_PLACES` is ignored. The same is true for usage of the `proc_bind` clause on the parallel region(s).

- `OMP_PROC_BIND=true` - Thread binding is enabled and the first thread is bound to the first place in the place list. No other guarantees regarding binding and placement are given.

  If the first thread cannot be bound, the behavior is implementation dependent.

  This is a legacy setting, available prior to OpenMP 4.0. We do not suggest to use it and specify a policy, or multiple policies, instead.

- `OMP_PROC_BIND=<comma separated list with policies>` - At each nesting level, the threads are placed according to the affinity policy in effect at that level. Threads are not allowed to migrate between the places.

As with all OpenMP environment variables, this variable defines the initial setting(s). At runtime an already defined policy may be overruled, or defined if not yet set, through the `proc_bind` clause supported on the `parallel` construct.

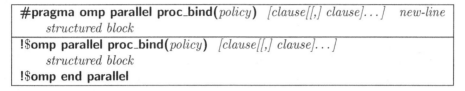

Figure 4.8: **Syntax of the proc_bind clause on the parallel construct in C/C++ and Fortran** – The thread affinity policy may be specified at each nesting level. It is only valid for the region it applies to. Choices for the policy are master, close, or spread.

This is a straightforward clause, taking one of the three affinity policies as an argument. The syntax in C/C++ and Fortran is given in Figure 4.8.

The affinity policy, as set through the proc_bind clause, is specified on each parallel region and not persistent. It is only valid for the duration of the particular region it applies to. In absence of the proc_bind clause, the corresponding setting through OMP_PROC_BIND takes effect. Be aware that the default setting for variable OMP_PROC_BIND is implementation dependent. In addition to define OMP_PLACES explicitly, it is recommended to set this variable as well.[7]

The policy defines in what way OpenMP threads are mapped onto the hardware threads. It can be adapted on every parallel region, but the setting is static for the duration of the execution of the parallel region it applies to. The supported policies are summarized in Figure 4.9.

Irrespective of the policy, once an OpenMP thread has been assigned to a place, it is not allowed to move to another place. This is called "thread binding."

To simplify the description of the affinity algorithms and the mappings, the notation defined in Figure 4.10 is used in the remainder of this chapter.

In all examples to follow, the generic multi-core architecture shown in Figure 4.1 on page 152 is the target system. The topology of this system can now be described in terms of OpenMP places. This system is relatively simple and the abstract names are sufficient, but to demonstrate the concepts, the resource numbers are used instead.

The system has two sockets with four cores each. A core supports four hardware threads. The threads within a core are fully symmetric in terms of memory access

---

[7]To easily verify the settings, environment variable OMP_DISPLAY_ENV is recommended to be set to true, or verbose.

Policy	Description
master	Each thread in the team is assigned to the same place as the master thread.
close	The threads in the team are placed close to the master thread. Threads are assigned to consecutive places in a round-robin way, starting with the place to the right of the master thread.
spread	Spread the threads as evenly as possible over the places.

Figure 4.9: **Supported policies for thread binding** – A specific policy is applied to a parallel region. In the case of nested parallelism, each parallel region has its own policy. The policy may be set through environment variable OMP_PROC_BIND, by using the proc_bind clause on a parallel region, or both. In case of the latter, the clause overrules the environment variable.

Symbol	Description
P	The number of places.
P_i	Place "i."
SP_i	Subpartition "i."
T	The number of threads in a team.
T_i	A thread with thread number "i" within a team.
ST_i	A subset of threads in a team, referred to with identifier "i."
$T_i \in P_j$	OpenMP thread "i" is scheduled to execute in place P_j.
$T_i \in SP_j$	OpenMP thread "i" is scheduled to execute in partition SP_j.

Figure 4.10: **Notation used in the affinity policy descriptions** – In the description of the various thread affinity policies the above notation is used. Places and subpartitions are considered as sets. This is why the mathematical $\in$ symbol is used to denote a thread is assigned to a place, or subpartition.

times. Memory access within a socket is uniform. In this respect, all cores within a socket are equal, but at the cache level there could be a difference in access times. From a memory access point of view, this system has four places ($P = 4$), symbolized by $P_0, \ldots, P_3$. Using the numbering for the hardware threads shown in Figure 4.1, the definition of each place is listed in Figure 4.11, where each place is defined to consist of the four hardware threads that are part of a core.

The place list consist of the four places $\{P_0, \ldots, P_3\}$ and is defined through environment variable OMP_PLACES as follows:

OMP_PLACES = "{0,1,2,3},{4,5,6,7},{8,9,10,11},{12,13,14,15}".

Place	Definition	
	Full List	**Interval Notation**
P_0	$\{0,1,2,3\}$	$\{0:4:1\}$
P_1	$\{4,5,6,7\}$	$\{4:4:1\}$
P_2	$\{8,9,10,11\}$	$\{8:4:1\}$
P_3	$\{12,13,14,15\}$	$\{12:4:1\}$

Figure 4.11: **Place definitions used in the examples in this section** – In the examples that illustrate the various affinity policies, the above definitions for the places are used. Both the full list expansions, as well as the equivalent interval notations are shown.

This may also be written in a more compact way, using the interval notation: `OMP_PLACES = "{0:4:1},{4:4:1},{8:4:1},{12:4:1}"`. Recognizing the regularity in this sequence, the definition may even be further condensed to `OMP_PLACES = "{0:4:1}:4:4"`. In the remaining subsections it is shown in what way this place list, in combination with the various affinity policies, is used to control where the OpenMP threads execute.

Before we go into the details, there are several comments to be made. They apply to all the placement policies and examples discussed below.

- The mapping of OpenMP threads onto the hardware is decided at the level of *places*. If a place consists of multiple resource numbers, the selection of a specific resource within the place depends upon the implementation.

- The phrase "a thread executes in a place" is a shortcut for the following scenario. The OpenMP runtime system selects an OpenMP thread to be scheduled onto the place. Next, the runtime scheduler selects a resource number within the place, to execute this thread.

- According to the specifications, the *initial placement* of the master thread of a team is inherited from the place where the parent thread of this master thread is running.

  There is a potential catch with this. Upon program start up, the OS decides on the placement of the process. At this point, the OpenMP runtime system is not involved and there is no concept of OpenMP places yet. Therefore, it may happen that the OS schedules the parent thread to run on a hardware resource that is not included in any of the places.

In case thread migration is supported on the system, the OpenMP runtime system first migrates the parent thread to a place in the place list and decides on the placement of the master thread next. If migration is not supported however, or the affinity request cannot be fulfilled for some other reason, the behavior is implementation-dependent.

We recommend to check the documentation of the specific runtime system used to verify the behavior in such cases.

- In the remainder, another shortcut is used. Whenever the place of the master thread is specified, it is implied that the selection of this place has been derived from the place where the parent of this master thread executes.

- To simplify the drawings, unless noted otherwise, in all examples, the parent of the master thread is assumed to execute in place P_0 defined in Figure 4.11.

4.6.1   The Master Affinity Policy

The most straightforward affinity policy is the `master` policy, where all threads in the team are scheduled to run in the same place the master thread executes in.

This policy is useful when efficient communication and data sharing between threads is important. This is under the assumption that the memory bandwidth requirements of the threads are modest. Otherwise, this policy may cause a bottleneck if all threads execute on the same socket, or core.

The `master` affinity policy is illustrated in Figure 4.12. The threads are symbolized by solid circles. The master thread has been colored black, while the gray circles represent the other threads in the team. If the master thread executes in the second place of the place list, $P_1 = \{4, 5, 6, 7\}$, the other threads in the team run there as well. Effectively, all threads in this team execute on the same core.

Because there are four threads in total, and four resources in this place, each OpenMP thread may execute on a different hardware thread, but this is not guaranteed.

The specifications require only that the other threads in the team to execute in the same place. Where they execute within this place, is an implementation-dependent choice. A good scheduler will exploit the presence of additional hardware threads and does not overload resources if this can be avoided.

If the number of OpenMP threads exceeds the number of resources within the place, multiple threads must share a resource. If there are eight threads in our

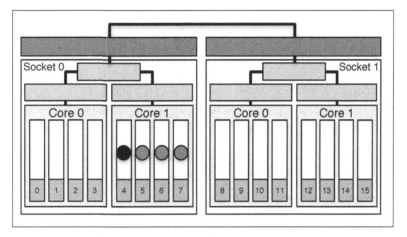

Figure 4.12: **An example of the master affinity policy** – With this policy, additional threads of the same team are scheduled to run in the same place where the master thread is executing. Threads are symbolized by solid circles. The master thread has a black color. The gray circles represent the other threads in the team. Because the master is assumed to execute in place P_1, the other threads execute in the same core.

example, each hardware thread in core 1 of socket 0 executes two OpenMP threads. This is probably not a good approach, because oversubscription of hardware threads usually degrades performance.

4.6.2 The Close Affinity Policy

The goal of the `close` affinity policy is to keep OpenMP threads close enough to take advantage of data locality, while still spreading the threads across the system as much as possible.

In a typical scenario, the cores (and hardware threads) within a single socket are used. Combined with the First Touch page placement policy, the data is located in the memory connected to the socket, and more expensive remote memory accesses are avoided.

Using the notation from Figure 4.10, the number of threads is denoted by T, and the number of places is symbolized by P. There are two cases to distinguish:

- If $T \leq P$, then there are sufficient places and each thread is assigned to a unique place.

Threads are selected by their thread number within the team, starting with the lowest numbered thread, and assigned to *consecutive* places in the place list. The first place selected is the one where the parent of the master thread executes.

For example, if $T = 3$ and $P = 4$, there are four places $P_0, \ldots, P_3$. Assuming the parent of thread T_0 executes in P_0, thread T_0 is assigned to place P_0 and the other threads T_i execute in place P_i, for $i = 1, \ldots, 3$.

- If $T > P$, then there are more threads than places and at least one place executes more than one OpenMP thread.

Each place gets assigned a *consecutive* subset of the total number of threads T in the team. There are P subsets and the number of threads ST_i in the subset is chosen, such that $floor(T/P) \leq ST_i \leq ceiling(T/P)$, $i = 0, \ldots P - 1$.[8]

The first subset includes the master thread and is assigned to the place where the parent of the master thread is running. The second subset is assigned to the place next to this place in the place list, and so on.

As an example, consider $T = 8$ and $P = 4$. Each subset contains $floor(8/4) = ceiling(8/4) = 2$ threads. Assuming the parent of the master thread executes in place P_0, threads T_0 and T_1 are assigned to P_0. Threads T_2 and T_3 are assigned to place P_1, and so on.

If P does not divide T evenly, the lower and upper bounds for ST_i differ by one and not all subsets contain the same number of threads. It is up to the implementation to assign subsets to places. In other words, at least one place gets assigned one more thread than other places and the implementation decides which place(s) to select for this.

Consider a case with seven threads ($T = 7$) and four places ($P = 4$). There is one subset with a single thread and three subsets have two threads each.[9] It is up to the implementation how to map the subsets onto the places. For example P_1, P_2 and P_3 may all execute two threads each, while the first place P_0 gets assigned one thread only.

---

[8]The Glossary contains the definitions of these functions.

[9]For the interested reader, "Computing the number of threads per subset" in the Glossary explains how these results may be obtained.

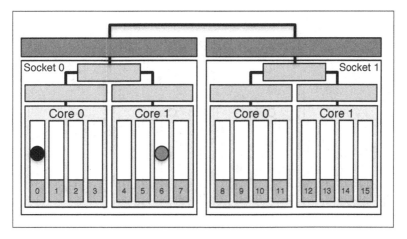

Figure 4.13: **An example of the close affinity policy using 2 threads** – With this policy, additional threads of the same team are scheduled close to the place where the master thread is executing. Threads are symbolized by solid circles. The master thread has a black color. The gray circle represents the other thread in the team. With the given place list, and assuming the master thread executes on core 0 of socket 0, the second thread executes on core 1 on the same socket.

The `close` affinity policy is illustrated in Figure 4.13 for a case with four places ($P = 4$) and two threads ($T = 2$). The $T \leq P$ algorithm applies.

The assumption is that the master thread executes in the place (P_0). This means the second thread is scheduled on a hardware thread from place P_1. Because each place spans a core, the threads effectively run on separate cores. In this case, both cores used are on the first socket, but if the parent of the master thread executes in place P_1, for example, the second thread executes on core 0 of the second socket.

The choice of a resource number within a specific place is determined by the runtime scheduler and the order within a single place is assumed to be irrelevant regarding scheduling preferences. This is illustrated in Figure 4.13. In this case, hardware threads 0 and 6 are selected.

If we increase the number of threads to three, the third place in the place list is added as a scheduling target and this third thread executes in core 0 on socket 1 (place P_2). Again the choice of a hardware thread within this core is determined by the scheduler. With four threads, core 1 on the second socket is also used.

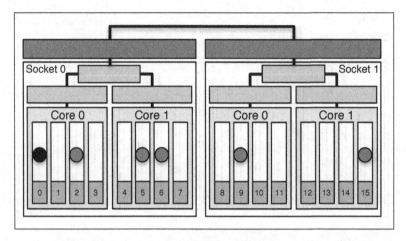

Figure 4.14: **An example of the close affinity policy using 6 threads** –
The master thread executes on core 0 of socket 0, that is, in place P_0. Four threads are
scheduled onto the four cores. The implementation selects the places for the remaining
threads. These are assumed to be P_0 and P_1 in this example.

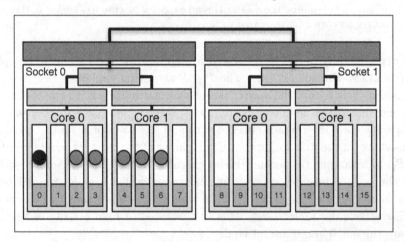

Figure 4.15: **Using the close affinity policy to force 6 threads onto 1 socket**
– With a modified place list spanning the first two cores only, the scheduler uses the two
cores on the first socket. Because there are two places, the six threads are balanced across
the two cores.

Once the number of threads exceeds the number of places in the place list ($T > P$), multiple threads are scheduled onto the same place. The details of the number of threads per place is implementation dependent. For example, if six threads are used, $floor(6/4) = 1$, $ceiling(6/4) = 2$ and two of the four places get assigned two threads. It is up to the implementation which places to select. A possible choice is shown in Figure 4.14.

This example illustrates another point. Although we used the `close` affinity policy, the threads are still spread over the entire system. This is because the place list spans all resources in the system.

When spreading the threads over the system is not desired, the solution is to modify the place list. As an example, assume all threads need to execute within the first socket only, but they should be balanced across the two cores. This is achieved by re-defining the place list to include only places P_0 and P_1. The `OMP_PLACES` environment variable must be set as follows: `OMP_PLACES = "{0,1,2,3},{4,5,6,7}"`. Alternatively, with the more compact interval notation, the same place list is given by `OMP_PLACES = "{0:4:1},{4:4:1}"`, or even shorter. `OMP_PLACES = "{0:4:1}:2:4"`. With this new place list, threads are assigned to only the two cores in the first socket. The assignment algorithm ensures load balancing across the two cores.

Figure 4.15 illustrates a case in which there are six threads. Because $T = 6$ and $P = 2$, the $T > P$ algorithm applies. There are two subsets and both contain $floor(6/2) = ceiling(6/2) = 3$ threads. Each subset gets assigned to a place.

As before, the mapping of OpenMP threads within a single place depends on the scheduler. It is guaranteed that only the first socket is used and each core executes three threads that are consecutively numbered.

If the parent of the master thread executes in place P_0, threads 0, 1 and 2 execute on core 0, while the three remaining threads 3, 4, and 5 execute in place P_1. This means they run on core 1.

As before, the selection of hardware threads within both places is up to the scheduler. It is a quality of implementation issue which hardware threads are selected. In this case, the ideal scenario is that all OpenMP threads execute on a different hardware thread.

4.6.3   The Spread Affinity Policy

The third policy, places the OpenMP threads as far apart as possible. As before, this is in the context of places.

One of the situations in which the `spread` policy can be of benefit, is in the case of an application that is memory-bandwidth demanding. The bandwidth provided by the various memories across the sockets, is best leveraged by distributing the threads over the sockets.[10]

Transparent to the user, the `spread` policy achieves its goal by splitting the place list into *subpartitions*. The OpenMP threads are mapped onto subpartitions, such that the distance between them is maximized.

The algorithm to define the subpartitions depends on the number of threads T and the number of places P in the place list:

- $T \leq P$ - The place list is split into T subpartitions. Each subpartition contains at least $floor(P/T)$, and at most $ceiling(P/T)$ *consecutive* places.

  Because there are T subpartitions, each thread is assigned to a subpartition, but a subpartition may consist of more than one place.

  Thread assignment starts with the master thread. It executes in the subpartition that contains the place where the parent thread runs. The thread with the next smallest thread number is assigned to the first place in the next subpartition, and so forth for subsequent threads. Relative to the starting point, the assignment wraps around.

  For example, if $T = 4$ and $P = 8$, there are four subpartitions $SP_0, \ldots, SP_3$ and each subpartition consists of $floor(8/4) = 2$ consecutive places.

  Using the notation from Figure 4.10, and assuming the parent of the master thread runs in place P_3, the subpartition definitions and thread assignments are described as follows:

$$SP_0 = \{P_0, P_1\} \text{ and } T_3 \in P_0$$
$$SP_1 = \{P_2, P_3\} \text{ and } T_0 \in P_2$$
$$SP_2 = \{P_4, P_5\} \text{ and } T_1 \in P_4$$
$$SP_3 = \{P_6, P_7\} \text{ and } T_2 \in P_6$$

---

[10]This of course assumes the data is also spread out over the various memories.

The master thread (T_0) is assigned to subpartition SP_1 and because the first place is used first, it executes in place P_2. As shown, subsequent threads are mapped onto the subsequent places, wrapping around. This is why thread T_3 executes in P_0.

There are four threads only and half of the eight places are used. When there are eight threads ($T = 8$), each subpartition consists of a single place: $SP_i = P_i$ for $i = 0, \ldots, 7$. In other words, each thread is assigned to a unique place.

When T does not divide P evenly ($floor(P/T) \neq ceiling(P/T)$), not all subpartitions contain the same number of places. All subpartitions have at least $floor(P/T)$ places, but at least one subpartition includes an additional place. The decision of which subpartition includes an additional place is implementation-dependent.

As an example, if $T = 5$ and $P = 8$, there are five subpartitions. Out of these, three contain $ceiling(8/5) - 2$ places and two consist of a single place each ($floor(8/5) = 1$). In such a case, an obvious choice is to assign places in a round-robin manner. In the scenario above, the first three threads may execute in a subpartition with two places, while the last two threads run in a subpartition with a single place.

If the parent of the master thread executes in place P_3 again, the following is a possible distribution of the threads over the subpartitions and places:

$$SP_0 = \{P_0, P_1\} \text{ and } T_4 \in P_0$$
$$SP_1 = \{P_2, P_3\} \text{ and } T_0 \in P_2$$
$$SP_2 = \{P_4, P_5\} \text{ and } T_1 \in P_4$$
$$SP_3 = \{P_6\} \text{ and } T_2 \in P_6$$
$$SP_4 = \{P_7\} \text{ and } T_3 \in P_7$$

Clearly, not all places are used. Such "leftover" places may be used in the case of nested parallelism.

- $T > P$ - The place list is split into P subpartitions. All subpartitions contain a single place and ST_i *consecutively* numbered threads are assigned to each subpartition. The number of threads in the subset is chosen, such that $floor(T/P) \leq ST_i \leq ceiling(T/P)$.

There are more threads than places and at least one place has more than one thread assigned to it.

Thread assignment to subpartitions is as follows. The first subset with ST_0 threads includes the master thread. It is assigned to the subpartition containing the place of the parent of the master thread. The next subset with ST_1 threads, is assigned to the next subpartition, and so on.

For example, if $T = 8$ and $P = 4$, there are four subpartitions $SP_0, \ldots, SP_3$. Each has $floor(8/4) = ceiling(8/4) = 2$ consecutive threads assigned to it.

If it is again assumed that the parent of the master thread executes in place P_3, the assignment of threads to places is as follows:

$$SP_0 = \{P_0\} \text{ and } T_2, T_3 \in P_0$$
$$SP_1 = \{P_1\} \text{ and } T_4, T_5 \in P_1$$
$$SP_2 = \{P_2\} \text{ and } T_6, T_7 \in P_2$$
$$SP_3 = \{P_3\} \text{ and } T_0, T_1 \in P_3$$

If P does not divide T evenly, the number of threads per subpartition is implementation-dependent.

Let's assume $T = 7$ and $P = 4$. In this case there are again 4 subpartitions and each consists of a single place. Because $floor(7/4) = 1$ and $ceiling(7/4) = 2$, two threads are assigned to three partitions, while one partition has a single thread assigned to it.

It is up to the implementation to decide how many threads there are in each subpartition. In the example below, only one thread is assigned to partition P_2. All other partitions have two threads:

$$SP_0 = \{P_0\} \text{ and } T_2, T_3 \in P_0$$
$$SP_1 = \{P_1\} \text{ and } T_4, T_5 \in P_1$$
$$SP_2 = \{P_2\} \text{ and } T_6 \in P_2$$
$$SP_3 = \{P_3\} \text{ and } T_0, T_1 \in P_3$$

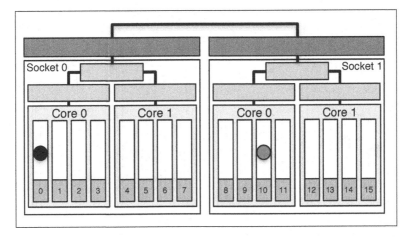

Figure 4.16: **An example of the spread affinity policy using 2 threads** – If the master thread executes on core 0 of socket 0, the second thread is scheduled to execute on core 0 of the other socket.

Before we continue, some more terminology needs to be explained. In the specifications, a subpartition is also referred to as a *place partition*. It is defined as an ordered list that corresponds to a contiguous list in the place list. In this book, we consistently use the word *subpartition* though.

An example of the `spread` affinity policy is illustrated in Figure 4.16. There are two threads ($T = 2$) and the place list from Figure 4.11 is used ($P = 4$).

There are fewer threads than places and the "$T \leq P$" algorithm applies. Two subpartitions, SP_0 and SP_1, are created. Both contain $floor(4/2) = 2$ consecutive places: $SP_0 = \{P_0, P_1\}$ and $SP_1 = \{P_2, P_3\}$. Assuming that the parent of the master thread executes in either place P_0, or P_1, the master thread is assigned to P_0 in subpartition SP_0. The second thread is scheduled onto place P_2, because this is the first place in the second subpartition SP_1. Given the definition of the place list, the two threads are scheduled on the first core of each socket, effectively spreading them over the two sockets.

If four threads are used, four subpartitions are created. Each of these spans the four threads in a different core, and a thread is assigned to one of the subpartitions. The result is that the four threads are spread over the four cores in the system. This is shown in Figure 4.17. As before, the selection of a resource number within a place is system dependent.

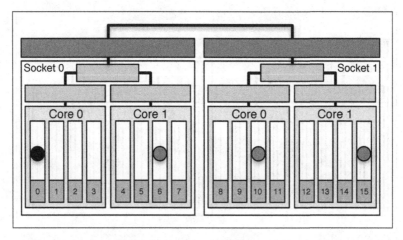

Figure 4.17: **An example of the spread affinity policy using 4 threads** – In this case, each core executes one thread. The mapping of the OpenMP threads onto the hardware threads within a core is implementation dependent.

Things get interesting if more than four threads are used. As an example, consider a scenario with six threads. This means that $T = 6$ and $P = 4$. The "$T > P$" algorithm applies and a total of four subpartitions are created. Each consists of a single place: $SP_i = P_i$ for $i = 0, \ldots, 3$. There are six threads to be distributed over these four subpartitions. Two of these subpartitions have two threads assigned to them, while the other two subpartitions contain one thread only. It is assumed that the parent of the master thread executes in place P_0. A possible assignment may be as follows:

$$SP_0 = \{P_0\} \text{ and } T_0, T_1 \in P_0$$
$$SP_1 = \{P_1\} \text{ and } T_2 \in P_1$$
$$SP_2 = \{P_2\} \text{ and } T_3, T_4 \in P_2$$
$$SP_3 = \{P_3\} \text{ and } T_5 \in P_3$$

Given the definitions and architecture, this is a very good placement. There is, however, no guarantee that this is what the runtime system does. How can it know what is best? It has visibility at the places level only and no understanding of the underlying architecture.

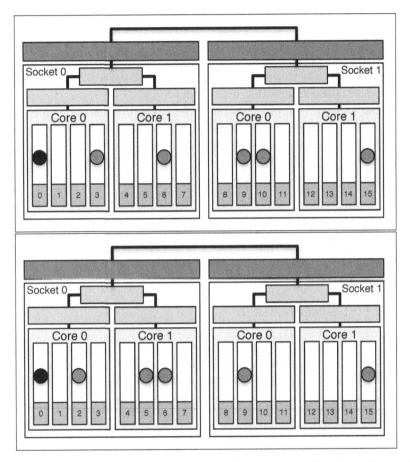

Figure 4.18: **Placement examples using the spread affinity policy with 6 threads** – In the first example, the placement is balanced and optimal, but there is no guarantee this is what the runtime system does. With the given place list, the second, unbalanced, distribution is equally valid.

The assignment below is equally valid for example, but now four threads execute within one socket, while only two threads execute in the other socket:

$$SP_0 = \{P_0\} \text{ and } T_0, T_1 \in P_0$$
$$SP_1 = \{P_1\} \text{ and } T_2, T_3 \in P_1$$

$$SP_2 = \{P_2\} \text{ and } T_4 \in P_2$$

$$SP_3 = \{P_3\} \text{ and } T_5 \in P_3$$

Both mappings are illustrated in Figure 4.18. As before, the scheduling of threads within one place is implementation dependent.

If this variation in the mapping is undesirable, the solution is to redefine the place list and eliminate undesired implementation-dependent choices. The most elegant solution is to define two places. Each place spans a socket:

$$P_0 = \{0 : 8 : 1\} = \{0, \ldots, 7\}$$

$$P_1 = \{8 : 8 : 1\} = \{8, \ldots, 15\}$$

The place list is defined as $\{P_0, P_1\}$. In this case, $T > P$ and there are two subpartitions. Each subpartition consists of a single place with $floor(6/2) = 3$ threads assigned to it. Assuming the parent of the master thread executes in P_0, the assignment is as follows:

$$SP_0 = \{P_0\} \text{ and } T_0, T_1, T_2 \in P_0$$

$$SP_1 = \{P_1\} \text{ and } T_3, T_4, T_5 \in P_1$$

This achieves load balancing over the two sockets with the guarantee that both sockets get assigned three threads each. The one uncertainty is whether the scheduler spreads these three threads over the two cores in each socket, or places all three in only one of the two cores on each socket.

The performance of the latter distribution is most likely sub-optimal, because the caches and bandwidths on the socket are not fully utilized. To avoid this scenario, a more complex place list must be constructed. The idea is to create more places in the place list. Define the following six places:

$$P_0 = \{0, 1\}$$

$$P_1 = \{2, 3\}$$

$$P_2 = \{4, 5, 6, 7\}$$

$$P_3 = \{8, 9\}$$

$$P_4 = \{10, 11\}$$

$$P_5 = \{12, 13, 14, 15\}$$

The place list is modified and consists of these six places, listed in the following order: $\{P_0, P_1, P_2, P_3, P_4, P_5\}$. With this new definition, the $T \leq P$ algorithm applies. There are six subpartitions and each consists of a single place only. Assuming that the parent of the master thread executes in place P_2, the mapping of threads onto places is as follows:

$$SP_0 = \{P_0\} \text{ and } T_4 \in P_0 = \{0, 1\}$$
$$SP_1 = \{P_1\} \text{ and } T_5 \in P_1 = \{2, 3\}$$
$$SP_2 = \{P_2\} \text{ and } T_0 \in P_2 = \{4, 5, 6, 7\}$$
$$SP_3 = \{P_3\} \text{ and } T_1 \in P_3 = \{8, 9\}$$
$$SP_4 = \{P_4\} \text{ and } T_2 \in P_4 = \{10, 11\}$$
$$SP_5 = \{P_5\} \text{ and } T_3 \in P_5 = \{12, 13, 14, 15\}$$

With these definitions, there are three threads per socket. It is guaranteed that one of the cores on each socket executes two OpenMP threads, while the other core on the same socket executes a single thread.

This is illustrated in Figure 4.19. In this example, it is assumed that the parent of the master thread executes in place P_2. As may easily be verified, regardless of where the parent of the master thread executes, the number of threads per core is always the same as above.

The places could have been defined differently to achieve a similar distribution. The two sockets, as well as the two cores within each socket, are symmetric. Within a socket, the number of threads per core could be interchanged, without an impact on the performance. All that is required is a slight change in the definition of the places.

Although any order of the places in the place list above achieves the same goal, there is a reason the place list is defined in the order shown here. If there are only two threads, they are scheduled onto a different socket. To be more specific, they are assigned to places P_0 and P_3.

Subpartitions are also used in the case of *nested parallelism*. At subsequent nesting levels, a subpartition defines the place list for a thread to be used. The subpartition serves as the starting point for the place list at the specific level.

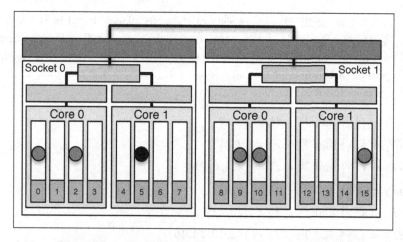

Figure 4.19: **The spread affinity policy with 6 threads and a different place list** – The place list has been modified to guarantee that core 0 on both sockets always executes two threads, while the other two cores execute a single thread. In this example it is assumed that the parent of the master thread executes in place P_2, but the number of threads per core does not depend on this. Regardless of where the master thread executes, the distribution is the same.

4.6.4 What's in a Name?

Despite their names, the `close` and `spread` affinity policies are not always as different as they may seem. Their differences depend on T, the number of OpenMP threads, and P, the number of places in the place list.

For example, in the above case with six threads and the modified place list ($P = 6$), the `close` policy may also be used to distribute the threads. The $T \leq P$ algorithm applies and each thread gets assigned to one of the six places. This results in the same mapping as shown in Figure 4.19 for the `spread` policy.

Upon closer inspection it is easy to see this is no coincidence. If the place list is the same and $T = P$, the `close` and `spread` policies result in identical mappings.

This may even be extended to the case $T \geq P$. The reason is that, if $T > P$, each of the subpartitions used by the `spread` policy, consists of a single place only. This is, however, exactly the same situation that arises if the `close` policy is applied. With both policies, the threads are distributed over the places in a consecutive way and the outcome is the same.

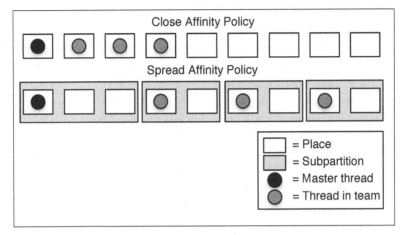

Figure 4.20: **Thread mappings in case there are four threads and nine places** – In this case, $T = 4$ and $P = 9$. Using the `close` affinity policy, the threads are mapped onto consecutive places. This is in contrast with the `spread` policy. There are four subpartitions and three of these contain two places, while one consists of three places. Threads are assigned to the subpartitions and mapped onto places as far apart as possible.

The one possible difference that may arise is if P does not divide T evenly. Then, not every subset of the threads has the same number of threads and the implementation determines how to map these subsets onto the place. This could be different for the two policies.

The policies are definitely different in the case of $T < P$. This is illustrated in Figure 4.20, when there are four threads and nine places. With the `close` policy, the four threads are scheduled onto the first four places. This is as close as possible within the context of places. In the case of the `spread` policy it is entirely different. Four subpartitions are created. One has three places, while the other three have two places. Threads are scheduled onto the subpartitions and within a subpartition the first place is selected. This maximizes the distance in terms of places, justifying the name "spread."

4.7   Making it Easier to Use the Thread Affinity Policies

The place list, places, and resource numbers may be used to provide full control over where threads execute. Now it is time to show a much easier, and more elegant way to control the placement of threads.

This ease-of-use is provided by using the *abstract names* to define the place list. These abstract names have already been touched upon in Section 4.5.3, but in this section, more details and several examples are given.

Recall there are three such names: `sockets`, `cores`, and `threads`. These names represent the various hardware execution elements in a contemporary parallel system. The interpretation of the abstract names is implementation-dependent, but it safe to assume they provide the functionality suggested by the names.

It is, however, conceivable that an architecture has additional, or different, elements not easily described by these names. This is why an implementation has the freedom to support additional abstract names, but these are system-dependent. Refer to the documentation of the specific OpenMP compiler and runtime system for a description of such extensions, if any.

The abstract names provide less control over the placement, but in often that is not needed. The considerable advantages are portability and robustness against errors in the place list. For example, setting `OMP_PLACES=cores`, is a generic choice and may be used on any system that supports the concept of cores.

This is why usage of the abstract names should be considered first, before using the system-dependent resource numbers to control the placement. These two approaches are mutually exclusive.

The abstract name is specified through the same environment variable `OMP_-PLACES`, that is used to define the place list with the resource numbers. The difference is that, instead of using places defined through resource numbers, an abstract name is used. This is an example of how to use all cores in the system: `OMP_PLACES=cores`.

The abstract name is handled by the OpenMP system and transparently translated into a place list. This is why the term "place list" is used sometimes in combination with the abstract name(s).

The generated place list is not visible to the user. It is created by the system and spans all corresponding hardware scheduling elements specified. In the above example, the (hidden) place list consists of all cores in the system.

When not all elements must be used, the abstract name may be appended by a positive number in parentheses. This number is used as the length of the place list. For example, this restricts the place list to four cores: `OMP_PLACES=cores(4)`

If fewer execution units (for example cores) than available are specified, the decision of which one(s) to select is determined by the implementation. If the number exceeds the number of units available, the length of the resulting place list to be used is implementation-dependent.

This is why usage of a specific number with the abstract name may be at odds with portability. The selection of cores depends on the OpenMP runtime system, and the number of cores requested may not be available on a different system. There is nothing wrong with that, but it is good to keep in mind, in case one needs to run the same application on a system with a different configuration.

As with the explicit place list, the abstract name may be used in conjunction with the environment variable `OMP_PROC_BIND`, or the `proc_bind` clause on the parallel region. Through these controls, the affinity policy (`master`, `close`, or `spread`) is defined. In the next three subsections, it is shown how to use the abstract names in combination with the affinity policies.

As before, the generic, multi-core system described in Figure 4.1 on page 152 is the target and the notation introduced in Section 4.6 is used.

To simplify the examples and diagrams, the assumption is that the parent of the master thread *always* executes in the first place of the (hidden) place list.[11]

4.7.1   The Sockets Abstract Place List

The `sockets` abstract name is used to schedule OpenMP threads across the sockets in the system. It is specified as follows: `OMP_PLACES=sockets`. The generated place list consists of all the sockets in the system. A socket may have multiple cores and more than one hardware thread per core.

The next step is to decide upon the affinity policy to control where the OpenMP threads are scheduled to run. This is illustrated with an example using the generic, multi-core system. It has two sockets and, in this case, the place list consists of two places ($P = 2$). Assume there are six OpenMP threads ($T = 6$).

The `master` policy is very straightforward. All six threads are scheduled to run on the same socket where the master thread executes. Because in this example the

---

[11]In the remainder of this section, it is no longer explicitly mentioned that this list is generated by the system and hidden to the user.

parent of the master thread is assumed to run on socket 0, all threads execute on this socket. It is up to the scheduler to decide which of the available eight hardware threads to select for the six OpenMP threads to run on.

In the case of the `close` policy, the "$T > P$" algorithm, described in Section 4.6.2, applies. Following the algorithm for this case, there are two thread subsets ST_0 and ST_1. They contain the following OpenMP thread numbers:

$$ST_0 = \{0, 1, 2\}$$
$$ST_1 = \{3, 4, 5\}$$

The threads in ST_0 execute in socket 0, while the threads in ST_1 are scheduled to run on socket 1. As mentioned earlier, it is up to the scheduler to select the cores and hardware threads. This means various mappings are allowed.

This is illustrated in Figure 4.21. In the first mapping, the threads within a socket execute in the same core. This is not the case in the second mapping, where the OpenMP threads are scattered over all cores. Again, both are valid mappings and also not the only ones possible.

As shown in Section 4.6.4, the mapping using the `spread` affinity policy is the same, as long as $T \geq P$, which is the case here. In the case of $T < P$, these policies lead to a different mapping, but in this particular scenario that is a corner case. There are only $P = 2$ places and only if $T = 1$, does this condition apply. If so, the mapping is again the same.

Whether or not the variation in the mapping of threads onto the hardware resources is acceptable, is decided by the user. What if a finer-grained level of control is desired? This is covered in the next two sections.

4.7.2   The Cores Abstract Place List

The `cores` abstract name indicates to the system that a core should be used as the scheduling entity for the OpenMP threads. This choice is specified in the following way: `OMP_PLACES=cores`.

The generated place list consists of all the cores in the system. Although a core may have more than one hardware thread, this is not considered for the mapping policy. It can be taken into account by the runtime scheduler though.

The `cores` abstract name is used on the generic, multi-core system. The difference compared to the previous case with the `sockets` name, is that there are now

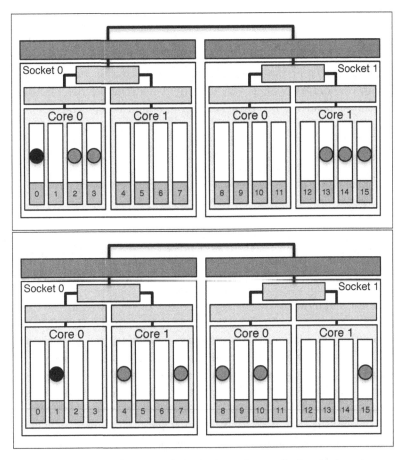

Figure 4.21: **Two possible mappings using the sockets abstract name with the close policy** – In the first mapping, the three threads per socket execute within the same core. This is, however, not guaranteed. The second mapping is equally valid, but the threads are scattered over all four cores.

four places $(P = 4)$. They span across the four cores in the system. Assume six OpenMP threads $(T = 6)$ again.

If the `master` affinity policy is applied, all six threads are scheduled to run on a single core. This is the same core where the parent of the master thread runs.

With the `close` policy, the "$T > P$" algorithm, described in Section 4.6.2, applies. There are $P = 4$ subsets, ST_0 through ST_3, with consecutive thread numbers, but because $floor(T/P) = 1$ and $ceiling(T/P) = 2$, not all subsets contain the same number of threads. To be more precise, two subsets contain two threads and the other two subsets contain a single thread only. The details of this distribution are implementation-dependent. For this example, assume the following:

$$ST_0 = \{0, 1\}$$
$$ST_1 = \{2, 3\}$$
$$ST_2 = \{4\}$$
$$ST_3 = \{5\}$$

These four subsets are assigned to the four places. Per the definition of the `close` policy, the threads in ST_0 are scheduled in the place where the parent of the master thread is running, which is a core in this case. The threads in ST_1 are scheduled in the next place in the place list, and so forth.

There are no requirements regarding the order of the cores in the (generated) place list, leaving a degree of freedom as to how to map the thread subsets onto the cores. In the generic, multi-core system for example, one socket may end up executing four threads, while two threads are running on the other socket.

This is actually what may be desired using the `close` policy, but an equally valid mapping is to execute three threads per socket. Both scenarios are illustrated in Figure 4.22.

The thing to note is that there is overlap between the mappings. The mapping shown in the second diagram in Figure 4.21 is the same as the second diagram in Figure 4.22. The difference in the hardware threads used illustrates the freedom the runtime scheduler has in assigning OpenMP threads to hardware resources. There is a difference, however. The mapping shown in the first diagram in Figure 4.21 is not possible here. Each core *must* execute at least one thread.

As explained in Section 4.6.4, in this case ($T \geq P$), the `spread` affinity policy has the same mapping characteristics. A difference arises if $T < P$. Assume the place list contains the cores in the left to right order, as shown in the generic, multi-core architecture. If two threads are used ($T = 2$), and the `close` policy is applied, each core on one of the two sockets executes a thread. If the `spread` policy is used, each socket executes one thread. Although not guaranteed by the OpenMP

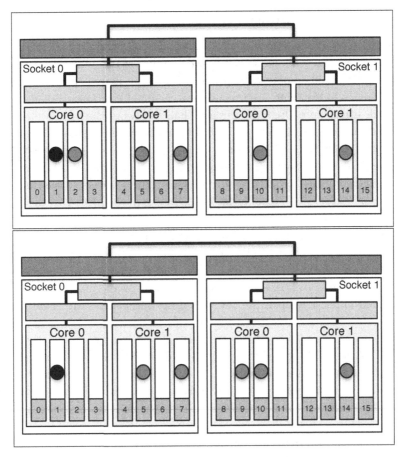

Figure 4.22: **Two possible mappings using the cores abstract name with the close policy** – In the first mapping, the first socket executes four threads, while there are only two threads running in the second socket. The second mapping is equally valid, but the threads are more balanced over the system.

4.5 specifications, one may assume that implementations generate topology-aware place lists. This is at least what is assumed to be the case here.

Although we have narrowed down where the OpenMP threads are allowed to run, there is still an uncertainty. The next section shows how the `threads` abstract name provides full control over the mapping.

4.7.3   The Threads Abstract Place List

The `threads` abstract name expands to a place list that contains all the hardware threads in the system. This name is selected as follows: `OMP_PLACES=threads`.

Most likely, the `master` policy is not very meaningful here, because it implies all OpenMP threads in the team are executing on a single hardware thread.

In general, using more OpenMP threads than hardware threads, is likely to degrade performance. This means that with the `threads` abstract name, the practical scenarios are for the "$T \leq P$" case only. These are the ones discussed here.

With the `close` policy, there are sufficient places for the OpenMP threads to run. Using the notation from Figure 4.10 on page 170, it is easy to see that $T_i \in P_i$ for all threads $i = 0, \ldots, T-1$. In terms of the places in the place list, the OpenMP threads execute back-to-back and are indeed "close" in this sense.

As before, the `spread` policy has T subpartitions in the case of $T \leq P$. With the choice of `threads` for the abstract name, the subpartitions consist of one or more hardware threads. Assignment of OpenMP threads to places is at this granularity. The lower the number of threads, the more they are spaced apart.

As observed in Section 4.6.4, the `close` and `spread` policies are equal if $T \geq P$.

Consider an example with six threads ($T = 6$) on the two-socket, generic, multi-core system. There are 16 hardware threads ($P = 16$), so consequently, $T < P$. Assume the places in the generated place list follow the left to right numbering of the hardware threads in the system.

If the `close` policy is applied, OpenMP threads are assigned to consecutive hardware threads, starting with the hardware thread in which the parent of the master thread runs. This is shown in Figure 4.23, where the parent of the master thread of the team executes on hardware thread 0.

With the `spread` policy there are six subpartitions ($T = 6$). Four of these contain $ceiling(16/6) = 3$ places, while the remaining two subpartitions contain $floor(16/6) = 2$ places. Each OpenMP thread is assigned to a subpartition. A possible mapping is the following:

$$SP_0 = \{P_0, P_1, P_2\} = \{0, 1, 2\} \text{ and } T_0 \in SP_0$$

$$SP_1 = \{P_3, P_4, P_5\} = \{3, 4, 5\} \text{ and } T_1 \in SP_1$$

$$SP_2 = \{P_6, P_7, P_8\} = \{6, 7, 8\} \text{ and } T_2 \in SP_2$$

$$SP_3 = \{P_9, P_{10}, P_{11}\} = \{9, 10, 11\} \text{ and } T_3 \in SP_3$$

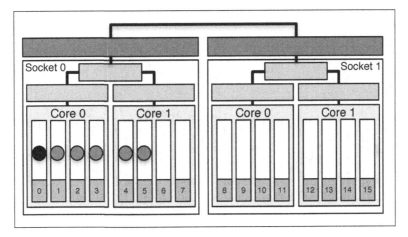

Figure 4.23: **Mapping using the threads abstract name with the close policy** – If the parent of the master thread executes on hardware thread 0, the six OpenMP threads execute on hardware threads 0   5.

$$SP_4 = \{P_{12}, P_{13}\} = \{12, 13\} \text{ and } T_4 \in SP_4$$

$$SP_6 = \{P_{14}, P_{15}\} = \{14, 15\} \text{ and } T_5 \in SP_5$$

The reason the word "possible" is used here is, because the implementation determines which subpartitions have three places and which one has two places. See also Section 4.6.3, starting on page 178.

Figure 4.24 illustrates two mappings for the subpartitions given above. As mentioned several times before, the assignment of OpenMP threads within a place is implementation-dependent.

In the first case, the distribution of the threads over the system is optimal. The second example, although valid as well, is less favorable. One core is not used at all and socket 1 executes twice as many OpenMP threads as socket 0.

Although the number of undesirable mappings has been reduced, there are still less optimal scenarios. If more control over the placement is required, the solution is to define an explicit place list. Figure 4.19, on page 186 shows such an example.

For a different number of threads, things may work out very well. For example, with eight threads ($T = 8$), each of the eight subpartitions contains $16/8 = 2$ consecutive hardware threads. The OpenMP threads are mapped symmetrically

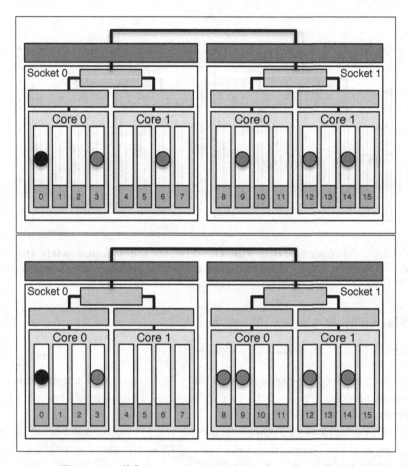

Figure 4.24: **Two possible mappings using the threads abstract name with the spread policy** – The distribution shown in the first picture is optimal. Each core executes one, or two, threads and the threads are well-balanced over the system. The second mapping, although possible, is not optimal. One core is not used at all and the number of threads per socket is not balanced.

onto these subpartitions, effectively spreading them out equally. An example of this is shown in Figure 4.25.

This is not a coincidence. In general, placement is more precisely defined if the number of threads T and the number of places P divide equally. If this is not

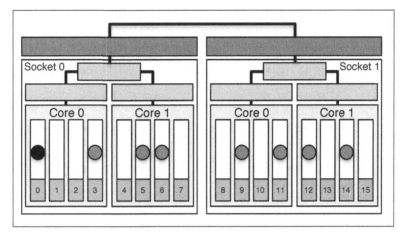

Figure 4.25: **The threads abstract name with the spread policy and eight threads** – In this case, the OpenMP threads are spread equally over the hardware threads in the system, maximizing the bandwidth.

the case, a load balancing issue arises and the implementation needs to make more decisions where to place the threads.

4.8 Where Are My Threads Running?

So far, the examples, have been theoretical. The time has come to show how thread affinity works in practice, but first some background information needs to be provided.

As of the OpenMP 4.5 specifications, diagnostic runtime functions to query the thread affinity environment and placement information, are supported. These are introduced and discussed in Section 2.3.2, starting on page 64.

These functions may be used to instrument the application and print the affinity information to verify where a thread executes. The drawback is that these calls must be included in the source code.

For the purpose of demonstrating how affinity works in practice, we prefer to do this without instrumenting the code.[12] This is why for this section, we turned to

---

[12]Most likely, the next release of the specifications supports an environment variable to print diagnostic thread affinity information at runtime.

Reference	Place List	Places	Coverage
PL_1	{0:128:1}	1	All hardware threads in socket 0.
PL_2	{0:8:1}:16:8	16	All hardware threads in socket 0.
PL_3	{0:8:1}:32:8	32	All hardware threads in the system.

Figure 4.26: **Definitions and references for the place lists used** – Throughout this section, several place lists are used. They are defined in this table and a reference for easy identification is assigned to each of them. The third column lists the number of places in the place list. The last column describes which of the hardware threads are included in the place list.

DTrace, a tool that allows the user to obtain runtime diagnostics at the OS-level, without the need to explicitly instrument the application. It is available on the Oracle Solaris, Oracle Linux, and macOS operating systems.[13] More information on DTrace can be found in the Glossary at page 340.

A DTrace script to monitor the mapping of the OpenMP threads onto the hardware threads was developed. The results are shown in the examples below, but the details of this script are beyond the scope of this book. Two tables are printed. The interpretation of these is given in Section 4.8.1 on page 200.

The system used in all the thread placement monitoring experiments has two sockets. Each socket has 16 cores, with eight hardware threads per core. This means it has a total of 32 cores and 256 hardware threads. The output listed in Figure 4.6 on page 163, was obtained using this system.

In this section, several place lists are used. For ease of reference they have been given a name and are listed in Figure 4.26. Note the difference between PL_1 and PL_2. Although both span all the hardware threads in socket 0, the first list has a single place only, while the second list consists of 16 places.

4.8.1 Affinity Examples for a Single-Level Parallel Region

The DTrace script has been used to obtain affinity statistics for a single-level parallel region. Within this parallel region there is only one `single` region with a print statement. The relevant code fragment is shown in Figure 4.27. This simple test program has been used to verify several affinity scenarios.

---

[13]Linux has a similar tool called *SystemTap* [25], but this has not been explored further.

```
1 #pragma omp parallel
2 {
3    #pragma omp single
4    {
5       printf("Single region executed by thread %d\n",
6               omp_get_thread_num());
7    } // End of single region
8 } // End of parallel region
```

Figure 4.27: **Single-level parallel region used to demonstrate the thread affinity settings** – There is one single-level parallel region. Only one thread prints a message.

We start with an explicit OpenMP place list. The numbering scheme depends on the system, as well as the OS, and suitable commands must be used to obtain this information. On this system, hardware threads $0 - 127$ are on socket 0, while threads $128 - 255$ are on socket 1.

The interval notation is used to define the list: OMP_PLACES="{0:128:1}".[14] This is place list PL_1, as defined in Figure 4.26. It consists of a single place only and spans the first half of the 256 hardware threads of the target system. These are all the threads in socket 0.

The next choice to be made is the thread affinity policy. In this first example, the close policy is selected by setting environment variable OMP_PROC_BIND as follows: OMP_PROC_BIND=close.

Four OpenMP threads are used ($T = 4$). Because there is a single place only ($P = 1$), the algorithm for the "$T > P$" case, as given in Section 4.6.2, applies. The thread subset ST_0 includes all four OpenMP threads ($T/P = 4$), and they are assigned to the single place spanning all hardware threads in socket 0.

Following this algorithm, and assuming the parent of the master thread executes on hardware thread 0, one may expect the other three threads to execute on hardware threads $1-3$, respectively. There is, however, *no guarantee* this happens. The order within a place list does not matter, and the implementation is free to select any hardware thread in the place list.

In Figure 4.28, the runtime statistics from the DTrace script are shown. Here, and in all subsequent figures in this section, two tables are listed. Together, they show

---

[14]How to set the environment variable, depends on the OS and shell used.

Thread	On HW Thread	Node	Created Thread
0	0	1	1
0	0	1	2
0	0	1	3

Thread	Running on HW Thread	Bound to HW Thread
0	178	0
1	0	1
2	0	2
3	0	3

Figure 4.28: **Affinity statistics for the PL_1 place list and the close policy**
– The first table shows that thread 0 creates the other three threads. It was running on
hardware thread 0 when it did so. The second table shows it did not start there, but was
migrated from hardware thread 178. This table also shows that the other threads started
on the same hardware thread 0, but were then bound to hardware threads $1 - 3$.

what has happened both at the OpenMP thread level, as well as which hardware
threads are involved.

The first table shows thread creation statistics and has four columns. The first
column gives the OpenMP thread ID. The second column, called "On HW Thread,"
lists the ID of the hardware thread this OpenMP thread was running on when it
created other threads. Column "Node" gives the memory node reference ID.

In Linux, this is called a "NUMA Node," while Solaris calls it a "Locality Group,"
or "lgroup" for short. In both cases, such a node has a uniform memory access
time for the hardware thread(s) connected to it. It is considered to be local to
those threads. Column four, "Created Thread," lists the OpenMP thread that was
created by the thread in the first column.

The second table indicates whether an OpenMP thread moved ("migrated") from
one hardware thread ("Running on HW Thread") to another ("Bound to HW
Thread"). Interpretation of these results sometimes requires cross checking the
two tables. One thing missing from these tables is a timestamp. The full script
includes this information, and in some examples this is used to explain the sequence
of events.

The first table shows that thread 0 created the other three threads. At the time
of thread creation, this thread was executing on hardware thread 0. Apparently,
this hardware thread is connected to memory node 1.

Thread	On HW Thread	Node	Created Thread
0	0	1	1
0	0	1	2
0	0	1	3

Thread	Running on HW Thread	Bound to HW Thread
0	244	0
1	0	8
2	0	16
3	0	24

Figure 4.29: **Affinity statistics for the PL_2 place list and the close policy**
– The results demonstrate this policy and how it relates to the place list. With four
threads, the first four places are used to schedule the OpenMP threads. In this case, each
thread is placed onto the first hardware thread within a place, but as explained earlier,
which hardware thread to select is an implementation-dependent choice. Effectively, each
thread is executing on a different core.

The second table shows that thread 0 started on hardware thread 178 but migrated to hardware thread 0. This is interesting, because this demonstrates that
the master thread started on the second socket, and was moved to socket 0. The
other three OpenMP threads started on hardware thread 0, but were moved, or
migrated, to hardware threads $1 - 3$.

These results show the implementation does what the close policy is meant to
achieve. Given the definition of the place list, any hardware thread ID in the range
$0 - 127$ is actually valid.

In the second example, place list PL_2 is used. There are 16 places and each
spans the hardware threads within a different core in socket 0. This results in the
following expansion for the place list: $P_0 = \{0, 1, \ldots, 7\}$, $P_1 = \{8, 9, \ldots, 15\}, \ldots,$
$P_{15} = \{120, 121, \ldots, 127\}$.

The same example has been executed using this second place list and the close
policy. Because there are four OpenMP threads ($T = 4$) and 16 places ($P = 16$),
the algorithm for the "$T \leq P$" case for the close policy applies. This implies
that the OpenMP threads are assigned to consecutive places, starting with the
place where the parent thread of the master thread runs. Each place spans a core,
and the threads must be assigned to the individual cores in socket 0. The affinity
statistics are shown in Figure 4.29.

As before, OpenMP thread 0 creates the other threads. It apparently started at hardware thread 244. From there, it migrated to thread 0. Threads $1 - 3$ started on hardware thread 0, but migrated to hardware threads 8, 16 and 24 respectively. This shows that all OpenMP threads are indeed scheduled onto successive places. Per the definition of the places, each thread executes on its own core on socket 0, and the implementation selected the first hardware thread on each core.

There is an important question to address: *"Why was the first place from the place listed selected, and not the place containing hardware thread 244?"*

The reason is that this hardware thread is not part of the place list. It is a thread on core 30, which is on socket 1. Upon program start-up, the OS has no notion of the OpenMP affinity settings and apparently decided to start the application on hardware thread 244. The OpenMP runtime system is, however, well aware of the affinity settings and moved the thread to hardware thread 0 *before* executing the parallel region.

The specifications do not guarantee this, though. Not all systems support thread migration, and the action taken in the above scenario is system-dependent. In general, if an affinity request cannot be fulfilled, the affinity of threads in the team is implementation-defined.

On this system, thread migration is supported, however, and the runtime system may move the master thread to the right location, which in this case is place P_0 of the place list. This marks the starting point of the places to be assigned to subsequent threads.

The same code and place list were used in the next experiment. The difference is that the spread affinity policy is selected. Following the algorithm for the "$T \leq P$" case, it follows there are $T = 4$ subpartitions with $P/T = 4$ consecutive places each:

$$SP_0 = \{P_0, P_1, P_2, P_3\}$$
$$SP_1 = \{P_4, P_5, P_6, P_7\}$$
$$SP_2 = \{P_8, P_9, P_{10}, P_{11}\}$$
$$SP_3 = \{P_{12}, P_{13}, P_{14}, P_{15}\}$$

Expanding the individual places to their lists of hardware threads, results in the table shown in Figure 4.30.

The mapping algorithm guarantees that the four OpenMP threads are assigned to the first place in each of the subpartitions selected for that thread. For example, because of the assumption of where the parent of the master thread executes, thread

Subpartition	Places			
SP_0	$\{0,\dots,7\}$	$\{8,\dots,15\}$	$\{16,\dots,23\}$	$\{24,\dots,31\}$
SP_1	$\{32,\dots,39\}$	$\{40,\dots,47\}$	$\{48,\dots,55\}$	$\{56,\dots,63\}$
SP_2	$\{64,\dots,71\}$	$\{72,\dots,79\}$	$\{80,\dots,87\}$	$\{88,\dots,95\}$
SP_3	$\{96,\dots,103\}$	$\{104,\dots,111\}$	$\{112,\dots,119\}$	$\{120,\dots,127\}$

Figure 4.30: **The expanded subpartition definitions** – This table shows the four subpartitions and their place list with hardware thread numbers. This is for the scenario with $T = 4$ threads, a place list defined by `OMP_PLACES="{0:8:1}:16:8"`, and the spread affinity policy.

```
Thread    On HW Thread    Node    Created Thread
   0             0           1           1
   0             0           1           2
   0             0           1           3


Thread    Running on HW Thread    Bound to HW Thread
   0              208                     0
   1                0                    32
   2                0                    64
   3                0                    96
```

Figure 4.31: **Affinity statistics for the PL_2 place list and the spread policy** – As before, the application is migrated to hardware thread 0. From there, the other threads are created and migrated to their destination hardware thread. Each thread is indeed scheduled onto the first place in its subpartition.

2 is assigned to SP_2 and it is scheduled onto a hardware thread in the range $64 - 71$ within this subpartition.

The runtime affinity results for this setup are shown in Figure 4.31 and clearly demonstrate how this policy works. As seen before, the application starts at a different hardware thread than the target. In this case, it starts at hardware thread 208. From there it is migrated to hardware thread 0 and creates the other three threads on the same hardware thread. From there, these threads migrate to their destination hardware threads.

Thread	Running on HW Thread	Bound to HW Thread
0	111	0
1	0	16
2	0	32
3	0	48
4	0	64
5	0	80
6	0	96
7	0	112

Figure 4.32: **Affinity statistics for the PL_2 place list, the spread policy, and 8 threads** – In this case, all eight subpartitions contain two consecutive places. Each OpenMP thread is mapped onto the first hardware thread in the first place of the corresponding subpartition.

As expected, those three threads are scheduled onto subpartitions SP_1, SP_2 and SP_3 respectively. Comparing the destination hardware threads with those listed in Figure 4.30 it is shown that they are scheduled onto the first hardware thread from the first place in the respective subpartition.

To further demonstrate this policy, the experiment was repeated, but with the number of threads set to eight ($T = 8$). This results in 8 subpartitions, containing $P/T = 2$ consecutive places each. For example, subpartitions $SP_0 = \{P_0, P_1\}$ and $SP_1 = \{P_2, P_3\}$. As before, the first OpenMP thread is assigned to SP_0, the second thread to SP_1, and so on. The affinity results of this experiment are given in Figure 4.32.

In the next two figures the first table with the thread creation statistics is omitted. It is similar to what we have seen in the previous experiments.

The results confirm the settings work as expected. Each OpenMP thread is mapped onto the first place of its subpartition. For example, thread 4 is assigned to subpartition $SP_4 = \{P_8, P_9\}$, and it executes on hardware thread 64, which is the first hardware thread in P_8.

Until now, the place list was restricted to span a single socket only. To demonstrate how to use both sockets, the following place list is defined: OMP_PLACES= "{0:8:1}:32:8". This place list consists of 32 places with 8 hardware threads per place: $P_i = \{i * 8, i * 8 + 1, \ldots, i * 8 + 7\}$ for $i = 0, \ldots, 31$. It is place list PL_3 from Figure 4.26.

Thread	Running on HW Thread	Bound to HW Thread
0	162	0
1	0	32
2	0	64
3	0	96
4	0	128
5	0	160
6	0	192
7	0	224

Figure 4.33: **Affinity statistics for the PL_3 place list, the spread policy and 8 threads** – There are again eight subpartitions, but this time with four consecutive places each. The OpenMP threads are mapped onto the first hardware thread in the first place of the corresponding subpartition.

With the `spread` policy, the algorithm for the "$T \leq P$" case applies. This results in eight subpartitions $SP_0, \ldots, SP_7$. Each subpartition contains $P/T = 4$ consecutive places. It is easy to see that the first place in subpartition SP_j is P_{j*4} for $j = 0, \ldots, 7$. It follows from the algorithm that OpenMP thread j is assigned to this place.

The observed runtime results for the `spread` affinity policy and eight threads are listed in Figure 4.33. The first hardware thread within place P_{j*4} has number $j*4*8 = j*32$ ($j = 0, \ldots, 7$). The results show that each OpenMP thread is scheduled onto this hardware thread. As mentioned before, this is an implementation-dependent choice. Every hardware thread selected from the correct place is equally valid.

4.8.2 Affinity Examples for a Nested Parallel Region

In this section, several examples for a two-level nested parallel region are presented and discussed. The relevant code fragment used in the experiments is listed in Figure 4.34.

The outer-level parallel region spans lines $1 - 16$. Only one thread prints a message. The second-level parallel region starts at line 8 and ends at line 15. Within this region, a single thread prints a message.

```
1 #pragma omp parallel
2 {
3    #pragma omp single
4    {
5      printf("First single region executed by thread %d\n",
6             omp_get_thread_num());
7    } // End of single region level 1
8    #pragma omp parallel
9    {
10       #pragma omp single
11       {
12         printf("Second single region executed by thread %d\n",
13                omp_get_thread_num());
14       } // End of single region level 2
15    } // End of parallel region level 2
16 } // End of parallel region level 1
```

Figure 4.34: **Nested parallel region used to demonstrate the thread affinity settings** – The nesting level is two. Regardless of the number of threads used, only two messages are printed, one from each nesting level.

In the first scenario, place list PL_1 (see also Figure 4.26 on page 198) is used. This list consists of a single place that spans all the hardware threads on socket 0 of the two-socket system.

This is a nested parallel region and, unless it is acceptable to rely on the implementation-dependent defaults, the affinity policy on both levels must be specified. In this case, we set OMP_PROC_BIND="spread,close". For the outer parallel region, two threads are used. The second-level parallel region has four threads. This is set as follows: OMP_NUM_THREADS="2,4".

The place list contains one place only ($P = 1$). At the outer level, there are two threads and the algorithm for the "$T > P$" scenario of the spread affinity policy applies. This implies there is only a single subpartition (the entire place) and all threads are assigned to it. In other words, two hardware threads on socket 0 are selected at runtime.

At the second level, the close policy applies. Each of the two threads creates its own team of threads and have the role of the master thread in their respective teams. The place list has one place only and in both cases, the same original

Thread	On HW Thread	Node	Created Thread
0	0	1	1
0	0	1	3
0	0	1	5
0	0	1	7
1	1	1	2
1	1	1	4
1	1	1	6

Thread	Running on HW Thread	Bound to HW Thread
0	191	0
1	0	1
2	1	6
3	0	7
4	1	2
5	0	3
6	1	5
7	0	4

Figure 4.35: **Affinity statistics for a nested parallel region using place list PL_1** – There are $2x4$ threads and the "`spread,close`" policy is applied. The two outer-level threads are mapped onto hardware threads 0 and 1. The other six threads at the second level are executed on hardware threads $2 - 7$.

place list is used. There are four threads per team and again the algorithm for the "$T > P$" scenario applies. Because there is one place only, the additional three threads per team are mapped onto the same place list.

The results in Figure 4.35 show that the program started execution on hardware thread 191 and from there migrated to hardware thread 0. OpenMP thread 1 was created on hardware thread 0 and moved to hardware thread 1. Both are part of the same node.

These two threads created their own team with three additional threads each. The first team consists of OpenMP threads $0, 3, 5$, and 7. Threads $1, 2, 4$, and 6 constitute the second team. Although these new threads were created on the hardware thread that their master thread was running on, they were moved to their destination. In the end, the eight threads are executing on hardware threads $0 - 7$.

It is interesting to note that this is a degenerate case. The `spread` and `close` policies are not really doing anything different. Actually, setting `OMP_PROC_-BIND="master,master"` results in the same mapping of the OpenMP threads onto the hardware threads.

In the second example, the mapping is very different. The program, the number of threads per level, and the affinity policies are the same, but the place list is set to `PL_2`. There are 16 places ($P = 16$) now and each place spans a core in socket 0. For both policies, the "$T \leq P$" scenario applies.

At the first level there are two subpartitions and they contain $16/2 = 8$ consecutive places:

$$SP_0 = \{P_0, \ldots, P_7\} = \{\{0:8:1\}:8:8\}$$
$$SP_1 = \{P_8, \ldots, P_{15}\} = \{\{64:8:1\}:8:8\}$$

The `spread` policy is applied to the outer level. Following the algorithm for this case, it is easy to see that OpenMP thread 0 executes in place P_0. Thread 1 is scheduled to run in place P_8. Given the definitions of these places, this means that thread 0 runs on core 0 and thread 1 executes on core 8.

At the second level, the two place lists are SP_0 and SP_1. Each has eight places ($P = 8$) and there are four threads per team ($T = 4$). Again, the "$T \leq P$" scenario applies, but now for the `close` policy. As a result, successive threads in a team are scheduled onto consecutive places in their respective place list.

For example, the four threads in the second team are mapped onto places P_8, $\ldots$, P_{11}, and they execute on cores $8, \ldots, 11$. As always, the choice of a hardware thread within a place is system-dependent.

The results of the experiment are shown in Figure 4.36. The mappings show that the settings work as expected. After the initial migration from hardware thread 143 to the destination hardware thread 0, OpenMP thread 0 creates thread 1. Both threads execute in the same socket, but far apart.

Although not explicitly clear from this overview, thread 0 then creates threads 3, 5, and 7 at the start of the second-level parallel region. Thread 1 creates threads 2, 4, and 6. The threads in the first team are scheduled onto hardware threads $i * 8$ for $i = 0, \ldots, 3$. The threads in the second team execute on hardware threads $64 + i * 8$ for $i = 0, \ldots, 3$.

The place list $P_i = \{i * 8, i * 8 + 1, \ldots, i * 8 + 7\}$ for $i = 0, \ldots, 7$. It follows that the hardware thread numbers used correspond to the first hardware thread in places $P_0, \ldots, P_3$ for the first team and $P_8, \ldots, P_{11}$ for the second team.

Thread	On HW Thread	Node	Created Thread
0	0	1	1
0	0	1	3
0	0	1	5
0	0	1	7
1	64	1	2
1	64	1	4
1	64	1	6

Thread	Running on HW Thread	Bound to HW Thread
0	143	0
1	0	64
2	64	72
3	0	8
4	64	80
5	0	16
6	64	88
7	0	24

Figure 4.36: **Affinity statistics for a nested parallel region using place list PL_2** – There are 2x4 threads and the "spread,close" policy is applied. The two outer-level threads are spread out as much as possible, and mapped onto hardware threads 0 and 64. The threads at the second-level are executed as close as possible to their respective master thread.

The third and last example is based upon the previous case, but this time, place list PL_3 is used. This means there are 32 places, and each place spans the hardware threads in a core.

Following the same algorithms, there are again two subpartitions at the first level ($T = 2$) and 16 consecutive places in each subpartition. This time, a subpartition spans all the cores and hardware threads in a socket. As a result, each outer-level thread executes in its own socket. The threads in the two teams, created at the second level, are kept close. Per the definitions of the place list and subpartitions, this means that each OpenMP thread executes on a separate core.

The runtime affinity statistics in Figure 4.37 confirm the above. There are 2x4 threads and the "spread,close" policy is specified. The two outer-level OpenMP

Thread	On HW Thread	Node	Created Thread
0	0	1	1
0	0	1	2
0	0	1	4
0	0	1	6
1	128	2	3
1	128	2	5
1	128	2	7

Thread	Running on HW Thread	Bound to HW Thread
0	255	0
1	0	128
2	0	8
3	128	136
4	0	16
5	128	144
6	0	24
7	128	152

Figure 4.37: **Affinity statistics for a nested parallel region using place list PL_3** – There are 2x4 threads and the `"spread,close"` policy is specified. The two outer level threads are spread out as much as possible and the threads at the second level are executed as close as possible to their respective master thread.

threads execute on hardware threads 0 and 128. These are in a different socket.[15] The two thread teams at the second level execute on four consecutive cores on each socket.

4.8.3   Making Things Easier Again

The previous two examples demonstrated how the thread placement in a nested parallel region may be controlled. In this section, it is demonstrated how the abstract names may be used to define the mappings. The example code, and all settings except for the place list definition, are the same. The place list definitions for all three cases discussed next are given in Figure 4.38.

---

[15]This is consistent with the difference in the node number.

Reference	Place List	Places	Coverage
Case I	sockets(1)	1	One socket in the system.
Case II	sockets(2)	2	Two sockets in the system.
Case III	cores	32	All cores in the system.

Figure 4.38: **Place list definitions and properties** – The second column contains the setting for environment variable OMP_PLACES.

Thread mappings for Case I In the first case, there is only a single place, spanning all hardware threads within a socket. The runtime affinity statistics shown in Figure 4.39, are similar to those from Figure 4.35, because in both cases the place list spans all hardware threads in a single socket.

The only possible difference is the selection of the socket. With place list PL_1, this was hardcoded to socket 0, while the OpenMP runtime system selects a socket. The output shows that the master thread at the first level was initially running on hardware thread 43 and was moved to its destination, hardware thread 0. Both hardware threads are on socket 0 of this system. Apparently the runtime system selected the first socket on which to run. This is the same starting point as the example shown in Figure 4.35, and the mapping is the same as in this earlier case.

Thread mappings for Case II The place list in the second case specifies two sockets to be used.[16] This definition expands to a place list consisting of two places ($P = 2$). Each place spans the hardware threads within one socket.

At the outer-level, there are two subpartitions ($T = 2$), containing one place each ($P/T = 1$). As each place spans a socket, the two outer-level threads are scheduled onto a different socket. Which socket they run on depends on where the parent of the master thread is running.

Upon encountering the second-level parallel region, each of these two threads creates a team of four threads. The place list is inherited from the (new) master thread and contains a single place. In this case, the place spans the socket where the respective master thread is running.

---

[16]On the target system this is equivalent to simply using "sockets," because this system has two sockets only.

Thread	On HW Thread	Node	Created Thread
0	0	1	1
0	0	1	2
0	0	1	4
0	0	1	6
1	1	1	3
1	1	1	5
1	1	1	7

Thread	Running on HW Thread	Bound to HW Thread
0	43	0
1	0	1
2	0	2
3	1	5
4	0	3
5	1	6
6	0	4
7	1	7

Figure 4.39:   **Affinity statistics for a nested parallel region using OMP_PLACES="sockets(1)"** – The initial mapping is the same as in the case where the explicit place list PL_1 was used. In both examples, the first-level master thread was bound to hardware thread 0. The details are somewhat different, but to the application, this should not matter and the final mapping to the hardware threads is the same.

At this second level, the close policy is in effect. There are four threads ($T = 4$) and one place ($P = 1$). Following the placement algorithm for the "$T > P$" case, there is only one subset of threads (ST) per team and each contains all four threads in the respective team. It also follows from the algorithm that the three additional threads in each team are scheduled on the same socket where their master thread is running.

The runtime results in Figure 4.40 show that the application started on hardware thread 138, but migrated to hardware thread 128. As mentioned before, there is no notion of time in these tables, but with the full output (not shown here), the following thread creation and migration was reconstructed.

While executing on hardware thread 128, thread 0 created OpenMP thread 1. This thread was moved to hardware thread 0. At this point, the two threads execute

Thread	On HW Thread	Node	Created Thread
0	128	2	1
0	128	2	3
0	128	2	5
0	128	2	6
1	0	1	2
1	0	1	4
1	0	1	7

Thread	Running on HW Thread	Bound to HW Thread
0	138	128
1	128	0
2	0	2
3	128	129
4	0	1
5	128	130
6	128	131
7	0	3

Figure 4.40:   **Affinity statistics for a nested parallel region using OMP_PLACES="sockets(2)"** – The other settings are the same as for the previous case. The two first-level OpenMP threads are scheduled onto a different socket. Each of these threads creates a team, and the threads in the team execute on a hardware thread in the same core as their master.

the outer-level parallel region. Both encounter the second-level region and act as the master thread for the teams created.

The tables show that thread 0 created threads 3, 5, and 6. These subsequently moved to hardware threads 129, 130, and 131. The four hardware threads $128, \ldots, 131$ are on socket 1. OpenMP thread 1 created threads 2, 4, and 7 on hardware thread 0. These migrated to hardware threads 2, 1, and 3 respectively.

The hardware thread numbers and the numbering in Figure 4.6 on page 163, confirm that the two outer threads are spread over the sockets and that their teams are executing on consecutive hardware threads within a core. They are truly "close."

Thread mappings for Case III   In the last example of this section, it is shown how to use the abstract names to guarantee each OpenMP thread executes on its own core.

This is achieved by setting `OMP_PLACES=cores`. On the target two-socket system, this expands to a place list with 32 elements ($P = 32$).

As before, the `spread` policy applies to the first-level parallel region. There are two threads ($T = 2$), and the "$T \leq P$" algorithm applies. This results in 2 subpartitions, both with $P/T = 32/2 = 16$ consecutive places. Each place spans a full core.

OpenMP thread 0 executes in the subpartition where its master thread runs. Thread 1 executes in the other subpartition.

There are two sockets with 16 cores each and two subpartitions both with 16 places. One may expect each subpartition to exactly span a socket, but *there is no guarantee*. The assignment of places/cores to subpartitions is implementation-defined.[17]

Each of the OpenMP threads executes in a separate core, and they are at a distance of 16 in terms of resource numbers.

At the second level, the `close` policy is in effect for both teams. The subpartition of the respective master thread serves as the place list. There are 16 places in each list ($P = 16$) and four threads ($T = 4$). The algorithm for "$T \leq P$" applies and each OpenMP thread is assigned to a unique place, which is a core in this case.

With this, the goal has been achieved. All eight threads in the nested parallel region execute on their own core.

The runtime results in Figure 4.41 show that OpenMP thread 0 starts on hardware thread 66 and migrates to its destination thread (64). There, it creates OpenMP thread 1.

Thread 0 also creates the other threads in its team. In this case, threads 3, 5, and 7 are created. These threads start on the same hardware thread that their master thread is running on (64) and from there migrate to their destination hardware threads: 72, 80, and 88.

After thread 1 migrated from hardware thread 64 to 192, it created OpenMP threads 2, 4, and 6 on hardware thread 192. These migrated to hardware threads 200, 208, and 216 respectively.

---

[17]It is reasonable to expect that an implementation makes sensible choices in this case, though.

Thread	On HW Thread	Node	Created Thread
0	64	1	1
0	64	1	3
0	64	1	5
0	64	1	7
1	192	2	2
1	192	2	4
1	192	2	6

Thread	Running on HW Thread	Bound to HW Thread
0	66	64
1	64	192
2	192	200
3	64	72
4	192	208
5	64	80
6	192	216
7	64	88

Figure 4.41: **Affinity statistics for a nested parallel region using OMP_PLACES=cores** – The other settings are the same as before. The eight OpenMP threads are distributed over the two sockets. On each socket, four cores execute the four OpenMP threads from the second-level parallel region.

The placement of the OpenMP threads confirms that the implementation spreads the two outer-level threads over the two sockets. The other three threads in each team run on the same socket as their master thread, and the cores used are next to each other. The specific mapping onto the sockets and cores is an implementation-dependent feature, however.

4.8.4 Moving Threads Around

So far, thread placement for a single (nested) parallel region has been the only consideration. In this section we show what happens when there are two separate single-level parallel regions with a *different* affinity policy.

The code fragment is shown in Figure 4.42. There are two single-level parallel regions. On the first region, the proc_bind clause is used to set the policy to spread. This is changed to the close policy on the second region.

```
1 #pragma omp parallel proc_bind(spread)
2 {
3    #pragma omp single
4    {
5        printf("First single region - spread policy\n");
6    } // End of single region
7 } // End of parallel region 1
8
9 #pragma omp parallel proc_bind(close)
10 {
11    #pragma omp single
12    {
13        printf("Second single region - close policy\n");
14    } // End of single region
15 } // End of parallel region 2
```

Figure 4.42: **Two parallel regions with different affinity settings** – There are two single-level parallel regions. The first region uses the **spread** affinity policy, while the second region sets it to **close**. This causes the threads to migrate in between the execution of the two regions.

The number of threads is set to four for both regions (OMP_NUM_THREADS=4) and the place list is defined using the **cores** abstract name: OMP_PLACES=cores. The policies are activated at runtime by setting OMP_PROC_BIND=true.

The place list contains 32 places ($P = 32$), which is the number of cores in this system. There are four threads ($T = 4$), and for the first parallel region the "$T \leq P$" algorithm applies. There are four subpartitions with $P/T = 8$ consecutive places. Each thread is assigned to one of these subpartitions: $T_i \in SP_i$ for $i = 0, \ldots, 3$.

Although not guaranteed, it is reasonable to assume that the subpartitions are defined as shown in Figure 4.43. There are eight places per subpartition and each place spans the hardware threads within a single core. If we denote the set of hardware thread numbers in core i by C_i, the following holds: $C_i = \{8 * i, 8 * i + 1, \ldots, 8 * i + 7\}$ for $i = 0, \ldots, 31$. For example, $C_2 = \{16, \ldots, 23\}$.

Sub-partition	All 32 places (each spanning one core)			
SP_0	$\{0, \ldots, 7\}$	$\{8, \ldots, 15\}$	$\{\mathbf{16}, \ldots, 23\}$	$\{24, \ldots, 31\}$
	$\{32, \ldots, 39\}$	$\{40, \ldots, 47\}$	$\{48, \ldots, 55\}$	$\{56, \ldots, 63\}$
SP_1	$\{64, \ldots, 71\}$	$\{72, \ldots, 79\}$	$\{\mathbf{80}, \ldots, 87\}$	$\{88, \ldots, 95\}$
	$\{96, \ldots, 103\}$	$\{104, \ldots, 111\}$	$\{112, \ldots, 119\}$	$\{120, \ldots, 127\}$
SP_2	$\{128, \ldots, 135\}$	$\{136, \ldots, 143\}$	$\{\mathbf{144}, \ldots, 151\}$	$\{152, \ldots, 159\}$
	$\{160, \ldots, 167\}$	$\{168, \ldots, 175\}$	$\{176, \ldots, 183\}$	$\{184, \ldots, 191\}$
SP_3	$\{192, \ldots, 199\}$	$\{200, \ldots, 207\}$	$\{\mathbf{208}, \ldots, 215\}$	$\{\mathbf{216}, \ldots, 223\}$
	$\{\mathbf{224}, \ldots, 231\}$	$\{\mathbf{232}, \ldots, 239\}$	$\{240, \ldots, 247\}$	$\{248, \ldots, 255\}$

Figure 4.43: **Places definitions for four threads and the cores place list** – The table shows in which way the hardware thread numbers map onto all 32 places when using four OpenMP threads and the **cores** place list. Each place spans the hardware threads within one core. The first column identifies the four subpartitions. The hardware threads used during execution of the example code are marked in boldface font.

The second parallel region uses the **close** affinity policy. There are again $T = 4$ threads and $P = 32$ places. These are all shown in Figure 4.43, including the hardware thread numbers for each place. Following the algorithm for the "$T \leq P$" case, the threads are assigned consecutive places, starting with the place where the master thread executes.

The first table in Figure 4.44 shows that OpenMP thread 0 executed on hardware thread 208 when it created the other three threads. Although there are two parallel regions, the threads are created only once and re-used for the second parallel region.

The first line in the second table shows that thread 0 migrated from hardware thread 212 to hardware thread 208 and then stayed there. After the three OpenMP threads 1, 2, and 3 were created there, they migrated twice. This is why there are two lines for each of these threads.

Initially these threads moved to hardware threads 16, 80, and 144, respectively. They are on cores C_2, C_{10}, C_{18}, and C_{26} respectively. The threads are evenly spread: the "distance" between consecutive cores is always 8.

Thread	On HW Thread	Node	Created Thread
0	208	2	1
0	208	2	2
0	208	2	3

Thread	Running on HW Thread	Bound to HW Thread
0	212	208
1	208	16
1	16	216
2	208	80
2	80	224
3	208	144
3	144	232

Figure 4.44: **Affinity statistics for the two parallel regions using the cores place list** – The results confirm that the threads are first spread, executing on hardware threads 208, 16, 80, and 144. On the next parallel region, the master thread remains on hardware thread 208, while the other three threads migrate to hardware threads 216, 224, and 232.

On the second parallel region, the master thread continued to run on hardware thread 208, but the other threads migrated to hardware threads 216, 224, and 232 on cores C_{26}, C_{27}, C_{28}, and C_{29}, respectively. These have a distance of 1. This is the close affinity policy in action.

4.9   Concluding Remarks

Thread affinity support allows the user to completely control where in the system the OpenMP threads should run. This is not a static placement and threads may move around in the system.[18]

The key concepts are the *OpenMP places* and the *affinity policies*. The latter defines the desired proximity (master, close, or spread) of the threads. This may be used to match the resource requirements of the application.

The places are used to control the scheduling granularity. When setting up the places and the place list, the user has the choice of either having full control using the resource numbers, or leveraging the symbolic names sockets, cores, or threads.

---

[18]Not all systems support thread migration. It is good practice to check this.

Both come with their pros and cons. The resource numbers are precise. There are no uncertainties as to where the threads execute, but the numbers depend on the OS, as well as the system characteristics. Most likely, they would need to be adapted when a different OS, or system is used. This is in sharp contrast with the symbolic names. They are guaranteed to be supported and provide portability, but a possible downside is that there may be some room for implementation-dependent behavior in the thread placement.

Below are several tips and tricks on how to make best use of this feature and to reduce the risk of making mistakes:

- A first step to optimize for performance on a cc-NUMA system is to use the First Touch placement policy to distribute the data in such a way that the threads mostly access their data from a nearby memory. Parallel data initializations are often sufficient to achieve this.

- If First Touch cannot be leveraged, for example when reading data, a redundant parallel initialization may help to distribute the data and avoid a single memory to become the bottleneck.

- If none of this is applicable, it is worth checking the documentation for a system call, for example `madvise()`, to specify a different placement policy.

- The `OMP_PLACES` and `OMP_PROC_BIND` environment variables have default settings. We strongly recommend setting these explicitly, or checking the documentation for the defaults.

- The use of environment variable `OMP_DISPLAY_ENV` is strongly recommended to verify the affinity settings.

- The place list is static. It is defined upon program startup and cannot be modified.

- Threads are not allowed to migrate between places.

- If a place contains multiple resource numbers, all numbers in the list are equal from a scheduling point of view.

- The affinity policy may be adapted on each parallel region.

- The abstract names are preferred when specifying the place list.

- An implementation may support additional abstract names to support specific architectural features.

- When more control over the placement is needed, the interval notation provides for a compact way to define the places. This is not only less error-prone, but also easier to adapt to other platforms.

5   SIMD – Single Instruction Multiple Data

According to Flynn's taxonomy [9], a Single Instruction Multiple Data (SIMD) processor exhibits data parallelism by providing instructions that operate on entire blocks of data, called *vectors*. This is in contrast with scalar instructions that operate on single data items, one at a time.

In the early 1970s, vector supercomputers were designed around this concept. Through a single instruction, they performed the same basic operation on an entire vector. Nowadays, this vector technology is mainstream and is more commonly known as "SIMD," but the underlying principles are the same. With a single instruction, multiple elements are updated concurrently.

Through the SIMD support in OpenMP, the user has an easy and portable way to express this instruction-level parallelism. SIMD is tightly integrated with the OpenMP threading model, supporting multi-level parallelism. In this chapter, the OpenMP SIMD constructs are covered in detail.

5.1   An Introduction to SIMD Parallelism

In OpenMP, vectorization is referred to as *SIMD parallelism*, or "SIMD" for short. SIMD provides data-parallelism at the instruction level: a single instruction operates upon multiple data elements concurrently. SIMD instructions use special *SIMD registers* containing multiple data elements. The width of these registers determines the *vector length*, which is the number of scalar data items that can be processed in parallel by a SIMD instruction.

Figure 5.1 illustrates the SIMD concept. Two arrays b and c are added together, and the result is stored into the array a. For the purpose of this example, the arrays have 16 elements only. The loop that implements this operation requires 32 load instructions, 16 add instructions, and 16 store instructions.[1] On a system with SIMD instructions with a vector length of four, it takes only 8 load instructions, 4 add instructions, and 4 store instructions.

The advantage is that the SIMD instructions are (almost) as fast as their scalar counterpart. In other words, the number of processor cycles needed to add 4 elements in SIMD mode is the same as the time it takes to execute one scalar add instruction. This means that, in this case, the processor time is reduced by a factor

---

[1] The few instructions needed to execute the loop, the "loop overhead," are not considered here.

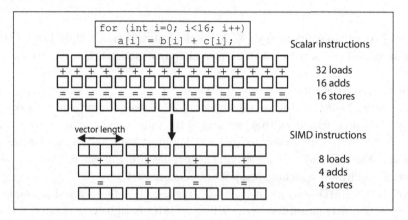

Figure 5.1: **An example of vectorization** – Vector instructions improve the performance by processing multiple data items concurrently.

of four. This is an upper limit, however. In practice, the improvement also depends upon the time it takes to move the data.

A compiler may be able to identify which operations are suitable for optimization using SIMD instructions, but it must prove that it is safe (or legal) to do so. Some of the challenges that a compiler encounters when trying to automatically generate SIMD instructions include: imprecise dependence information, data layout and alignment, conditional execution, packing and unpacking of scalar data items into vectors, calls to functions, and loop bounds that are not always an even multiple of the vector length.

In particular, C/C++ pointer variables pose a challenge to a compiler's dependence analysis. Different pointers may be aliases for the same memory block, resulting in seemingly independent operations having an implied dependence. Compilers must start with an assumption that a dependence exists between two accesses to memory and then attempt to prove that there is not one.[2]

Once it has been determined that a loop is safe to vectorize, there are some more issues to consider. To get the full benefit from SIMD, the starting address of the vectors may need to be aligned on the correct boundary. This means that the address in memory must be a multiple of the vector length in bytes.

---

[2]This is explained in more detail in the Glossary.

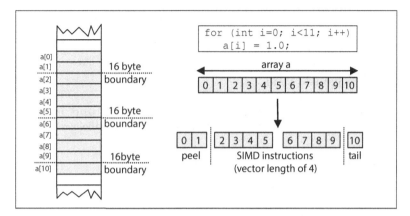

Figure 5.2: **Loop modifications needed to vectorize a loop using SIMD instructions** – To enforce alignment and ensure the remaining loop length is a multiple of the vector length, the compiler may need to peel off iterations and also treat the tail end separately.

If this is not the case, the compiler uses *loop peeling* to process the first element(s) separately, such that the first element processed with SIMD instructions starts on the correct boundary in memory. The vector is then processed in chunks that are a multiple of the vector length. If the number of loop iterations that remain after loop peeling is not a multiple of the vector length, the remaining items are processed in the *tail* part of the loop.

This is illustrated in Figure 5.2, where the array **a** with 11 elements is processed. This array is of type **float** and each element takes 4 bytes in memory. On a system with a SIMD register width of 16 bytes and with the memory-layout shown here, the first two elements need to be processed separately. The next 8 elements require two SIMD instructions. The remaining last element is handled separately.

The parts of the array processed separately are relatively inefficient. In most cases, the need to handle these situations can only be detected during program execution. In Section 5.2.5 it is shown which controls OpenMP provides to pass on more information to the compiler, which it can use to generate more efficient code.

```
#pragma omp simd [clause[[,] clause]. . . ] new-line
    for-loops
!$omp simd [clause[[,] clause]. . . ]
    do-loops
!$omp end simd
```

Figure 5.3: **Syntax of the simd construct in C/C++ and Fortran** – The simd construct is the fundamental construct to express SIMD parallelism in a loop.

5.2 SIMD loops

The OpenMP compiler may transform a loop that is marked with the simd construct, into a *SIMD loop*. As a result, multiple iterations of the loop may be executed concurrently by a single thread. A SIMD loop of length n, consists of the logical iterations $0, 1, \ldots, n - 1$. The numbering denotes the sequential order in which loop iterations are executed.

A *SIMD chunk* refers to the set of iterations that are executed concurrently by a SIMD instruction in a single thread. Within a chunk, each iteration is executed by a *SIMD lane*, which refers to the mechanism that a SIMD instruction uses to process one data element. The number iterations in a SIMD chunk is the vector length.

5.2.1 The Simd Construct

The simd construct applies to one or more subsequent loops. The structure of the loops on which the simd construct is placed must conform to the same restrictions that are required by the for (do in Fortran) construct. The simd construct syntax in C/C++ and Fortran is given in Figure 5.3. The clauses that are supported by the simd construct are listed in Figure 5.4.

The OpenMP specification describes the execution model of the simd construct as follows: "When an OpenMP thread encounters a simd construct, the iterations of the loop associated with the construct may be executed concurrently using the SIMD lanes that are available to the thread." Intentionally, this allows for much freedom in the implementation.

The code in Figure 5.5 sums the two arrays pointed to by b and c and stores the result in the array pointed to by a. All three arrays are of length n. For this operation, all loop iterations are independent and may be executed concurrently.

private *(list)* **lastprivate** *(list)* **reduction** *(reduction-identifier : list)* **collapse** *(n)* **simdlen** *(length)* **safelen** *(length)* **linear** *(list[:linear-step])* **aligned** *(list[:alignment])*

Figure 5.4:   **Clauses supported by the simd construct** – The semantics of the `private`, `lastprivate`, `reduction`, and `collapse` clauses have been extended to the `simd` construct and are described in the main text. The `simdlen` clause is described in Section 5.2.2. The `safelen` clause is described in Section 5.2.3, The `linear` clause is described in Section 5.2.4. The `aligned` clause is described in Section 5.2.5.

```
1 void simd_loop(double *a, double *b, double *c, int n)
2 {
3   int i;
4
5   #pragma omp simd
6   for (i=0; i<n; i++)
7     a[i] = b[i] + c[i];
8 }
```

Figure 5.5:   **Example of the simd construct** – The vectors b and c are added and the result is stored in vector a.

This can be exploited by threads, for instance with the `for` construct, or with a SIMD loop (or with both).

Adding the OpenMP `simd` construct instructs the compiler to generate a SIMD loop. If, in fact, the pointer variable b or c is an alias for the pointer variable a, adding the `simd` construct to this loop would be a user error, the resulting behavior would be undefined, and incorrect results should be expected.

In this particular case, no further clauses are necessary. Similar to the `for` construct, the loop iteration variable i is `private`. However, with the `simd` construct, one private instance will be created per SIMD lane. The memory pointed to by a, b, and c (the arrays) is shared. The compiler is free to select the appropriate vector length that is suitable for the target architecture.

```
1 void simd_loop_private(double *a, double *b, double *c, int n)
2 {
3   int i;
4   double t1, t2;
5
6   #pragma omp simd private(t1, t2)
7   for (i=0; i<n; i++)
8   {
9     t1 = func1(b[i], c[i]);
10    t2 = func2(b[i], c[i]);
11    a[i] = t1 + t2;
12  }
13 }
```

Figure 5.6: **Example using private variables in a simd construct** – The two function calls return intermediate results that must be stored in private variables to avoid a data race. Each SIMD lane has its own instance of a private variable.

A simd construct has a data environment with shared and private variables. The private and lastprivate clauses modify the simd construct's data environment. In Section 1.2.3, the concept of an "execution instance" was introduced. In the context of the simd construct, the execution instance is a SIMD lane, and one instance of each variable is created per SIMD lane.

The code fragment in Figure 5.6 illustrates the use of the private clause. The two function calls to func1() and func2() return intermediate results that are stored in the variables t1 and t2, respectively. Because loop iterations are executed simultaneously by SIMD lanes, both variables must be privatized in order to avoid data races. The privatization is accomplished by listing the variables t1 and t2 in the private clause. Note that in this particular example, the same effect may be achieved by declaring both variables inside the loop.

The loop iteration variable i is privatized by default. However, in a simd construct, it is treated as lastprivate. After the loop, the original loop iteration variable contains the final value of the private loop iteration variable that was computed in the last sequential iteration.

```
1 void simd_loop_collapse(double *r, double *b, double *c,
2                          int n, int m)
3 {
4   int i, j;
5   double t1;
6
7   t1 = 0.0;
8   #pragma omp simd reduction(+:t1) collapse(2)
9   for (i = 0; i<n; i++)
10      for (j = 0; j<m; j++)
11          t1 += func1(b[i], c[j]);
12   *r = t1;
13 }
```

Figure 5.7: **Example of the reduction and collapse clauses on the simd construct** – The two perfectly nested loops are collapsed into a single iteration space. The reduction clause is required to parallelize the accumulation into t1.

An instance of a private variable is not initialized and no assumption about its initial value can be made. Further, the lifetime of a private variable is restricted to the simd construct, and there is no method for accessing the value of a private variable after the region completes.

Variables that appear as list items in a lastprivate clause on a simd construct are private. As explained in Section 1.2.3, the final value of the private variable that is computed in the last sequential iteration is available after the construct in the original variable that the lastprivate variable corresponds to.

The reduction clause described in Section 2.4.3, on page 93 works similarly in the context of the simd construct. The reduction clause takes a list of variables and the reduction operator as its arguments. For each variable in the list, a private instance is used during the execution of the SIMD loop. The partial results are accumulated into the private instance. The reduction operator is applied to combine all partial results, such that the final result is returned in the original variable and made available after the SIMD loop.

The collapse clause described in Section 2.1.3, starting on page 43, works the same on the simd construct. The clause takes a positive integer number as its argument that indicates the number of loops that are collapsed into one iteration space. All the loop iteration variables in the associated collapsed loops are lastprivate.

```
1 unsigned int F(unsigned int *x, int n, unsigned int mask)
2 {
3     #pragma omp simd simdlen(32/sizeof(unsigned int))
4     for (int i=0; i<n; i++) {
5         x[i] &= mask;
6     } // End of simd region
7 }
```

Figure 5.8: **Example of the simdlen clause on the simd construct** – The simdlen clause is a hint to guide the compiler in the selection of a vector length for the loop.

The use of both the reduction and collapse clauses is illustrated in Figure 5.7. Through the collapse clause, the two loops are merged into a single loop. The reduction clause is used to correctly compute the variable t1.

The collapse clause should be used with caution in the context of vectorization, because it increases the complexity of the generated SIMD code. We recommend to verify that such a loop is vectorized as intended.

Many modern compilers provide a feature known as "compiler commentary," which provides information about the optimizations, or lack thereof, performed.[3] If vectorization is supported on the target processor, messages related to this may be helpful in determining how to effectively use the OpenMP simd constructs. We recommend checking the documentation of the compiler to determine if this feature is supported and, if so, how to enable it.

5.2.2 The Simdlen Clause

The simdlen clause takes a constant positive integer value as its argument. This value specifies the preferred number of iterations to be executed concurrently. It impacts the vector length used by the generated SIMD instructions.

The value in the clause is a preference. The compiler has the freedom to deviate from this choice and to choose a different length. In the absence of this clause, an implementation-defined default value is assumed for the vector length. The purpose of the simdlen clause is to guide the compiler. Perhaps the user has more informa-

---

[3]Success, or failure, of vectorization also depends on the compiler options used. Check the documentation of the compiler for relevant options to consider.

```
1 void dep_loop(float *a, float c, int n)
2 {
3   for (int i=8; i<n; i++)
4     a[i] = a[i-8] * c;
5 }
```

Figure 5.9: **Example of a loop-carried dependence** – The loop-carried dependence creates a limit on the vector length.

tion on the loop characteristics and knows that a specific length may be beneficial to performance. An incorrect choice may negatively impact the performance but will not lead to an incorrect result. Figure 5.8 is a code example that uses the `simdlen` clause on a `simd` construct.

5.2.3   The Safelen Clause

A limit on the vector length used by SIMD instructions is sometimes required. An example of this is when vectorizing a loop with loop-carried dependences. As shown in the code in Figure 5.9, an operation in a previous loop iteration must complete before an operation in the current loop iteration can execute. In this case, the read of `a[i-8]` on the current iteration i cannot execute until the write of `a[i]` on the previous $i - 8$ iteration is completed.

The *loop-carried dependence distance* is the number of loop iterations between a previous and current iteration, which in this example is 8. It is a distance between iterations, specifying how far a dependency is in the iteration space. When using SIMD parallelism, the vector length must be less than or equal to the distance of the smallest loop-carried dependence in the loop.

In this particular example, a vector length of up to 8 could be used. The maximum safe distance between loop iterations can be specified through the `safelen` clause.

The `safelen` clause takes a constant positive integer value as its argument. The value for `safelen` provides an *upper limit* on the vector length. This number specifies the length in which it is safe to vectorize the loop. The vector length ultimately selected by the compiler is still implementation-defined, but it does not generate SIMD code using a vector length that exceeds the `safelen` value.

```
1 void simd_loop_safelen(double *a, double *b, double *c, int n,
2                        int offset)
3 {
4   int i;
5   #pragma omp simd safelen(16)
6   for (i=offset; i<n; i++)
7     a[i] = b[i-offset] + c[i];
8 }
```

Figure 5.10:   **Example of the safelen clause on the simd construct** – The
`safelen` clause ensures that a vector length of up to 16 is correct.

The code fragment in Figure 5.10 illustrates the use of the `safelen` clause. The
accesses to the elements of array `b` use the variable `offset`. Unless the compiler
can determine the value of this variable, it may select a vector length that generates
incorrect results. In this case, the user has more knowledge of the value. The value
16 is specified in the `safelen` clause at line 4. This means that the user guarantees
that the loop can be safely vectorized using a vector length of 16 or less.

If the clause is not specified, the assumed value for `safelen` is the number of
loop iterations. Note the difference between the `safelen` and `simdlen` clauses.
The `safelen` clause is required for correctness while the `simdlen` clause indicates
a preference.

5.2.4   The Linear Clause

Scalar data elements are packed into vectors, operated on collectively as a vector
by SIMD instructions, and then unpacked. When the scalar data elements are
accessed in a linear fashion, it is easy to see how the vector is constructed. For
example, assuming that alignment restrictions have been satisfied, a single SIMD
load or store instruction may be used to read and write consecutive scalar data
elements as vectors.

In situations in which the scalar data elements are arranged consecutively in
memory, the accesses to the scalar data elements are said to occur with a stride
of one (*unit stride*). If the scalar data elements are not arranged consecutively in
memory, but instead are at a regular offset from each other, then the data elements
may be accessed with a stride greater than one. In this case, the stride is equal to
the offset between the scalar data elements.

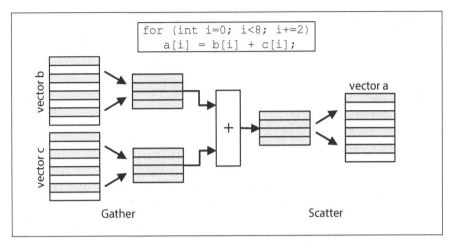

Figure 5.11: **Gather and scatter scalar data elements in and out of a vector** – Scalar data elements are gathered into vectors, operated on as a vector, and then scattered back to their destination locations.

To construct a vector, a *gather* operation reads scalar data elements from memory linearly but with a stride greater than one. Likewise, a *scatter* operation writes the scalar data elements in a vector back to memory linearly with a stride greater than one. The gather and scatter vector operations are illustrated in Figure 5.11. Some architectures have SIMD load and store instructions that support gather and scatter operations.

The best situation is when the vectors are accessed with a linear stride of one. The next best scenario is when the access pattern is linear but with a stride that is greater than one and gather and scatter instructions may be used. The worst case scenario is when no linear access pattern can be determined and the scalar data elements must be individually packed into and unpacked from vectors.

The `linear` clause is provided for the user to indicate the linear behavior of a variable in a loop. The compiler may use this information to determine the most efficient way to pack and unpack scalar data elements into vectors.

The `linear` clause is a data-sharing clause that provides a *superset* of the functionality of the `private` clause. On a loop or `simd` construct, the syntax of the clause is `linear` *(list[:linear-step])*. The `linear` clause accepts a list of variables as its argument. An optional, colon-separated, *linear-step* (stride) is supported.

```
1 void simd_loop_linear(double *a, double *b, double *c, int n,
2                          int offset)
3 {
4   int i, j = 0;
5
6   #pragma omp simd linear(j:1)
7   for (i=offset; i<n; i+=2)
8     a[i] = b[j++] + c[i];
9 }
```

Figure 5.12:   **Example of the linear clause on the simd construct** – The
`linear` clause defines how the j index variable relates to the loop variable i that is used
as an index into some of the arrays.

The `linear` clause may appear on the `simd` or `for` (do in Fortran) constructs.
In C, a variable that appears in the clause must have an integral or pointer type.
In C++, the variable must either have an integral or pointer type or be a reference
to an integral or pointer type. In Fortran, the variable must have an **integer** type.
If a *linear-step* expression is specified, it must be invariant during the execution of
the associated loop.

The semantics for the `private` clause apply: every variable listed in the clause is
private in the associated construct. For the `simd` construct, it is private to a SIMD
lane. In addition, this clause asserts that a variable has a linear relationship with
the iteration space of the loop to which the clause applies. The value of the private
variable in each loop iteration is defined as the value of the original variable, before
the construct was entered, plus the logical number of the loop iteration times the
linear-step or 1 if no *linear-step* is given. After the loop, the original variable has
the final value of the private variable from the sequentially last iteration.

A common use case of the `linear` clause is a loop, where in addition to the loop
variable, additional variables are used to index into arrays. If such variables have
a linear relationship with the loop variable, this clause may be used. A simple
example that demonstrates the use of this clause is shown in Figure 5.12.

Arrays a and c are accessed through the loop variable i, but array b is indexed
through another variable, j. The variable j has a linear relationship with the
loop iteration variable i, which is incremented by 2 in each iteration, while j is
incremented by 1. Variable i takes the values `offset`, `offset+2`, `offset+4`,....

The sequence for j is 0, 1, 2, ... By asserting the linear properties of the variable j, the compiler can more easily determine the access pattern for the array b and thus generate a SIMD instruction that reads b as a vector. Notice that a gather operation may be use to read the array c and that a scatter operation may be used to write to the array a.

The user may ask if the `linear` clause is necessary because a compiler can very often easily determine the linear behavior of a variable in a loop. The `linear` clause may also appear on `declare simd` directive, where it is used to specify the linear behavior of a function parameter (see Section 5.2.2). It is perhaps more useful in this capacity where the compiler may not be able to automatically determine the linear behavior of a function parameter.

5.2.5   The Aligned Clause

Data alignment is important for good performance. If a data element is not aligned on an address in memory that is a multiple of the size of the element in bytes, an extra cost is incurred when accessing the element. For example, on some architectures it may not be possible to load or store from a memory address that is not aligned to the size of the object being accessed. Instructions that do this are sometimes referred to as non-aligned loads and stores. Even if an architecture has non-aligned load and store instructions, they may execute with a higher cost to performance.

In many cases, alignment is handled by the compiler, but in certain scenarios this is impossible. As an example, consider processing a stream of data at the bit level. The program interprets this stream in terms of 32-bit integers. Depending on where in the stream the processing begins, the data may or may not be aligned.

Often, there are ways to enforce the correct alignment. For example, if two arrays are used in a loop, their relative alignment may be improved by adjusting the dimensions. There are also specific functions to enforce a certain alignment. An example is the `posix_memalign()` function from the POSIX standard. It allocates a memory block on a specific boundary. Other options are to consider vendor-specific features. We recommend checking the vendor's documentation for the details.

The alignment issues are the same when using SIMD instructions to vectorize loops. Figure 5.2 on page 223 illustrates the difference between aligned and unaligned data access in a vector loop. As explained there, in the case of a misalignment, iterations need to be "peeled off" to enforce alignment.

If vectorization is requested through the use of the OpenMP `simd` construct, but the resulting performance is poor, or the compiler commentary indicates issues in the vector code generation, then adjusting the data alignment may improve the performance.

The `aligned` clause is supported on both the `simd` construct, as well as the `declare simd` directive. This clause requires a list of variables as its argument, and an optional, colon-separated, *alignment*. The alignment must be a constant positive integer, and an implementation-defined default value is assumed if it is not given in the clause. In C, a variable that appears in the clause must have an array or pointer type. In C++, a variable that appears in the clause must have array, pointer, reference to array, or reference to pointer type. In C/C++, all the variables in the list are guaranteed to point to an object that is aligned in memory at an address that is a multiple of the number of bytes specified by the alignment. In Fortran, all the variables in the list are guaranteed to be aligned in memory at an address that is a multiple of the number bytes specified by the alignment.

If the alignment assumption is invalid and one or more variables do not have the alignment attributes specified, the behavior is implementation-dependent. It is highly recommended to avoid this type of error.

In the example code shown in Figure 5.13, the `align` clause appears on the `simd` construct at line 5. It asserts that the value of the pointer variable x is always aligned to a 16-byte boundary. Assuming that the size of the `float` data type is 4 bytes and knowing the alignment of the address in x is 16 bytes, the compiler has the information it requires to generate aligned 128-bit vector load and store instructions. It is important to note that the code is dependent on the assertion that value of `x` is always aligned to at least a 16-byte boundary.

5.2.6   The Composite Loop SIMD Construct

One of the main reasons for OpenMP to include support for SIMD parallelism is to cleanly define the interaction between vectorization through SIMD and thread-level parallelism, such as with the loop construct. Before support for SIMD was introduced in OpenMP 4.0, vendor-proprietary constructs had to be mixed with OpenMP. This not only violated portability, but there were also unwanted side-effects on performance.

```
1 void f_aligned(float *x, float scale, int n)
2 {
3   int i;
4
5   #pragma omp simd aligned(x:16)
6   for (i=0; i<n; i++)
7     x[i] = x[i]*scale;
8 }
```

Figure 5.13: **Example of the aligned clause on the simd construct** – The `aligned` clause asserts that the value of the pointer variable x is always aligned on a 16 byte boundary. With this information, the compiler may generate wider and more efficient vector load and store instructions.

#pragma omp for simd *[clause[[,] clause]...]* *new-line*
for-loops
!$omp do simd *[clause[[,] clause]...]*
do-loops
!$omp end do simd

Figure 5.14: **Syntax of the loop simd construct in C/C++ and Fortran** – The composite construct combines thread and SIMD parallelism. Chunks of loop iterations are distributed to the threads in a team. The chunks of iterations are then executed with a SIMD loop. A clause that may appear on either the loop construct or the `simd` construct may appear on the composite clause.

In OpenMP, the `simd` construct may be combined with the loop construct, resulting in the `for simd` (`do simd` in Fortran) composite construct.[4] In the same way as the OpenMP `simd` construct, the `for simd` construct applies to the subsequent loop, and the same restrictions outlined earlier must be adhered to, in addition to possible restrictions from the `for` or `do` construct. The syntax for the `for simd` construct in C/C++ and the `do simd` construct in Fortran is given in Figure 5.14.

The composite construct addresses the following question: which is performed first, vectorization and then thread-level parallelism, or vice versa?

With the `for simd` construct, chunks of loop iterations are first distributed across the threads in a team by a method that is determined by any clauses that apply

---

[4]The difference between a composite and a combined construct is explained in Section 6.5.2 starting on page 283.

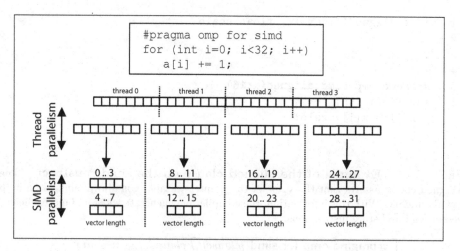

Figure 5.15: **Combining thread and SIMD parallelism** – Thread and SIMD parallelism are used to execute a loop.

to the `for` construct. Then, the chunks of loop iterations may be converted into SIMD loops in a way that is determined by any clauses that apply to the `simd` construct. The process is the same when using the `do simd` construct in Fortran. The distribution of loop iterations across threads and then SIMD loops is illustrated in Figure 5.15.

When using the composite construct, the user must be aware that both the number of threads, as well as the scheduling of the worksharing construct, may influence the efficiency of the resulting SIMD loop. Furthermore, the user must consider the effect of a private variable in the context of a composite construct. There is a private instance of the variable per SIMD lane.

Each loop has a certain amount of work associated with it. If the number of threads is increased, the amount of work performed per thread is reduced. Adding SIMD parallelism to this does not necessarily improve the efficiency. Especially if the SIMD loops that each thread works on reduce in length as the thread count increases. Most likely, some experimentation to find the optimal combination may be required.

The loop schedule of the worksharing construct affects the opportunities for vectorization. For good performance this must be taken into account. If the `static` schedule is used with a small chunk size, or if the `dynamic`, or `guided`, schedule is

```
1 void func_1(float *a, float *b, int n)
2 {
3   #pragma omp for simd schedule(static, 5)
4   for (int k=0; k<n; k++)
5   {
6     // do some work on a and b
7   }
8 }
9
10 void func_2(float *a, float *b, int n)
11 {
12   #pragma omp for simd schedule(simd:static, 5)
13   for (int k=0; k<n; k++)
14   {
15     // do some work on a and b
16   }
17 }
```

Figure 5.16: **SIMD loops without and with the simd schedule modifier** – The simd schedule modifier in func_2() guarantees that a preferred implementation-defined vector length is respected when distributing the loop

used, the SIMD efficiency may not be optimal. The reason is that the number of iterations per thread may be too small for SIMD to be beneficial. The compiler may not be able to generate the most efficient SIMD code because of loop tails and poor memory access patterns. Ideally, the selected chunk size for the threads is a multiple of the vector length.

The code in function func_1() in Figure 5.16 shows an example of a problematic chunk size. Each thread gets assigned a loop with only 5 iterations. This loop is vectorized, but it is very short, and depending on the vector length of the target architecture, this may lead to inefficiencies.

To address this issue, the simd schedule modifier is used at line 12 in Figure 5.16. For the loop in function func_2(), the modifier results in an adjustment of the chunk size. If chunk_sz denotes the chunk size, the formula to adjust this for a given vector length is given by: $ceiling(\text{chunk\_sz}/\text{simd\_len}) \times \text{simd\_len}$, with simd_len the vector length of the target architecture. For example, if the vector length is eight float elements, the resulting chunk size is increased from 5 to 8.

```
1 double compute_pi(int n)
2 {
3   const double dH = 1.0 / (double) n;
4   double dX, dSum = 0.0;
5
6   #pragma omp parallel for simd private(dX) \
7                         reduction(+:dSum) schedule(simd:static)
8   for (int i=0; i<n; i++) {
9     dX = dH * ((double) i + 0.5);
10    dSum += (4.0 / (1.0 + dX * dX));
11  }
12  // End parallel for simd region
13
14  return dH * dSum;
15 }
```

Figure 5.17:   **Example that uses the composite for simd construct** – The numerical solution for integration has a compute-intensive loop that is parallelized and vectorized.

An example that combines many of the topics covered in this section is shown in Figure 5.17. The number π can be approximated by computing the integral $\int_0^1 \frac{4}{1+x^2}\, dx$ through numerical integration. The compute_pi() function implements a simple numerical solution to this problem.

In Figure 5.17, the combined use of a **parallel** construct and the composite **for simd** construct is illustrated by placing the **parallel for simd** directive before the loop that spans lines $8 - 11$. Variable dX must be private, because it is modified in every loop iteration and the value differs for every SIMD lane. The computation of the summation at line 9 is a reduction operation that requires the **reduction** clause at line 7. This is an algorithm without load balancing issues and the simd:static schedule is most efficient.

5.2.7   Use of the Simd Construct with the Ordered Construct

The ordered clause is described in detail in Section 1.6.4. In short, the ordered region within a parallel loop is guaranteed to be executed in the original sequential order of the loop iterations. The code outside of this region is executed in parallel.

```
1 extern int x;
2 extern void global_update(int, int);
3 #pragma omp declare simd
4 extern int vec_work(int);
5
6 void F(int *a, int *b, int n)
7 {
8   #pragma omp simd
9   for (int i=0; i<n; i++)
10  {
11    // vectorize this part of the loop
12    a[i] = vec_work(b[i]);
13
14    // execute this part of the loop in sequential order
15    #pragma omp ordered simd
16    {
17      global_update(x, a[i]);
18    } // End ordered simd region
19  } // End simd region
20 }
```

Figure 5.18: **An ordered region within a SIMD loop** – The ordered region is executed with one SIMD lane in the original sequential order of the loop iterations.

Since OpenMP 4.5, the simd clause is supported on the ordered construct. Following the semantics of the loop construct, this clause has the effect that any encountering thread uses only one SIMD lane to execute the ordered region in the sequential order of the loop iterations. An example that uses the simd clause on the ordered construct is shown in Figure 5.18.

On line 12, the call to the function vec_work() is executed with SIMD parallelism. The call to the function global_update() at line 17 is executed in the original sequential loop iteration order by one SIMD lane at a time. This approach is efficient if the ordered region contains a small portion of the code that is not critical to the overall runtime.

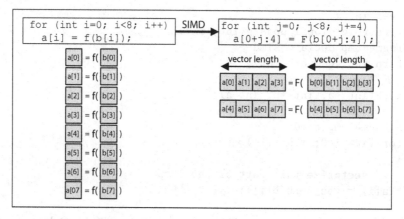

Figure 5.19: **Illustration of function calls with SIMD** – The scalar function
f() is modified and renamed to F() in this example. This function supports vector input
arguments and returns an entire vector.

5.3 SIMD Functions

Function calls inside a SIMD loop obstruct the generation of efficient SIMD instructions. In the worst case scenario, the call to the function must be done using
scalar data elements, which will most likely negatively impact the efficiency of the
generated code.

To fully exploit SIMD parallelism, a function called from within a SIMD loop
must be to a SIMD equivalent version of the function. This means that the compiler
must generate a special version of the function with SIMD parameters and code
that uses SIMD instructions.

The concept of a SIMD function is illustrated in Figure 5.19. The compiler
generates a SIMD version of the function f(). The function's scalar parameters
are converted to vector parameters. Scalar operations in the function body are
replaced with corresponding vector operations. If the function f() is called outside
the context of a simd region, the scalar variant is used.

This **declare simd** directive and its clauses are used to tell the compiler to
generate one or more SIMD versions of a function. These specialized versions of a
function may then be called from SIMD loops.

| #**pragma omp declare simd** *[clause[[,] clause]. . .] new-line* |
| *function declaration or definitions* |
| !**$omp declare simd***[(proc-name)]   [clause[[,] clause]. . .]* |

Figure 5.20: Syntax of the declare simd directive in C/C++ and Fortran
– The `declare simd` directive is used to declare that one or more versions of a SIMD function should be generated.

| **simdlen** *(length)* |
| **linear** *(list[:linear-step])* |
| **aligned** *(list[:alignment])* |
| **uniform** *(argument-list)* |
| **inbranch** |
| **notinbranch** |

Figure 5.21: Clauses supported by the declare simd directive – The `simdlen`, `linear`, `aligned`, and `uniform` clauses, discussed in Section 5.3.2, declare SIMD attributes for function parameters. The `inbranch` and `notinbranch` clauses, described in Section 5.3.3, specify that a SIMD function variant is always called under a conditional branch and never called under a conditional branch.

5.3.1 The Declare Simd Directive

The `declare simd` directive is used to declare that a SIMD variant of a function may be called from a simd region. The syntax for this directive in C/C++ and Fortran is shown in Figure 5.20. The clauses that may appear on the `declare simd` directive are listed in Figure 5.21.

When the `declare simd` directive is placed before a function declaration, it asserts that a SIMD variant of the function, with characteristics that are described by the clauses on the directive, may be called from within a loop in a simd region. The user may think of this like a special type of SIMD function prototype. If the `declare simd` directive is placed in the same translation unit as the definition of the function, then a SIMD variant of the function is generated by the compiler.

The compiler may generate multiple versions of a SIMD function and select the appropriate version to invoke at a specific call-site in a `simd` construct. The user may tailor a SIMD function variant by using clauses on the directive. For example, different SIMD versions of a function may be specialized for either different SIMD instruction widths or other function parameter attributes.

```
1 #pragma omp declare simd
2 double my_func(double b, double c)
3 {
4   double r;
5   r = b + c;
6   return r;
7 }
8
9 void simd_loop_function(double *a, double *b, double *c, int n)
10 {
11   int i;
12   #pragma omp simd
13   for (i=0; i<n; i += 2)
14   {
15     a[i] = my_func(b[i], c[i]);
16   }
17   // End simd region
18 }
```

Figure 5.22: **Example of the declare simd directive** – The function `my_func()` is called from within a `simd` construct. The `declare simd` directive declares that the compiler should generate a SIMD version of the function.

There are two restrictions. If a SIMD function has a side effect, the resulting behavior is undefined.[5] Furthermore, in C++, a function that appears under a `declare simd` directive is not allowed to throw any exceptions.

An example using the `declare simd` directive is shown in Figure 5.22. At line 1, the `declare simd` directive is used to inform the compiler that the function `my_-func()` may be called from a simd region. This instructs the compiler to generate at least one additional SIMD version of the function `my_func()`. Because of the `simd` construct at line 12, SIMD instructions are used to execute the loop that spans lines $13 - 16$. The call to `my_func()` at line 15 will be to a SIMD variant of the function that was declared at line 1.

---

[5]In the Glossary it is explained what a side effect is.

Note that in some examples in this section, the function call and the function definition are presented as if they were both in the same file (or translation unit). This is done to keep the examples simple.

Because the compiler can see the definition of the function and the place where the function is called, the user may wonder why the `declare simd` directive is needed. Depending on the compiler used, it may not be.

The `declare simd` directive is more critical when a function is defined in one file and called in another file. In that case, the compiler is instructed to generate a SIMD function variant even though it may not see the call to the function in a place where SIMD instructions are used.

5.3.2 SIMD Function Parameter Attributes

The `uniform`, `linear`, `simdlen`, and `aligned` clauses are used to specify attributes for SIMD function parameters. Except for the `simdlen` clause, the variables that appear in these clauses must be parameters of the function to which the directive applies.

When a parameter is listed in the `uniform` clause, it indicates that the parameter is passed an argument with the same value for all concurrent calls to the function in the execution of a single SIMD loop. This means that all SIMD lanes observe the same value for the parameter. If the arguments from consecutive loop iterations are passed as a vector to a SIMD variant of a function, then each element in the vector has the same value.

The `linear` clause has a different meaning when it appears on a `declare simd` directive. In this context, it is not a data-sharing clause as described in Section 5.2.4. Instead, it indicates that an argument passed to a function parameter has a linear relationship across the concurrent invocations of a function. Each SIMD lane observes the value of the argument in the first SIMD lane plus the offset of the SIMD lane from the first SIMD lane times the *linear-step*. For example, if the linear step is 2, there are 8 simd lanes, and the first simd lane observes the value 10, then the second lane observes the value 12, the third lane observes the value 14, and so on.

The example in Figure 5.23 shows the combined use of the `uniform` and the `linear` clauses on a function that is marked for vectorization with the `declare simd` directive. At line 14, the function `cosScaled` is called with the loop-invariant base address of the array `b`. The variable `c` is loop-invariant and the loop variable

```
1 #include <math.h>
2 #pragma omp declare simd uniform(ptr, scale) linear(idx:1)
3 double cosScaled(double *ptr, double scale, int idx)
4 {
5   return (cos(ptr[idx]) * scale);
6 }
7
8 void simd_loop_uniform_linear(double *a, double *b, double c,
9                               int n)
10 {
11   int i;
12
13   #pragma omp simd
14   for (int i=0; i<n; i++) {
15     a[i] = cosScaled(b, c, i);
16   }
17   // End simd region
18 }
```

Figure 5.23: **Example of the linear and uniform clauses on the declare simd directive** – The SIMD variant of the cosScaled function may assume that ptr and scale are loop invariant and that idx is incremented by 1 each time through the loop from where the function is called.

i is an offset into the b array. In the function cosScaled, the ptr parameter is a pointer and the scale parameter is a scalar.

The uniform(ptr, scale) clause informs the compiler to generate a SIMD function that assumes both of these parameters are passed arguments that are loop-invariant. The idx parameter appears in a linear clause, indicating to the compiler that the idx parameter is passed an argument that is incremented by 1 each time through the SIMD loop from where the function is called. By listing ptr in a uniform clause and k in a linear clause, the compiler can generate a unit stride SIMD load instruction for the write to ptr[idx].[6]

Figure 5.24 is another example that uses the uniform and linear clauses to optimize the access to a multi-dimensional array within a function that is called from a SIMD loop. If the index in the first dimension is always the same, and the

---

[6]In [26], the vector code generated by the Intel compiler for a similar example is discussed.

```
1 #pragma omp declare simd uniform(x, y, d1, i, a) linear(j)
2 void saxpy_2d(float *x, float *y, float a, int d1, int i, int j)
3 {
4   y[(d1*i)+j] = a*x[(d1*i)+j] + y[(d1*i)+j];
5 }
```

Figure 5.24: **Example using the uniform and linear clauses for multi-dimension array access** – Access in the first dimension is uniform. The loop that calls the saxpy_2d() function indexes linearly through the second dimension via the variable j.

```
1 #pragma omp declare simd simdlen(16)
2 char F(char x, char y, unsigned char mask)
3 {
4     return (x + y) & mask;
5 }
6
7 void img_mask(char *img1, char *img2, int n, unsigned char *m)
8 {
9   #pragma omp simd simdlen(16)
10   for (int i=0; i<n; i++) {
11     img1[i] = F(img1[i], img2[i], m[i]);
12   } // End simd region
13 }
```

Figure 5.25: **Example of the simdlen clause on the declare simd directive** – Use the simdlen clauses on the declare simd directive to generate a SIMD variant of the function F() that has a vector length of 16.

outer (SIMD) loop progresses over the second dimension, then the index variable of the first dimension may appear in a uniform clause to assert that this variable has an invariant value.

A simdlen clause may appear on a declare simd directive and has a similar meaning as it does for the simd construct. The constant value that appears in the clause specifies a length for vectorized arguments. The clause is treated as a hint on the simd construct; on the declare simd directive, it is not. The compiler generates a SIMD version of the function, which expects its vector arguments to have a length specified in the clause. The function variant may be called from

```
1 #pragma omp declare simd linear(src,dst) \
2                        aligned(src,dst:16) simdlen(32)
3 void copy32x8(char *dst, char *src)
4 {
5    *dst = *src;
6 }
7
8 #pragma omp declare simd uniform(x,y) linear(i) \
9                        aligned(x,y:64) simdlen(16)
10 float saxpy(float a, float *x, float *y, int i)
11 {
12   return a * ((x[i]) + (y[i]));
13 }
```

Figure 5.26: **Example of the aligned clause on the declare simd directive** – Use the `aligned` clauses on the `declare simd` directive to generate SIMD variants of the functions `copy32x8()`, and `saxpy()` that expect the addresses passed in pointer arguments to have a specific byte alignment.

a SIMD loop whose corresponding `simd` construct has a `simdlen` clause with the same value. An example that does this is shown in Figure 5.25.

When a pointer variable appears in an `aligned` clause on a `declare simd` directive, it declares that the value of the pointer variable argument has the specified byte alignment. The SIMD version of the function may then use aligned vector memory accesses for the pointer variable. When the SIMD function is called from a simd region, the object pointed to by the pointer variable argument must be aligned to the specified byte boundary. This can be ensured by using the `aligned` clause on the `simd` construct that encloses the call to the SIMD function. Examples that use the `aligned` clause combined with other clauses on `declare simd` directives are shown in Figure 5.26.

The `linear` clause supports a *modifier* that provides additional capabilities for C++ and Fortran. The following description focuses on the semantics of the modifier in C++.[7] The syntax of the `linear` clause with a modifier is `linear`*(modifier(list)[:linear-step])*. The modifier may be `uval` or `ref`. The `uval`

---

[7]See the OpenMP 4.5 specifications for more details on using the `linear` clause with a modifier in Fortran.

```
 1 #pragma omp declare simd linear(ref(x)) linear(uval(c))
 2 void increment(int& x, int& c)
 3 { x += c; }
 4
 5 void Fref(int *a, int n)
 6 {
 7   #pragma omp simd
 8   for (int i=0; i<n; i++) {
 9     increment(a[i], i);
10   } // End simd region
11 }
```

Figure 5.27: **Example of the ref and uval modifiers in the linear clause –** The `ref` modifier declares that the address of x is linear. The `uval` modifier declares that the address of c is uniform, and its value is linear.

or `ref` modifier can be used only if the function parameter has a reference type. The modifier defines how the address and the value of a variable are observed across SIMD lanes as follows:

- `uval(x)`: The storage address of x is uniform. The value in the storage location x is linear.

- `ref(x)`: The storage address of x is linear.

A simple C++ example that uses the `ref` and `uval` modifiers in the `linear` clause on a `declare simd` directive is shown in Figure 5.27.

5.3.3   Conditional Calls to SIMD Functions

The `inbranch` and the `notinbranch` clauses declare whether or not a SIMD variant of a function is called conditionally from a simd region. There are no arguments for these clauses.

A conditional branch is a point in a program in which the execution control may be transferred to another point within the program. An example is an `if-then-else` statement. The `if` part is the branch (instruction). If the condition evaluates to `false`, execution is transferred to the `else` part.

In the presence of conditional branches, the generation of SIMD instructions using the full vector length may not be possible. Because a conditional branch

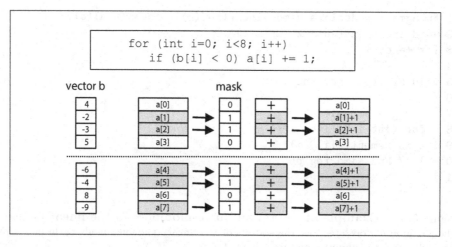

Figure 5.28: **Conditional control flow converted to masked vector instructions** – A vector mask predicate is used to enable or disable an operation on a given vector element. If the indexed mask is 1, the operation occurs. When it is 0, the operation is masked off.

creates an uncertainty regarding the number of consecutive elements available, it is more difficult for the compiler to generate SIMD instructions that use the full vector.

Depending on the target architecture, a compiler may generate *masked* vector code. Masked vector instructions use a bit vector, called "the mask," to ensure that the vector operation is applied only to those elements for which the mask bit is set to true. This concept is illustrated in Figure 5.28.

The inbranch clause asserts that the function is always called from within a conditional branch in a SIMD loop. With the inbranch clause present, the compiler must restructure the code to handle the possibility that a SIMD lane may not execute the code in the function. One approach to doing this is to pass the vector mask as an extra argument to the SIMD function variant.

The notinbranch clause may be used when the function is never called from within a conditional branch in a SIMD loop. The notinbranch clause enables the compiler to be more aggressive at optimizing the code in the function to use SIMD instructions. It can do this, because it does not need to consider the conditional execution of the instructions that execute in a SIMD lane.

```
 1 #pragma omp declare simd inbranch
 2 float do_mult(float x)
 3 {
 4   return (-2.0*x);
 5 }
 6
 7 #pragma omp declare simd notinbranch
 8 extern float do_pow(float);
 9
10 void simd_loop_with_branch(float *a, float *b, int n)
11 {
12   #pragma omp simd
13   for (int i=0; i<n; i++) {
14     if (a[i] < 0.0 )
15       b[i] = do_mult(a[i]);
16
17     b[i] = do_pow(b[i]);
18   } /* --- end simd region --- */
19 }
```

Figure 5.29: **Example of the inbranch and notinbranch clauses on the declare simd directive** – The inbranch clause tells the compiler to generate a SIMD variant of the function do_mult() that must be called conditionally within a SIMD loop. The notinbranch clause on the declaration of the do_pow() function tells the compiler that there is a SIMD variant of the function that must be called unconditionally within a SIMD loop.

If neither clause is specified, then the SIMD version of the function may or may not be called from within a branch, and the code the compiler generates must handle either situation.

The code in Figure 5.29 illustrates the use of the inbranch and notinbranch clauses. At line 1, the inbranch clause is used on the declare simd directive to tell the compiler to generate a SIMD variant of the function do_mult() that assumes it is always called conditionally. At line 15, the function do_mult() is called only when the condition computed at line 14 evaluates to 1 (true). The compiler generates a call to the SIMD variant of the function declared at line 1. If the compiler uses masking, the function is called unconditionally with an extra argument that passes the condition mask.

```
1 #pragma omp declare simd linear(pixel) uniform(mask) inbranch
2 #pragma omp declare simd linear(pixel) notinbranch
3 #pragma omp declare simd
4 extern void compute_pixel(char *pixel, char mask);
```

Figure 5.30: **Example of multiple declare simd directives for a function –**
Multiple SIMD versions of the function are generated. The invocation of a specific version
of the function is determined by where it is called.

At line 7, the `notinbranch` clause is used on the `declare simd` directive to tell
the compiler that there is a SIMD variant of the function `do_pow()` that is optimized
to assume it is never called conditionally. At line 17, the function `do_pow()` is called
unconditionally. The compiler generates a call to the SIMD variant of the function
declared at line 7, which does not pass a vector mask to the function.

5.3.4 Multiple Versions of a SIMD Function

As shown in Figure 5.30, multiple consecutive `declare simd` directives with different clauses may appear before the declaration of a function. When the declaration
is in the same file as the definition of the function, the SIMD function variants are
generated for each `declare simd` directive.

The multiple consecutive `declare simd` directives must appear on a function
declaration that is visible when the function is called in a `simd` construct. This
enables the compiler to select the best SIMD function variant for the function call.

5.4 Concluding Remarks

This chapter has covered how to use the OpenMP SIMD constructs to exploit
SIMD instructions, which are present in several contemporary microprocessors.
The performance improvements from using SIMD instructions can be substantial.
In [15], the authors proposed a draft version of what became the OpenMP SIMD
constructs and evaluated the performance improvement for selected benchmarks.
In [14], the authors discuss vectorization for a specific architecture.

The SIMD constructs in OpenMP may be used as a stand-alone feature to vectorize loops, but in many cases, we expect the SIMD constructs to be used to further improve the performance of an application already parallelized using OpenMP

threads. This is achieved by adding the `simd` constructs presented here to the time-consuming loops.

The capabilities of modern compilers to successfully vectorize code differ. Check the compiler's documentation for the relevant options to consider and to see if it supports a compiler commentary feature.

The SIMD loop body should not contain complex nested conditional branches, and the `if` clause should be avoided. When possible, align objects on byte boundaries that match an architecture's vector length. Use the `aligned` clause to indicate a variable's alignment. Use the `safelen` clause to vectorize loops with dependences, but care needs to be taken to use it the correct way. Use the `schedule(simd:static)` on the `for simd` and `do simd` constructs to balance thread and SIMD parallelism.

Utilize the `linear`, `uniform`, `simdlen`, and `aligned` clauses on the `declare simd` directive to generate specialized SIMD function variants. Add the `inbranch` and `notinbranch` clauses to the `declare simd` directive to generate SIMD versions of functions that may be called conditionally or unconditionally depending on the function call site. Be careful when using multiple `declare simd` directives for the same function. Each directive may result in another version of the function, which can increase the size of a program.

The `simd` and `for simd` (`do simd` in Fortran) constructs are combined with other OpenMP constructs. The `taskloop simd` construct is discussed in Chapter 3. The `distribute parallel for simd`, `distribute parallel do simd`, and `distribute simd` constructs are discussed in Chapter 6. This underlines the strength of OpenMP. In a consistent, portable, and integrated way, multiple levels of parallelism are supported.

6 Heterogeneous Architectures

Specialized accelerator processors, which dramatically improve the performance of some computations, are proliferating, and general-purpose processors are now very often connected to some type of accelerator. The popularity of these heterogeneous architectures across all types of computing has had a noticeable impact on the development of software.

To exploit these systems, developers must write software that executes various regions of code on different types of devices. There are many reasons for wanting to do this but very often the motivation is to accelerate computationally intensive loop nests.

However, the programming models for these systems are difficult to use. Often code modules are written twice, once for the general-purpose processor and then again for the accelerator. The accelerator version is often written in a lower-level, accelerator-specific language. The result is the undesirable software maintenance problem of keeping two versions of code, which implement the same algorithm, synchronized.

The OpenMP Language Committee recognized the need to make it easier to program heterogeneous architectures and set about to extend OpenMP to support these types of systems [3]. The results of this work were initially released in OpenMP 4.0 and updated in OpenMP 4.5.

Software developers can use OpenMP to program accelerators in a higher-level language and maintain one version of their code, which can run on either an accelerator or a general-purpose processor. In this chapter, we present the syntax for and describe how to use the OpenMP *device constructs* and related runtime functions that were added to support heterogeneous architectures.

6.1 Devices and Accelerators

Typically, the motivation for running code on a heterogeneous architecture is to execute parts of a program on an *accelerator*. As the name implies, the desire is to dramatically improve the performance of a program by leveraging the specialized hardware capabilities of accelerator devices.

OpenMP provides the means to distribute the execution of a program across different devices in a heterogeneous architecture. A device is a computational resource where a region of code can execute. Examples of devices are GPUs, CPUs, DSPs, FPGAs or other specialized processors. OpenMP makes no distinction about the

```
1 #pragma omp target map(a,b,c,d)
2 {
3   for (i=0; i<N; i++) {
4     a[i] = b[i] * c + d;
5   }
6 } // End of target
```

Figure 6.1: **Code fragment with one target region** – The target region is executed by a thread running on an accelerator.

specific capabilities or limitations of a device. Devices have their own threads which cannot migrate across devices. Program execution begins on the *host device*. The host device offloads the execution of code and data to accelerator devices.[1] Devices have access to memory where variables are stored. The memory may or may not be shared with other devices.

As shown in the code fragment in Figure 6.1, the **#pragma omp target** directive defines the target region spanning lines $1 - 6$. When a host thread encounters the **target** construct on line 1, the target region is executed by a new thread running on an accelerator.

By default, the thread that encounters the **target** construct waits for the execution of the target region to complete before it can continue executing the code after the **target** construct.

Before the new thread starts executing the target region, the variables a, b, c, and d are *mapped* to the accelerator. Mapped is the concept that OpenMP uses to describe how variables are shared across devices.

Very often the code that we wish to accelerate already includes OpenMP pragmas. We can place a **target** directive before a structured block that contains OpenMP constructs. In the code fragment shown in Figure 6.2, the target region is executed by a new thread on an accelerator. However, the new thread immediately encounters a **parallel for** construct and a team of threads is created that work together to execute the iterations of the subsequent loop.

The heterogeneous features of OpenMP fall into two general categories: program execution and data management. In the following sections, we will cover each of these categories in more detail.

---

[1]OpenMP uses the term *target* devices.

```
1 omp target map(a,b,c,d)
2 {
3   #pragma parallel for
4   for (i=0; i<N; i++) {
5     a[i] =  b[i] * c + d;
6   }
7 } // End of target
```

Figure 6.2: **Augmented code fragment with a parallel region** – The parallel region is executed by a team of threads running on an accelerator.

6.2 Heterogeneous Program Execution

This section describes the OpenMP heterogeneous program execution model. The device constructs, clauses, and new environment variable listed below are used to determine where (on which device) and how regions of a program are executed on a heterogeneous architecture:

- Target Construct

- Target Teams Construct

- Declare Target Construct

- Distribute Construct

- Device and Nowait Clauses

- `OMP_DEFAULT_DEVICE` Environment Variable

Of these, the `target` and `target teams` constructs are the most important as they are used to select which parts of a program are run on an accelerator. When a function name appears in a `declare target` construct, it indicates that the function is expected to be called from code executing on an accelerator, thus causing the compiler to generate a device-specific version of the function.

The heterogeneous execution model concepts are covered in this section. The complete syntax and semantics of the `target`, `target teams`, and `declare target` constructs are covered in detail in Sections 6.4, 6.5, and 6.7, respectively.

On a heterogeneous architecture with multiple accelerators, the `device` clause, `OMP_DEFAULT_DEVICE` environment variable, and runtime functions listed in Section 2.3.4 starting on page 70 are used to choose among and query about the different devices. Selecting a device using these clauses and functions is described in Section 6.10.

By default, the thread that encounters a device construct waits for the construct to complete. However, when a `nowait` clause is added to a device construct, the encountering thread does not wait, but instead continues executing the code after the construct. Task scheduling constructs are used to synchronize with the completion of the device construct's execution. The relationship between the device constructs and tasking is discussed in this section. The `nowait` clause is covered in Section 6.9.

The `target teams` construct starts multiple thread teams running in parallel on an accelerator. The `distribute` construct is a worksharing construct that schedules the iterations of a loop across the teams that are started by a `target teams` construct.

Combined with the `parallel for` and `simd` constructs, the `distribute` construct expresses a three-level hierarchy of parallelism across which loop iterations are spread. Loop iterations are first distributed to teams of threads, then to the threads in each team and, then to the SIMD vector lanes within each thread. This pattern of nested parallelism is executed efficiently by many types of accelerators.

The syntax and details of the `distribute` construct, and its combination with other constructs are covered in Sections 6.5.1 and 6.5.2.

6.2.1 A New Initial Thread

Recall that the thread that starts the execution of a program and executes all of the sequential code outside of any parallel regions is the *initial thread* (see Section 1.2.2). The OpenMP heterogeneous execution model is host-centric. The initial thread that starts the execution of a program is running on the host device. In other words, the program starts running on the host device. Prior to OpenMP 4.0 there was only one initial thread.

After OpenMP 4.0 and the addition of the `target` construct, multiple initial threads could arise during the execution of a program. A *target region* is all of the code that is dynamically encountered during the execution of a `target` construct. As shown in Figure 6.3, the thread that encounters a `target` construct does not

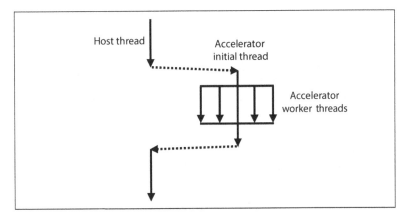

Figure 6.3:   **The heterogeneous programming model supported by OpenMP** – Program execution begins on the host device. When a host device thread encounters a `target` construct, a new initial thread executes the target region. When the initial thread encounters a `parallel` construct it becomes the master of a teams of threads.

itself execute the target region. Instead, a new initial thread begins the execution of the target region. Each target region acts as an OpenMP sub-program where an initial thread begins the execution of the sub-program. The initial thread may encounter other parallel constructs and spawn teams of threads.

The initial thread that executes a target region is potentially running on an accelerator. We say potentially because it's possible that the OpenMP program is running on a system that has no accelerators, in which case, the target region is executed by an initial thread running on the host device. Even on systems where accelerators are available, if the `target` construct has an `if` clause whose conditional expression evaluates to *false* then the initial thread executes on the host device (see Section 6.10.2). If there are multiple accelerators available, the `device` clause can be used to select one of them. When a `device` clause is not present, the initial thread executes on the default device specified by the *default-device-var* ICV. By default, the thread that encounters the `target` construct waits for the execution of the target region to complete and then continues executing the code after the `target` construct. Note how this is different from a `parallel` construct where the thread that encounters the construct becomes the master thread in a team of threads that is created to execute the parallel region.

6.2.2   Contention Groups

A *contention group* is the set of all threads that are descendants of an initial thread. An initial thread is never a descendant of another initial thread. Each dynamically encountered `target` construct starts a new contention group.

   Threads in different contention groups cannot synchronize with each other. This means that threads that arise from different target regions cannot synchronize with each other. Further, the threads in the contention group formed by the initial thread that started the execution of the program cannot synchronize with any threads that arise from target regions. This restriction effectively limits how threads in contention groups (often threads on different devices) can interact with each other.

   When threads from different contention groups execute in parallel, only variables[2] written to atomically (using an `atomic` construct) by a thread in one contention group can be read by a thread in another contention group, and only if both contention groups are executing on the same device.

6.2.3   A League of Teams

The `target teams` construct starts a *league* of teams executing on an accelerator. Each of these teams is a single initial thread executing in parallel the subsequent code statement. This is similar to a `parallel` construct but different in that each thread is its own team: a team of one. Threads in different teams are in different contention groups and, therefore, restricted in how they can synchronize with each other.

   When a `parallel` construct is encountered by a league, each initial thread in the league becomes the master of a new team of threads. The result is a league of teams where each team has one or more threads. Each team is a contention group. Each team of threads then concurrently executes the parallel region.

   Leagues are used to express a type of loosely connected parallelism where teams of threads execute in parallel but with very limited interaction across teams. We will explore this more later in Section 6.5.1 when we discuss how leagues are used in accelerated worksharing.

---

[2]The size of these variables must be less than or equal 64 bits.

6.2.4   The Target Task

Sometimes we don't want the host thread that encounters a target region to wait for the target region to complete. We want the target region to execute asynchronously so that the host thread can go off and do other work. OpenMP already has tasks that provide capabilities for launching and coordinating the asynchronous execution of code regions. Leveraging these features, the device constructs are formulated as OpenMP task generating constructs.

We have been talking in terms of threads up to this point, but recall that threads are the entities that do work; the actual work is a task. There is always a task (implicit or explicit) that a thread is executing. Tasks are executed only by threads running on the device where the tasks were generated.

The `target` construct is a task-generating construct. When a thread encounters a `target` construct, it generates an explicit task that manages the execution of the target region. The OpenMP 4.5 specification refers to this task as the *target task*. This is an unfortunate name as it seems to imply that the target task is running on an accelerator, but it is an explicit task generated on the host. The target task is complete when the enclosed target region is complete.

When the target task executes, the target region executes in the context of an implicit task, called an *initial task*, on the accelerator. The initial task is executed by the initial thread. Before OpenMP 4.0 there was only one initial task; the implicit task that enclosed the whole program. However, now each time a target region executes, a new initial task is generated on the target device. The target task is complete when the initial task, and thus the target region, is complete.

The task that the host thread is executing when it encounters the `target` construct is called the *generating task*. It generates the target task. Because the `target` construct results in a task, we now have available all of the asynchronous execution features from OpenMP tasking.

As shown in Figure 6.4, the target task is executed immediately by the thread that is executing the generating task. The thread suspends executing the generating task and begins executing the target task. The target task is by default an *included task*. It is a feature of the OpenMP tasking model that the task that generates an included task cannot be scheduled to execute until the included task is complete. For our purposes, the effect is that execution cannot continue after a `target` construct until the target region is complete.

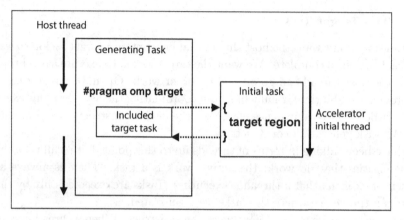

Figure 6.4: **The target task as an included task** – By default, the target task is an included task. The generating task cannot resume until the included target task is complete. The target task completes when the implicit task that contains the target region is completed by the initial thread running on an accelerator.

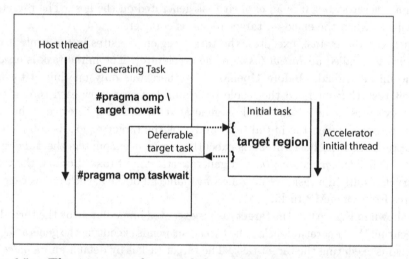

Figure 6.5: **The target task as a deferrable task** – The nowait clause makes the target task a deferrable task. The generating task may now be scheduled to execute before the target task is complete. The effect is that the generating task may execute in parallel with the target task.

However, sometimes we want the host device to do useful work in parallel with the accelerator device. Figure 6.5 shows how the `nowait` clause solves this problem. The `nowait` clause changes the default behavior of the target task so that it is no longer an included task With a `nowait` clause, the target task is like any other deferrable task.

Once a thread suspends execution of a target task, it is available to execute other tasks, including the original task that generated the target task. The effect is that execution of the generating task may continue past the `target` construct and before the associated target region has completed. The generating task is not stuck waiting for the target task (and thus the target region) to complete. The OpenMP task synchronization features, introduced in Chapter 3, may be used to determine when the target task is complete.

For example, in Figure 6.6 the thread that encounters the `target` construct generates a task and then continues after the construct to execute the function `F()`. The target task and the function `F()` are potentially executed in parallel. The host thread then waits at the `taskwait` construct to ensure that the target task has completed.

```
1 #pragma omp target map(a,b,c,d) nowait // Generate target task
2 {
3   #pragma parallel for
4   for (i=0; i<N; i++) {
5     a[i] =  b[i] * c + d;
6   }
7 } // End of target
8
9 F(b); // Execute in parallel with target task
10
11 #pragma omp taskwait // Wait for target task to finish
```

Figure 6.6: **Code fragment with a target nowait region** – The encountering thread generates a target task and then continues past the target construct to execute the function *F()*.

6.3   Heterogeneous Memory Model

This section provides an overview of the OpenMP heterogeneous memory model. The device constructs, clauses, and runtime functions that control how data is shared between threads executing on the host and an accelerator device are listed below:

- Map and Defaultmap Clauses

- Target Data Construct

- Target Enter and Exit Data Constructs

- Target Update Construct

- Declare Target Directive

- Use_device_ptr and Is_device_ptr Clauses

- Device Memory Functions

Of these, by far the most important is the `map` clause. Recall from Chapter 1 that variables are shared or private. As of OpenMP 4.0, variables can also be *mapped*, which is the concept that OpenMP uses to describe how data is shared across devices. The `defaultmap` clause can change the default rules for determining if certain variables are either private or mapped. The general concepts of mapped variables are discussed later in this section. The syntax and mechanics of the `map` and `defaultmap` clauses are covered in Section 6.6.

The host and accelerator may have different representations for the address of a variable. The `use_device_ptr` and `is_device_ptr` clauses are provided for the instances in which this difference in address representation must be dealt with explicitly. These device pointer clauses are covered in Section 6.11.

Variable's with static storage (for example, global variables) may be mapped for the entire program using the `declare target` directive, which is covered in Section 6.7.

The `target data`, `target enter data`, `target exit data`, and `target update` constructs are used to reduce the performance overhead of copying data between the host and an accelerator. These data-mapping constructs are covered in Section 6.8.

The device memory functions are described in detail in Section 2.3.4 starting on page 70. The `omp_target_is_present` function determines if a variable is mapped. Otherwise, the other device memory functions manage dynamically allocated device memory. Section 6.12 has examples that demonstrate how to use these functions.

6.3.1 Mapped Variables

Threads executing on an accelerator can have private variables. The initial thread that begins the execution of a target region gets a private instance of a variable that appears in a `private` or `firstprivate` clause on the `target` construct. For a `firstprivate` clause, the private variable is initialized with the value of the original variable from the host thread that encountered the construct. Likewise, any automatic (stack) variables that are declared in a scope contained within the construct are private to the initial thread.

OpenMP threads share variables that are stored in a single shared memory. However, heterogeneous architectures do not always have memory that is symmetrically shared between host and accelerator devices. A very common example of a heterogeneous architecture like this is one where the accelerator is a card and communication to the accelerator occurs over a PCIe bus.

As shown in figure 6.7, OpenMP supports heterogeneous architectures with both distributed and shared memory by *mapping* variables from the host to an accelerator. When the host and accelerator device do not share memory, a mapped variable is copied from the host's memory into the accelerator's local memory. Mapping hides whether or not a variable is shared by or copied to a device. Based on a heterogeneous architecture's memory system, the OpenMP implementation does what is required, either sharing or copying a variable when it is mapped.

How does one ensure that threads on different devices see the same value of a mapped variable and when? For the most part, the OpenMP memory consistency model as outlined in Chapter 1.2.3, starting on page 6, is extended to mapped variables.

A mapped variable is similar to a shared variable. Without some type of synchronization, two threads executing on different devices cannot simultaneously access the same mapped variable if either of the threads writes to the variable.

Threads executing on different devices may see a consistent value of a mapped variable at points that are determined by the effects of the `map` clause and the `target update` construct.

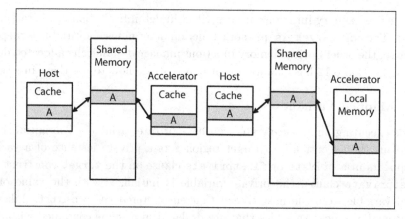

Figure 6.7: **A mapped variable in shared or distributed memory** – A mapped variable may be in either shared or distributed memory. The OpenMP implementation determines if copies are required.

If memory is distributed, then mapping a variable requires memory allocation, copy, and flush operations. The allocation and copy operations are not required (or are trivial) when memory is shared, but the flush operation is still necessary. Although the underlying machinations of variable mapping is handled by the OpenMP implementation, it is important to be aware of the dual-nature of mapped variables to write programs that achieve good performance across different architectures.

Because two devices may not share the same address space, the address of a mapped variable may not be the same on two devices When a pointer variable is mapped, only the pointer is synchronized, not the block of memory it points to. However, array sections may be used to map the pointed-to memory.

6.3.2   Device Data Environments

An accelerator has a *device data environment* that contains the set of all variables currently accessible by threads running on that device. As we discussed in the previous section, host threads share variables with target device threads by mapping them. Mapping a variable ensures that the variable is in the data environment of an accelerator.

An *original* variable in a host thread's data environment is mapped to a *corresponding* variable in the accelerator's data environment. Depending on the availability of shared memory between the host and target devices, the original and corresponding variables are either the same variable allocated in shared memory, or they are allocated in different memories and copy operations are required to keep the original and corresponding variables consistent. Whether a mapped variable uses shared or distributed memory is taken care of by the OpenMP implementation.

There only can be one instance of a variable in a device data environment. The OpenMP implementation keeps track of which variables are mapped. If a variable is already *present* in a device data environment, mapping it again will find the variable is already there and increment a reference count. It will not allocate another instance of the variable.

Minimizing the transfer of data between the host and an accelerator is often critical to getting good performance on heterogeneous architectures. Repetitively mapping a variable that is reused by multiple `target` constructs is potentially inefficient. The `target data`, `target enter data` and `target exit data` constructs amortize data transfers by mapping variables across the execution of multiple `target` constructs. Further, the `declare target` construct can map static and global variables for the whole program. Once a variable is mapped to an accelerator, situations can arise where the value of the variable must be updated from or to the device, and the `target update` construct fulfills this need. The `omp_target_is_present` runtime function is used to test if a variable is mapped.

6.3.3   Device Pointers

Because shared and distributed memory is supported, the OpenMP memory model assumes that the host and accelerator data environments are in different address spaces. However, this assumption creates some restrictions on accessing the address of the variable. With the OpenMP device constructs, the user must be aware of the different address spaces and be careful when using pointers. If the host and accelerator do not share memory, their local memories are in different address spaces. When a variable is mapped to an accelerator's data environment, a copy occurs, and the address of the variable on the accelerator is not the same as the address of the variable on the host.

Memory addresses are stored in pointer variables. A host thread cannot access memory via a pointer variable that contains an accelerator address. Likewise, an accelerator thread cannot access memory via a pointer variable that contains a host address. Further, the host and accelerator may have different representations for

```
1    char *hptr = malloc(N);
2
3    // Error - Accessing a host address on accelerator
4    #pragma omp target map(hptr)
5    for (int i=0; i<N; i++)
6      *hptr++ = 0;
```

Figure 6.8: **Illegal access of a host memory address** – A pointer variable containing a host memory address cannot be de-referenced by an accelerator thread.

```
1    char *dptr;
2    #pragma omp target map(dptr)
3    dptr = malloc(N);
4
5    // Error - Accessing a device address on host
6    for (int i=0; i<N; i++)
7      *dptr++ = 0;
```

Figure 6.9: **Illegal access of an accelerator memory address** – A pointer variable containing an accelerator memory address cannot be de-referenced by a host thread.

the address of a variable. For example, the value of a memory address might require 64 bits on a host and 32 bits on an accelerator.

In Figure 6.8, the host pointer variable hptr is assigned the address of a memory location in the host's address space. Mapping hptr copies the value of the pointer variable to the accelerator. The access to hptr at line 6 in the target region by an accelerator thread is illegal. The accelerator thread is attempting to access a host address.

Likewise in Figure 6.9, the accelerator pointer variable dptr is assigned the address of a memory location in the accelerator's address space. The access to dptr at line 7 by a host thread is illegal.

A *device pointer* is a pointer variable in the host data environment whose value is an object that contains the address of a storage location in an accelerator's device data environment.

Note that the value of a device pointer is an object. How the value of a device address is represented on a host is not necessarily the same way that it is represented

```
1    int dev = omp_get_default_device();
2    char *dptr = omp_target_alloc(dev, n);
3
4    #pragma omp target is_device_ptr(dptr)
5    for (int i=0; i<n; i++)
6      *dptr++ = 0;
```

Figure 6.10: **Legal access of an accelerator memory address using a device pointer** – A device pointer variable that appears in an is_device_ptr clause may be de-referenced in a target region.

on an accelerator. When a device pointer is referenced in a target construct, the compiler may need to transform the representation of the device address stored in the device pointer.

In Figure 6.10, the `omp_target_alloc` function returns a device address. The device pointer dptr must appear in an is_device_ptr clause on the **target** construct to correctly refer to it in the target region. The variable dptr is private in the target region. On entry to the region, the private dptr variable is initialized with the accelerator's memory address that corresponds to the original value of dptr before the region (the host's representation of the device address). See Section 6.11 for more details on device pointers.

6.3.4   Array Sections

Pointer variables are used extensively in C and C++. The value stored in a pointer variable is the address of another variable. As we saw in the last section, in order to support a variety of systems, the OpenMP model assumes that the host and accelerator may not share the same address space. Thus, mapping a pointer variable by itself is not very useful. We want to map the pointed-to variable (the memory that the pointer references). In order to map the pointed-to variable, we need to know its size.

For C and C++, we need something in the OpenMP syntax to express the concept of mapping the pointed-to variables. This is one of the reasons that OpenMP 4.0 added *array section* syntax for array and pointer variables.[3]

---

[3]Array sections may also appear in the depend clause.

An array section is a subset of the elements in an array. In OpenMP array sections are restricted to a contiguous set of elements. The C and C++ array subscript syntax is extended to support an array section expression. The array section syntax base[*offset* : *length*] is described below:

- The *base* is a C or C++ variable name with array, pointer type, or in C++, reference to array or reference to pointer type.

- The *offset* is an non-negative integer expression that is an offset from the start of the array. The *offset* is optional and, if not specified, defaults to 0.

- The *length* is a non-negative integer expression that is the length of the array section. If the *base* variable has a type of array or reference to array, then the *length* is optional and defaults to the number of elements in the array. If the *base* variable has a type of pointer or reference to pointer, then the *length* must be specified.

The value of a pointer variable used in an array section is the address of a pointed-to array variable. The pointed-to array variable may or may not have been dynamically allocated. Even if the pointed-to variable is a single scalar variable, when it's used in an array section, it is an array of one element.

An array section is *pointer-based* when the *base* is a pointer variable. A pointer-based array section is mapped using the following steps:

1. Create a pointer variable in the accelerator's data environment.

2. Map the host's pointed-to variable to the accelerator's data environment.

3. Initialize the accelerator's pointer variable with the address of the pointed-to variable in the accelerator's address space.

In Figure 6.11, the host pointer variable hptr is assigned the address of a storage location in the host's data environment. The array section hptr[0:1024] is then mapped to the accelerator's data environment. The 1024 element array pointed to by hptr is mapped to the accelerator. The hptr pointer variable is not mapped but is private in the target region and initialized with the address of the pointed-to array. Compare this to Figure 6.8.

```
1   char *hptr;
2
3   hptr = malloc(1024);
4
5   // Map an array section.
6   #pragma omp target map(hptr[0:1024])
7   for (int i=0; i<N; i++)
8     hptr[i] = 0;
9
```

Figure 6.11: **Map a pointer-based array section** – Use an array section to map pointed-to memory.

```
 1 float *p = malloc(N);
 2 float a[N];
 3
 4 // Map pointer based array section
 5 map(p[0:N:1])
 6 map(p[0:N])
 7 map(p[:N])
 8
 9 // Map array based array section
10 map(A[0:N:1])
11 map(A[0:N])
12 map(A[:N])
13 map(A[:]) // Size is N
14
15 // Map array section with offset
16 map(p[32:N-32]
17 map(A[N/2:N/4]
18
```

Figure 6.12: **Array section syntax examples** – Various usage of array section syntax in C and C++.

Array sections are available in the Fortran base language. In C/C++, an array section may appear only as a list item in an OpenMP map or depend clause. The C/C++ base language was not extended to support array sections. Some examples of array sections in C/C++ are shown in Figure 6.12

```
1 #define BIG 256
2 #define N (1024*1024)
3 int a[N*BIG];
4
5 void F(const int c, const int d)
6 {
7   for (int k=0; k<N*BIG; k+=N) {
8     #pragma omp target map(from:a[k:N]) firstprivate(c,d)
9     for (int i=0; i<N; i++) {
10       a[k+i] =  k+i * (c + d);
11     } // End of target
12   }
13 }
```

Figure 6.13: **Use array section to map a subset of an array** – Map a slice of the array **a** each time through the loop.

Array sections are also useful for mapping a slice of an array. It might be that mapping a very large array exceeds the storage capacity of the accelerator's local memory. In this case, we would like to map slices of the array and then compute on each slice. Figure 6.13 shows how this can be done. The rest of the sections in this chapter describe the syntax and semantics of the device constructs and clauses.

6.4   The Target Construct

The purpose of the `target` construct is to offload the execution of code to an accelerator. The code in a target region is executed by a new initial thread. The code in Figure 6.14 is a simple hello world example that uses the `target` construct.

The OpenMP runtime function `omp_is_initial_device` returns true if the code is executing on the host device. If there are no accelerators on the system where the code is running, then the initial thread that executes the target region runs on the host device.

Since the initial thread that executes the target region can always *fall back* to the host, programs that use device constructs are portable to systems that do not have accelerators. However, in the following description of the `target` construct it is assumed that the code is running on a system with at least one accelerator.

```
 1 #include <stdio.h>
 2 #include <omp.h>
 3 void hello(void)
 4 {
 5   #pragma omp target
 6   {
 7     if (!omp_is_initial_device())
 8       printf("Hello World from accelerator\n");
 9     else
10       printf("Hello World from host\n");
11   }
12 }
```

Figure 6.14: **Example of a target construct** – If the initial thread is running on an accelerator, it executes the first `printf()`. Otherwise, it is running on the host device and executes the second `printf()`. Note that some implementations may not support calling `printf()` on an accelerator.

#pragma omp target *[clause[[,] clause]...]*   *structured block*
!$omp target *[clause[[,] clause]...]*   *structured block*   **!$omp end target**

Figure 6.15: **Syntax of the target construct in C/C++ and Fortran** – A target region is executed by an initial thread running on an accelerator.

The `target` construct syntax in C/C++ and Fortran is given in Figure 6.15. The clauses that are available on the `target` construct are listed in Figure 6.16.

The `target` construct is a task generating construct. When a thread encounters a `target` construct a target task is generated on the host device. You can think of the target task as a task bound to the host device that wraps the execution of the target region. The target task is complete (on the host) when the target region is complete (on the accelerator). The `nowait` and `depend` clauses affect the type and asynchronous behavior of the target task.

By default, the execution of the target task is synchronous. The encountering thread cannot continue past the target construct until the target task is complete. The `nowait` clause makes the execution of the target region asynchronous. After

if *([target:] scalar-expression)*	(C/C++)
if *([target:] scalar-logical-expression)*	(Fortran)
map *([[map-type-modifier[,]] map-type:] list]*	
device *(integer-expression)*	(C/C++)
device *(scalar-integer-expression)*	(Fortran)
private *(list)*	
firstprivate *(list)*	
is_device_ptr *(list)*	
defaultmap(tofrom:scalar)	
nowait	
depend *(dependence-type: list)*	

Figure 6.16: **Clauses supported by the target construct** – The `if` and `device` clauses are discussed in Section 6.10. The `map` clause is discussed in Section 6.6.1. The `nowait` and `depend` clauses are discussed in Section 6.9. The `is_device_ptr` clause is discussed in Section 6.3.3 The `defaultmap` clause is discussed in Section 6.6.3.

generating the target task, the encountering thread does not wait for the target task to complete, but instead it can continue and execute the code after the `target` construct. Task scheduling via the `taskwait` construct or the `depend` clause may be used to synchronize with the completion of the target task. The execution model of the `target` construct is covered in detail in Section 6.2.

The target region is executed by an initial thread. Where the initial thread runs (the host or an accelerator) is determined by the *default-device-var* ICV. The `device` clause can be used to specify a device other than the default. The `if` clause is available to conditionally fall back to running the initial thread on the host.

The initial thread gets a private instance of a variable that appears in a `private` or `firstprivate` clause on a `target` construct. For a `firstprivate` clause, the private variable is initialized with the value of the original variable from the host thread that encountered the target construct. Likewise, any automatic (stack) variables that are declared in a scope contained within the target construct are private to the initial thread. Variables that appear in `map` clauses are mapped. Any assignments specified by a `map` clause occur when the target task executes. If a variable referenced in the `target` construct does not appear in a `map`, `private`, `firstprivate` or `is_device_ptr` clause, then default data-mapping rules determine if and how the variable is mapped (see Section 6.6).

C/C++ pointer variables that appear in `map` clauses as the base of an array section are private in the target region. The private variables are initialized with the value of the address of the array section's pointed-to memory in the accelerator's address space.

The code in Figure 6.17 illustrates how to use the `target` construct to offload to an accelerator the matrix times vector product example taken from [2]. By adding the `target` construct at line 6, the loop body is offloaded to an accelerator. When a host thread encounters the `target` construct at line 5, it generates an included target task, suspends the current task, and starts executing the target task. Because the target task is included, the host thread must wait for the target region, and thus the target task to complete, before continuing to execute the statement after the target construct. Scalar variables that do not appear in a `map` clause default to firstprivate, but for clarity the variables m and n are listed explicitly in a clause. Because the variables a, b, and c are pointers, array sections are required in the `map` clause to describe the size of the pointed-to memory. The pointer variables themselves are private in the target region.

The array sections' pointed-to memory is mapped to the accelerator's address space. If the host and accelerator do not share memory, storage is allocated in the accelerator's local memory, and the array sections are copied from the host's memory to the accelerator's local memory. The private pointer variables are assigned the address of the array section's pointed-to memory in the accelerator's address space. Because the variables i and j are declared in a scope enclosed in the target construct at line 7, they are private.

The target region is executed by an initial thread running on the default accelerator. The initial thread encounters the `parallel for` worksharing construct at lines 8 − 9 and becomes the master of a new team of threads that work together to execute the for-loop at line 10. The variables m, n, a, b, and c which were private to the initial thread are now shared among the threads in the team. The variables i and j are private to each thread in the team.

If the host and accelerator do not share memory, then when the target region is complete, the array sections are copied back from the accelerator's local memory to the host's memory. The storage allocated in the accelerator's local memory is then released. After the target region is complete, the target task completes and the host thread starts executing again at line 17 after the `target` construct.

```
1 void mxv(int m, int n, double * restrict a,
2          double * restrict b, double * restrict c)
3 {
4
5   #pragma omp target map(a[:n],b[:n],c[:n]) firstprivate(m,n)
6   {
7     int i, j;
8     #pragma omp parallel for default(none) \
9             shared(m,n,a,b,c) private(i,j)
10    for (i=0; i<m; i++)
11    {
12      a[i] = b[i*n]*c[0];
13      for (j=1; j<n; j++)
14        a[i] += b[i*n+j]*c[j];
15    } // End of parallel for
16  } // End of target
17 }
```

Figure 6.17: **Example using the target construct to execute the matrix times vector on an accelerator** – The host thread waits for the execution of the target region to finish before it continues after the construct.

The restrictions on the usage of the **target** construct are as follows:

- A **target** construct cannot be nested inside a target region.

- A **target data**, **target update**, **target enter data**, or **target exit data** construct cannot be nested in a target region.

- **threadprivate** variables cannot be accessed in a target region.

- In C++ a virtual member function cannot be invoked on an object that was not constructed on the accelerator. The object cannot be a mapped variable.

- In Fortran, if an array section is derived from a variable that has a **POINTER** or **ALLOCATABLE** attribute, then the variable cannot be modified in the target region.

#pragma omp teams *[clause[[,] clause]...]*   *structured block*
!$omp teams *[clause[[,] clause]...]*   *structured block* **!$omp end teams**

Figure 6.18:   **Syntax of the teams construct in C/C++ and Fortran –**
Create a league of initial threads each in its own team.

6.5   The Target Teams Construct

Strictly speaking, `target teams` is a combined construct made up of the `target`
and `teams` constructs. But since a `teams` construct may appear only nested immediately inside a `target` construct with no other intervening statements or declarations between the two constructs, the two constructs are inseparable. The `teams`
construct syntax in C/C++ and Fortran is shown in Figure 6.18.

Similar to the `parallel` construct, the `target teams` construct specifies that
the subsequent code block should be run in parallel. A `parallel` construct creates
a team of threads, where the thread that encountered the `parallel` construct
becomes the master thread. Each thread in the team executes the parallel region.
The `target teams` construct starts a *league* of initial threads where each thread
is in its own team. Each initial thread executes the teams region in parallel (see
Section 6.2.2). One can think of the `target` construct as a `target teams` construct
that creates a league with only one initial thread.

When a `parallel` construct is encountered by a league, each thread in the league
becomes the master of a new team of threads. The result is a league of teams where
each team has multiple threads. Each team of threads concurrently executes the
parallel region. The clauses that may appear on the `teams` construct are listed in
Figure 6.19. Clauses from both the `target` and `teams` constructs may appear on
the `target teams` construct.

The number of teams created by a `target teams` construct is implementation
defined or is specified by the `num_teams` clause. Each team is executing in its own
contention group. The maximum number of threads active in a contention group
is specified by the `thread_limit` clause.

The `target teams` and `parallel` constructs both fork multiple threads that
execute the subsequent block of code in parallel. The `target teams` construct is

num_teams *(integer-expression)*	(C/C++)
num_teams *(scalar-integer-expression)*	(Fortran)
thread_limit *(integer-expression)*	(C/C++)
thread_limit *(scalar-integer-expression)*	(Fortran)
default(shared | none)	(C/C++)
default(shared | firstprivate | private | none)	(Fortran)
private *(list)*	
firstprivate *(list)*	
shared *(list)*	
reduction *(reduction-identifier : list)*	

Figure 6.19: **Clauses supported by the teams construct** – The num_teams and thread_limits clauses are described below.

asserting a more restricted form of parallelism than the **parallel** construct allows. The compiler can take advantage of these restrictions and be much more aggressive at exploiting parallelism. These restrictions are as follows:

- Because the teams that are started by a **target teams** construct are each in their own contention group, threads from different teams cannot synchronize with each other.

- The only OpenMP constructs that can appear in a **teams** region are the **parallel**, **distribute** and any other **parallel** or **distribute** regions arising from related constructs. These are listed here:

  - parallel
  - parallel for (C/C++)
  - parallel do (Fortran)
  - parallel sections
  - distribute
  - distribute simd
  - distribute parallel for (C/C++)
  - distribute parallel do (Fortran)
  - distribute parallel for simd (C/C++)
  - distribute parallel do simd (Fortran)

```
1 #include <omp.h>
2 extern void do_team_work(int, int, int, int);
3 #pragma omp declare target(do_team_work)
4 void f()
5 {
6   #pragma omp target teams
7   {
8     int team = omp_get_team_num();
9     int nteams = omp_get_num_teams();
10    int tid = omp_get_thread_num(); // Always 0
11    int nthreads = omp_get_num_threads(); // Always 1
12    do_team_work(team, nteams, tid, nthreads);
13  } // End of target teams
14 }
```

Figure 6.20: **Example of the target teams construct** – Multiple initial threads execute the function do_team_work().

In Figure 6.20 the **target teams** construct at line 6 creates a league of initial threads. Each initial thread is in its own team. The initial threads (and therefore the teams) are numbered from 0 to $N-1$ where N is the number of initial threads created. The number of initial threads is returned by the OpenMP runtime function `omp_get_num_teams`. Calling the `omp_get_team_num()` in a teams region returns the team number of the initial thread. Since each team is a single initial thread, the calls to `omp_get_num_threads()` at line 11 and `omp_get_thread_num()` at line 10 will always return one and zero, respectively. Each initial thread calls the function `do_team_work()` at line 12 passing in the team number, the number of teams, the thread number and the number of threads in the team. Figure 6.21 diagrams the execution of the region assuming four initial threads.

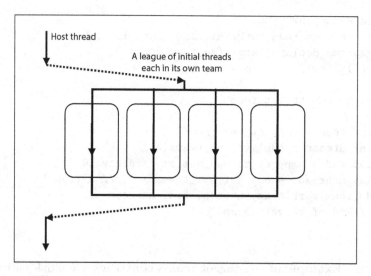

Figure 6.21: **The target teams construct creates a league of initial threads** – Each initial thread is a team of one thread. The initial threads execute the teams region in parallel.

In Figure 6.22, the `target teams` construct again creates a league of initial threads, but this time each initial thread immediately encounters the `parallel` construct at line 7. Each initial thread then becomes the master of a new team of multiple threads. The number of teams and a thread's team number are determined by the `omp_get_num_teams` and `omp_get_team_num` runtime functions, respectively. The call to the `omp_get_num_threads()` function at line 12 returns the number of threads in a team, which is 5. The call to `omp_get_thread_num` at line 11 returns the threads number in the range 0 to 4. Each thread in each team (a total of 20 threads) then calls the function `do_team_work()` passing in the team number, the number of teams, the thread number and the number of threads in the team. Figure 6.23 diagrams the execution of all the threads, assuming four teams with five threads per team. Note that if the thread calling `omp_get_team_num` is in a team that was initiated by a parallel region nested inside a teams region, the function still returns the number of the initial thread that is the ancestor of the thread.

```
1 void f()
2 {
3    #pragma omp target teams num_teams(4)
4    #pragma omp parallel num_threads(5)
5    {
6      int team = omp_get_team_num();
7      int nteams = omp_get_num_teams();
8      int tid = omp_get_thread_num();
9      int nthreads = omp_get_num_threads();
10     do_team_work(team, nteams, tid, nthreads);
11   } // End of target teams
12 }
```

Figure 6.22: **Example of a parallel construct nested in a target teams construct** – Multiple teams of threads execute the function `do_team_work()`.

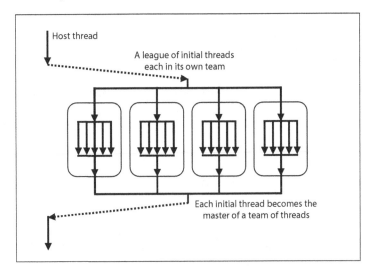

Figure 6.23: **The initial threads created by the teams construct each become the master of a new team of threads.** – Each initial thread starts execution as team of one thread. The initial threads execute the teams region in parallel and immediately encounter a parallel construct. Each initial thread then becomes the master of a new team of threads.

#pragma omp distribute *[clause[[,] clause]. . .]*
    for-loops

!$omp distribute *[clause[[,] clause]. . .]*
    do-loops

!$omp end distribute *[clause[[,] clause]. . .]*

Figure 6.24: Syntax of the distribute construct in C/C++ and Fortran –
Distribute loop iterations to the initial threads in a league.

---

private *(list)*
firstprivate *(list)*
lastprivate *(list)*
collapse *(n)*
dist_schedule *(kind[, chunk_size])*

Figure 6.25: Clauses supported by the distribute construct – The details for
the dist_schedule clause are given in the text.

6.5.1 The Distribute Construct

The `target teams` construct starts a league of initial threads where each thread
is in its own team. Similar to the loop construct, the `distribute` construct is a
worksharing construct that distributes the iterations of a loop to the initial threads
in a league. The loop iterations are divided into chunks, which are then scheduled across the initial threads in a league. The `distribute` construct syntax in
C/C++ and Fortran is shown in Figure 6.24. The clauses that are available on the
`distribute` construct are listed in Figure 6.25.

Variables that appear in the `private`, `firstprivate` or `lastprivate` clause are
private in each initial thread. The `distribute` construct has no implicit barrier at
the end of the construct. This is like having a loop construct with a `nowait` clause.
The initial threads do not synchronize at a barrier at the end of the region.

The `collapse` clause has the same behavior as it does on the loop construct. It
collapses the iterations of perfectly nested loops into a single iteration space. The
restrictions on the format of the loop to which the construct applies are the same
as those for the loop construct.

How the loop iterations are scheduled to execute across the initial threads in
the league is implementation-defined, unless the `dist_schedule` clause is present.
When the `dist_schedule(static)` clause is present, the loop iterations are divided

```
1 void saxpy(float *restrict y, float *restrict x, float a, int n)
2 {
3    #pragma omp target teams map(y[:n]) map(to:x[:n])
4    #pragma omp distribute
5    for (int i=0; i<n; i+=n)
6    {
7        y[i] = y[i] + a*x[i];
8    }
9 }
```

Figure 6.26: **Example of the distribute worksharing construct** – Each initial thread created by the target teams construct executes a subset of the iterations in the loop's iteration space.

into contiguous chunks. If *chunk_size* appears in the clause, then it specifies the size of the chunks. Otherwise, each thread is assigned no more than one chunk, and the chunks are roughly equal in size.

A version of the familiar saxpy (single precision $y = a * x + y$) function is shown in Figure 6.26. The `distribute` worksharing construct distributes the iterations of the loop to the initial threads in the league started by the `target teams` construct.

What is the difference between the execution of the `for` (or `do` in Fortran) and the `distribute` worksharing constructs? The `distribute` construct has the potential for better performance because of the restrictions on where it can be used and what other OpenMP constructs can appear inside the distribute region. This enables the compiler to be more aggressive with optimizations. The `for` and `do` constructs are more versatile but may not perform as well.

The idea behind the `target teams` and `distribute` constructs is to spread the execution of a loop coarsely across hardware compute units and then more finely to the threads that execute within those compute units. What we have shown so far is how to distribute the loop iteration to the compute units.

The code in Figure 6.27 converts the saxpy loop into a doubly nested loop.

The `distribute` construct at line 5 assigns the execution of two iterations in the outer loop to a league of two initial threads. The `parallel` construct at line 8 is then encountered by each initial thread with different values for j. Each initial thread becomes the master thread in a team of four threads. The first team executes the first half of the loop iterations and the second team executes the other half.

```
1 void saxpy(float *restrict y, float *restrict x, float a, int n)
2 {
3    // Assume n is even
4    #pragma omp target teams map(y[:n]) map(to:x[:n]) num_teams(2)
5    #pragma omp distribute
6    for (int j=0; j<n; j+=n/2)
7    {
8      #pragma omp parallel num_threads(4)
9      #pragma omp for
10     for (int i=j; i<n/2; i++)
11        y[i] = y[i] + a*x[i];
12   }
13 }
```

Figure 6.27: **Example of worksharing a loop across two levels of parallelism** – Use team level parallelism on the outer loop and thread level parallelism on the inner loop. Distribute the loop iterations to two teams. Each team then uses four threads to execute the iterations that are assigned to it.

The loop iterations scheduled to execute on an initial thread are then scheduled according to the for worksharing construct at line 9, to execute on the team of threads that the initial thread is now the master of.

In accelerated worksharing, loops are first scheduled at a coarse level to teams and then more finely to the threads in each team. We rewrote the saxpy loop in order to schedule it across two levels of parallelism: teams and threads. However, rewriting loops is tedious and is something we want to avoid.

Section 6.5.2 introduces *composite* accelerated worksharing constructs. When composite accelerated worksharing constructs are used, loop iterations are distributed across multiple levels of parallelism without having to rewrite the loop as we did in Figure 6.27.

6.5.2   Combined and Composite Accelerated Worksharing Constructs

Recall that combined constructs are short-hand notation for specifying the individual constructs in which one construct is immediately nested inside another. For example, the `parallel for` combined construct is equivalent to a `parallel` construct with a `for` construct nested immediately inside the `parallel` construct. The combined construct has the same execution behavior as the two separate constructs. However, in some instances, depending on the compiler, the combined constructs may achieve better performance than the individual constructs.

With some exceptions, the clauses that may appear on a combined construct are any of the clauses that may appear on the individual constructs that make up the combined construct. There are many new combined constructs involving the device constructs. They are presented in this section in two groups.

The first group is the *combined target* constructs. The constructs in this group combine the `target` construct with other constructs. The second group is the *combined target teams* constructs. They combine the `target teams` construct with new worksharing constructs. This second group is discussed at the end of this section after the new worksharing constructs are presented.

The syntax for the combined target constructs in C/C++ and Fortran are shown in Figure 6.28. The combined target constructs that include a `parallel` directive create a team of threads where the initial thread is the master of the team. The target simd region is executed by an initial thread that uses SIMD parallelism to execute the iterations of the subsequent loop.

A composite construct is different than a combined construct. Composite constructs combine multiple constructs, but the combination has execution behavior that is different from when the constructs are specified separately.

The `distribute parallel for` construct is a composite accelerated worksharing construct that distributes the iterations of a loop across two levels of parallelism. Each initial thread in the league that encounters the construct becomes the master thread of a team. The iterations of a loop are first distributed to the master threads. The subset of loop iterations assigned to the master thread are then again distributed to the threads in the team.

The code in Figure 6.29 shows how the `distribute parallel for` accelerated worksharing construct is used to distribute the iterations of the saxpy loop to teams and then to the threads in those teams.

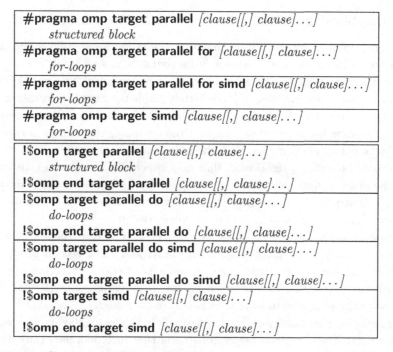

Figure 6.28: **Syntax of the combined target constructs in C/C++ and Fortran** − Constructs combining `target` with other constructs. A `copyin` clause may not appear on any of the combined target constructs.

Another way to look at this type of construct is to consider the nested version of the C/C++ saxpy loop from Figure 6.27. We had to rewrite the loop to distribute its iterations across two levels of parallelism.

The `distribute parallel for` (or `distribute parallel do` in Fortran) construct tells the compiler to create the second level of parallelism and to distribute loop iterations across the two levels of parallelism. So, now we don't have to rewrite loops!

The first level of parallelism is created by a `target teams` construct. When the resulting league of initial threads encounters the `distribute parallel loop` construct, the following steps occur:

1. By the `distribute` part of the construct, each initial thread is assigned loop iterations according to the `distribute` construct's scheduling algorithm.

```
1 void saxpy(float *restrict y, float *restrict x, float a, int n)
2 {
3   #pragma omp target teams map(y[:n]) map(to:x[:n])
4   #pragma omp distribute parallel for
5   for (int i=0; i<n; i++)
6     y[i] = y[i] + a*x[i];
7 }
```

Figure 6.29: **Example of the distribute parallel loop accelerated work-sharing construct** – Create multiple thread teams executing in parallel. Distribute loop iterations to the teams and then to the threads in each team.

2. By the `parallel` part of the construct, each initial thread becomes the master thread of a thread team. This creates the second level of parallelism. Now multiple teams of threads are executing in parallel.

3. By the `for` part of the construct, the subset of iterations assigned to each initial thread (the master thread) are then distributed across the threads in each team.

The composite accelerated worksharing constructs and their syntax in C/C++ and Fortran are shown in Figure 6.30. With a few exceptions, all clauses that may appear on the individual directives that make up the construct, may appear on the composite construct.

The `distribute simd` construct distributes loop iterations across two levels of parallelism. Loop iterations are assigned to the initial threads in a league according to the `distribute` constructs scheduling algorithm. Each initial thread then uses SIMD parallelism to execute the loop iterations assigned to it.

The `distribute parallel for simd` (or `distribute parallel do simd` in Fortran) construct distributes loop iterations across three levels of parallelism. Loop iterations are first assigned to the initial threads in each team. Each initial thread becomes the master of a new team of threads. The loop iterations assigned to an initial thread are then distributed to the threads in the master thread's team. Each thread then uses SIMD parallelism to execute the iterations assigned to it.

The composite accelerated worksharing constructs may be combined with the `target teams` construct. As mentioned at the beginning of this section, these are

`#pragma omp distribute parallel for` *[clause[[,] clause]...]*   *for-loops*
`#pragma omp distribute simd` *[clause[[,] clause]...]*   *for-loops*
`#pragma omp distribute parallel for simd` *[clause[[,] clause]...]*   *for-loops*

`!$omp distribute parallel do` *[clause[[,] clause]...]*   *do-loops* `!$omp end distribute parallel do` *[clause[[,] clause]...]*
`!$omp distribute simd` *[clause[[,] clause]...]*   *do-loops* `!$omp end distribute simd` *[clause[[,] clause]...]*
`!$omp distribute parallel do simd` *[clause[[,] clause]...]*   *do-loops* `!$omp end distribute parallel do simd` *[clause[[,] clause]...]*

Figure 6.30: **Syntax of the composite accelerated worksharing constructs in C/C++ and Fortran** – Distribute loop iterations across multiple levels of parallelism: teams, threads and SIMD lanes.

called combined target teams constructs. The combined target teams constructs and their syntax in C/C++ and Fortran are shown in Figure 6.31.

Because the `target teams` construct is a combined construct, the `target` construct may be separated out of a combined target teams construct (see Section 6.5). For example, a `target teams distribute` construct may be separated into a `target` construct with an immediately nested `teams distribute` construct. Typically, this is simply a syntax preference, but there are some instances when `target` must be a separate construct. This can occur when a variable must be `private` in the teams region and mapped in the target region.

A variable cannot appear in both a `map` clause and a data-sharing attribute clause on the same construct. For example, in Figure 6.32 the variable `sum` appears in a `reduction` clause, and therefore, cannot also appear in a `map` clause. Because `sum` is not mapped, its reduced value is lost after the `target teams` region completes.[4]

The solution, as shown in Figure 6.33, is to use a separate `target` construct that explicitly maps the variable `sum`. Each initial thread that executes the teams region

---

[4]The same problem can occur when using a `reduction` clause on the target combined constructs.

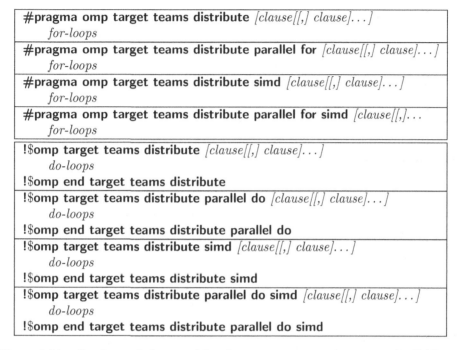

Figure 6.31: **Syntax of the combined target teams constructs in C/C++ and Fortran** – Constructs that combine `target teams` and accelerated worksharing constructs.

gets a private instance of `sum`. Once the teams region is complete, the mapped `sum` variable contains the reduced value. In the map-exit phase for the target region, the reduced value is assigned to the host's original `sum` variable.

6.6 Data Mapping Clauses

Recall from Section 6.3.2 that an accelerator has a *device data environment*, which contains the set of all variables that are available to the threads executing on that accelerator. When an *original variable* in the host's data environment is mapped to an accelerator, a *corresponding variable* is allocated in the accelerator's device data environment. During the execution of a program, the set of corresponding

```
1 int dotp(int *restrict a, int *restrict b, int n)
2 {
3   int sum = 0;
4
5   #pragma omp target teams distribute map(to:a[:n],b[:n]) \
6                                       reduction(+:sum)
7   for (int i=0; i<n; i++)
8     sum += a[i] * b[i];
9
10   return sum;  // Sum is always 0
11 }
```

Figure 6.32: **A variable cannot appear in both map and reduction clauses on the same construct** – The reduction clause is associated with the teams directive. The variable sum is not mapped, and therefore, the reduced value of sum is lost after the region.

```
1 int dotp(int *restrict a, int *restrict b, int n)
2 {
3   int sum = 0;
4
5   #pragma omp target map(sum) map(to:a[:n],b[:n])
6   #pragma omp teams distribute reduction(+:sum)
7   for (int i=0; i<n; i++)
8     sum += a[i] * b[i];
9
10   return sum;
11 }
```

Figure 6.33: **Use a separate target construct to map reduction variables** – The variable sum is private in the teams region, but now mapped in the target region.

variables in an accelerator's device data environment will change as variables are mapped and unmapped from it.

Depending on the memory architecture of the heterogeneous system, the original and corresponding variables may or may not share the same storage location. Because of this, a user must consider these two aspects of mapped variables:

- Because the original and corresponding variables *may* share the same storage location, a mapped variable should be thought of like a shared variable. This means that if either the original or the corresponding variable is written to by a thread, synchronization and memory consistency operations are required to avoid data races.

- Because the original and corresponding variables *may not* share the same storage location, copy operations might be required to make the original and corresponding variables consistent. These copy operations can be costly in regards to performance and should be avoided if possible.

If a variable is accessed in a target region, but the variable does not appear as a list item in a `map` clause on the construct then there are default rules to determine if the variable is mapped or private. These rules and the `defaultmap` clause are covered in Section 6.6.3. Structure members may appear as list items in a `map` clause but with some limitations that are described in Section 6.6.2. Section 6.6.4 shows how to access previously mapped memory using pointer-based array sections with a length of zero.

6.6.1   The Map Clause

Variable names, array sections, and structure elements may appear as list items in a `map` clause. An optional *map-type* and `always` *map-type-modifier* control how the list items are mapped. The syntax of the `map` clause is shown in Figure 6.34. If no *map-type* is specified, the default is `tofrom`.

There are three phases that occur when mapping a variable in a `target` region:

1. The *map-enter* phase occurs on entry to the `target` region when the variable is mapped to the accelerator.

2. The *compute* phase occurs when, during the execution of the `target` region, threads executing on the accelerator access the mapped variable.

3. The *map-exit* phase occurs on exit from a `target` region when the variable is unmapped from the accelerator.

The map-enter and map-exit phases manage the storage allocation and copy operations for a mapped variable. In the map-enter phase storage is allocated for the variable in the accelerator's address space, and then the value of host's original variable is copied to the accelerator's corresponding variable. In the map-exit phase, the value of the accelerator's corresponding variable is copied to the host's original variable, and then the storage for the corresponding variable in the accelerator's address space is released.

In Figure 6.35, the map-enter phase occurs on entry to the target region at line 3. Storage is allocated for the three corresponding arrays a, b and t in the accelerator's address space. The values of the host's original a, b and t array variables are then copied to the accelerator's corresponding array variables.

The map-exit occurs on exit from the target region at line 14. The values of the accelerator's corresponding array variables are copied back to the host's original array variables, and the storage for the three variables in the accelerator's address space is then released.

Notice that, in the compute phase, the arrays a and t are only written to and that array b is only read from. Let's assume that t is a temporary variable, and that the values written to it are never used after the target region. It is apparent then that the copies for a and c that occur during the map-enter phase are not needed. Further, the copies that occur during the map-exit phase for b and c are not needed.

The map clause's *map-type* is used to optimize the copies that occur during the map-enter and map-exit phases. On many heterogeneous systems, it is costly to copy variables between the host and an accelerator. The *map-type* is used to disable these copies as shown in Figure 6.36.

map *([[map-type-modifier[,]] map-type:] list)*
where the optional *map-type* is one of:
alloc
to
from
tofrom
release
delete
where the optional *map-type-modifier* is:
always

Figure 6.34: **Syntax of the map clause in C/C++ and Fortran** – The map clause controls how variables are mapped.

In Figure 6.37 the code from Figure 6.35 is updated to use explicit map-types. The map-enter phase occurs on entry to the target region at line 4 and storage is allocated for the three corresponding arrays a, b and t in the accelerator's address space. Only the value of the host's original b array variable is copied to the accelerator's corresponding b array variable. The corresponding a and t array variables are left uninitialized. The map-exit phase occurs on exit from the target region at line 15. Only the value of the accelerator's corresponding a array variable is copied

```
 1 #include <stdlib.h>
 2 void func(float a[1024], float b[1024], int t[1024])
 3 {
 4   #pragma omp target map(a, b, t) // Map-enter
 5   {
 6     int i;
 7
 8     for (i=0; i<1024; i++)
 9       t[i] = rand()%1024;
10
11     for (i=0; i<1024; i++)
12       a[i] =  b[t[i]];
13
14   } // End of target, map-exit
15 }
```

Figure 6.35: **Example of the map clause** – Copies occur for the arrays a, b, and t at the entry to and exit from the target region.

map-type	Perform map-enter copies	Perform map-exit copies
alloc	No	No
to	Yes	No
from	No	Yes
tofrom	Yes	Yes
release	–	No
delete	–	No

Figure 6.36: **Map-type effect on mapping variables** – The default *map-type* is tofrom. The release and delete *map-types* apply only to the map-exit phase and can only appear in a map clause on a **target exit data** construct (See Section 6.8.3).

```
1 #include <stdlib.h>
2 void func(float a[1024], float b[1024], int t[1024])
3 {
4   #pragma omp target map(from:a) map(to:b) \
5                       map(alloc:t) // Map-enter
6   {
7     int i;
8
9     for (i=0; i<1024; i++)
10      t[i] = rand()%1024;
11
12    for (i=0; i<1024; i++)
13      a[i] = b[t[i]];
14
15  } // End of target, map-exit
16 }
```

Figure 6.37: **Example of the map clause with map-types** – Eliminate superfluous copies by using map-types.

to the host's original a array variable. The storage in the accelerator's address space for all three variables is then released. Using map-types, unnecessary copy operations have been eliminated.

On entry to a `target`, `target data`, or `target enter data` construct, a map-enter phase occurs. Likewise, on exit from a `target`, `target data`, or `target exit data` construct, a map-exit phase occurs. The `target data`, `target enter data`, and `target exit data` data mapping constructs only map variables and do not execute any code on an accelerator (see Section 6.8).

What happens when a construct maps a variable, but that variable has already been mapped by a `target enter data` construct or by an enclosing `target data` construct? There can be only one instance of a corresponding variable in an accelerator's device data environment. A reference count is associated with each corresponding variable. When a variable is *present* in an accelerator's device data environment, its corresponding variable's reference count is greater than or equal to one. The map-enter and map-exit phases increment or decrement the corresponding variable's reference count. The point of the reference count is to keep track of the number of times a variable has been mapped and to only remove it from the

```
 1 #include <stdlib.h>
 2 #include <stdio.h>
 3 void func(float a[1024], float b[1024], int t[1024])
 4 {
 5   #pragma omp target data map(from:a) map(to:b) \
 6                           map(alloc:t) // Map-enter
 7   {
 8     #pragma omp target map(always,from:t) // Map-enter
 9     for (int i=0; i<1024; i++) {
10       t[i] = rand()%1024;
11     } // Map-exit
12
13     for (int i=0; i<1024; i++)
14       printf("t[%d]=%d\n", i, t[i]);
15
16     #pragma omp target map(a,b,t) // Map-enter
17     for (int i=0; i<1024; i++) {
18       a[i] = b[t[i]];
19     } // Map-exit
20
21   } // End of target data, map-exit
22 }
```

Figure 6.38: **Example of a variable appearing in nested map clauses –** There is only one instance of a variable in an accelerator's address space.

accelerator device data environment after it has been unmapped the same number times.

In the code in Figure 6.38 **target data** construct at line 5 maps the variables a, b and t according to their respective map-types. However, the variables a, b and t are mapped again by the enclosed **target** constructs at lines 8 and 16.

The **target data** construct's map-enter phase at line 5 allocates storage in the accelerator's address space for the variables a, b and t. Only the corresponding variable a is assigned the value of the host's original a variable. The b and t corresponding variables are uninitialized.

The target construct's map-enter phase at line 8 does not allocate storage for the variable t, because t is already present in the accelerator's device data environment.

The `always` *map-type-modifier* combined with the `from` *map-type* forces a copy of `t` from the accelerator to the host during the map-exit phase at the end of the target region at line 11.

The target construct's map-enter phase at line 16 does not allocate storage or copy the variables `a`, `b` and `t` to the accelerator, because they are already present in the accelerator's device data environment. Likewise, the map-exit phase at line 19 does not copy the variables back to the host or release the storage on the accelerator. In this case, it is as if the effects of the `map` clause are ignored.

Finally, at line 20 the map-exit phase for the `target data` construct copies the value of the `b` from the accelerator and then releases the storage for all three variables.

At the start of the map-enter phase, if a corresponding variable's reference count is greater than or equal to one, then no new storage is allocated, and the value of the original variable is not copied to the corresponding variable. The only effect is that the reference count is incremented.

Likewise, at the start of a map-exit phase, if a corresponding variable's reference count is greater than one, then the value of the corresponding variable is not copied back to the original variable, and its storage is not released. The only effect is that the reference count is decremented.

The `always` *map-type-modifier* asserts that the map-enter and map-exit copies should occur regardless of the reference count. It provides a way to force a copy to occur.

The steps associated with the map-enter and map-exit phases are updated to incorporate the reference count, *map-type*, and *map-type-modifier* as shown below:

The map-enter phase:

1. If a corresponding variable is not present in the accelerator's device data environment then:

    - Allocate storage in the accelerator's address space for the corresponding variable, and initialize its reference count to zero.

2. Increment the corresponding variable's reference count by one.

3. If the `to` or `tofrom` map-type is specified then:

    - If the corresponding variable's reference count is one or the `always` *map-type-modifier* is specified, then assign the value of the host's original variable to the accelerator's corresponding variable.

The map-exit phase:

- If a corresponding variable is present in the accelerator's device data environment then:

  1. If the `from` or `tofrom` *map-type* is specified then:
     - If the corresponding variable's reference count is one or the `always` *map-type-modifier* is specified, then assign the value of the accelerator's corresponding variable to the host's original variable.
  2. Decrement the corresponding variable's reference count by one.
  3. If the `delete` *map-type* is specified and the corresponding variable's reference count is not infinite, then set it to zero.
  4. If the corresponding variable's reference count is zero, then release the storage for the corresponding variable in the accelerator's address space.

Although the `alloc` and `release` *map-types* do not appear explicitly above, their effect is to either decrement or increment the reference count. The `delete` *map-type* sets the reference count to zero. It provides a way to force the removal of a variable from an accelerator's device data environment. Globally mapped variables and device memory associated to host memory by the `omp_target_associate_ptr()` function have an infinite reference count and cannot be removed. Both the `delete` and `release` *map-types* may appear only in `map` clauses on the `target exit data` construct (see Section 6.8.3).

6.6.2   Mapping Structure Members

Similar to how an array section can map a subset of the elements in an array, individual structure members can appear in `map` clauses in order to map a subset of the members in a structure variable. The restrictions on mapping structure members are as follows:

- Structure members must explicitly appear in `map` clauses, otherwise a reference to a structure member in a `target` construct implicitly maps the whole structure.

- To map a subset of the members in a structure variable, all structure members in the subset must appear in a `map` clause(s) on the same construct.

- If a subset of members of a structure variable are mapped, only the structure members in the subset can be referenced in a `target` region.

- When a subset of members of a structure variable are mapped, the subset may not be increased by additionally mapping other members of the structure variable.

- C/C++ structure members with type pointer may appear as the base of an array section, but only the rightmost structure member can specify an array section. For example, `S.a[:100]` is legal syntax, but `S.b[:100].z` is not.

To illustrate these concepts, some simple use cases are presented in Figure 6.39. A structure type `Stype` is declared at line 1. Lines 3 − 4 use the `declare target` construct to declare that `f1()`, `f2()`, and `f3()` are mapped functions and may be called from a target region (see Section 6.7).

For the `target` construct at line 8, the whole structure variable S is mapped even though only the members `S.x` and `S.y` are referenced in the construct. The structure members `S.x` and `S.y` appear explicitly in a `map` clause on the `target` construct at line 11, and now only these two members are mapped instead of the whole structure variable S. The `map` clause on the `target` construct at line 14 has an array section where `S.p` is used as the base of the array section.

On line 17, only `S.x` is mapped, but the call at line 18 refers to the address of `S`. This is allowed as long as the code inside the function `f3()` accesses only `S.x`. In the last example that spans lines 20 − 24 the structure member `S.x` is mapped by the `target data` construct at line 20. The `target` construct then maps `S.y`. This is an error because it tries to change the subset of mapped structure members (the fourth restriction above). This may be remedied by adding `S.y` to the `map` clause on line 20.

6.6.3   The Defaultmap Clause and Data-mapping Attributes

If and how a variable is mapped is determined by the variable's data-mapping attributes. The rules for determining the data-mapping attributes for a variable are either explicitly or implicitly determined.

The data-mapping attributes for variables that appear in clauses or are declared in a scope inside the `target` construct are explicitly determined according to the following rules:

```
 1 typedef struct { int x, y, size, *p; } Stype;
 2 extern Stype S;
 3 extern int f1(int,int), f2(int*,int), f3(Stype *);
 4 #pragma omp declare target to(f1, f2, f3)
 5
 6 void foo1(Stype S)
 7 {
 8    #pragma omp target
 9    f1(S.x, S.y);
10
11    #pragma omp target map(S.x, S.y)
12    f1(S.x, S.y);
13
14    #pragma omp target map(S, S.p[:S.size])
15    f2(S.p, S.size);
16
17    #pragma omp target map(S.x)
18    f3(&S);
19
20    #pragma omp target data map(S.x)
21    {
22       #pragma omp target map(S.y) // Error
23       f1(S.x, S.y);
24    }
25 }
```

Figure 6.39: **Example of mapping structure members** – Structure members may appear in map clauses and array sections with some restrictions.

- A variable that appears in a **map** clause is mapped according to the *map-type*.

- A variable that appears in a **private**, **firstprivate**, or **is_device_ptr** clause is private.

- A variable that is declared in a scope inside the **target** construct is private.

The data-mapping attributes for all other variables referenced in a **target** construct are implicitly determined according to the following rules:

- If the variable is not a scalar variable, the variable is mapped with a *map-type* of `tofrom`.

- If the `target` construct does not have a `defaultmap(tofrom:scalar)` clause, then a *scalar* variable is `firstprivate`.

- If the `target` construct has a `defaultmap(tofrom:scalar)` clause, then a *scalar* variable is mapped with a *map-type* of `tofrom`.

- A pointer variable that appears in a pointer based array section in C/C++ is `private`.

In general, variables with implicitly determined data-mapping attributes are treated as if they had appeared in a `map` clause with a *map-type* of `tofrom`. The exception is scalar and C/C++ pointer variables. Scalar variables have a base language built-in type (for example, `int` or `float` in C/C++).[5]

The performance overhead of a mapped variable can be higher than a `private` variable. A mapped variable requires a presence check to see if the variable is already present in the accelerator's device data environment. Variables that are `private` do not require this check. The overhead of performing the presence check is more pronounced for the smaller variables, such as scalars. For these reasons, the implicit data-sharing attribute for scalar variables referenced in a `target` construct is `firstprivate`. However, the `defaultmap(tofrom:scalar)` clause is provided to change the implicit data-mapping attribute for these variables to mapped with a *map-type* of `tofrom`.

In the `saxpy()` function shown in Figure 6.40, the scalar variables `a` and `n` are `firstprivate`. Because they are used in array sections, the pointer variables `y` and `x` are `firstprivate` and initialized with the address of the corresponding array section in the accelerator's device data environment (see Section 6.3.4).[6] Each initial thread created by the `target teams` construct at line 3 gets a private instance of `a`, `n`, `y` and `x`.

Notice that if a variable is `firstprivate`, then any changes to that variable in the target region will not be reflected back to the original variable. This can result in unexpected results. For example, in Figure 6.41 the variable `sum` is `firstprivate`. After the target region completes at line 8, the computed value of `sum` is lost, and the

---

[5]The precise definition of a scalar variable is determined by the base language.
[6]The original pointer value is discarded when the host and accelerator do not share the same address space.

```
 1 void saxpy(float *restrict y, float *restrict x, float a, int n)
 2 {
 3   #pragma omp target teams map(y[:n]) map(to:x[:n])
 4   {
 6     #pragma omp distribute
 7     for (int i=0; i<n; i++) {
 8         y[i] =  y[i] + a*x[i];
 9     } // End of distribute
10   } // End of target teams
11 }
```

Figure 6.40: **Example of default data-mapping attribute rules** – The pointer variables x and y are private. The scalar variables a and n are firstprivate.

```
 1 float dotp(float *restrict y, float *restrict x, int n)
 2 {
 3   float sum = 0.0;
 4   #pragma omp target map(y[:n]) map(to:x[:n])
 5   {
 6     for (int i=0; i<n; i++)
 7       sum += y[i] * x[i];
 8   } // End of target
 9
10   return sum;
11 }
```

Figure 6.41: **Example of problems with implicit firstprivate variables** – Because the variable sum is firstprivate, the computed value of sum is lost at the end of the target region.

dotp() function always returns 0.0. To correct the problem with the sum variable, either place it in a map clause or add a defaultmap(tofrom:scalar) clause to the target construct. It is recommended to not rely on implicit behavior and instead list variables explicitly in map, private, or firstprivate clauses as appropriate.

6.6.4   Pointers and Zero-length Array Sections

In Section 6.3.4, we showed how array sections are used to map memory that a pointer variable points to. Recall that an array section has a length. If the length of an array section is zero, then it is a *zero-length array section*.

A pointer-based zero-length array section has a special meaning in a **map** clause on a **target** construct. The pointer variable is **private** in the target region. If the value of the original pointer is an address that is already mapped, then the corresponding **private** pointer variable in the **target** region is assigned the corresponding device address. If the value of the original pointer is an address that is not mapped, then the corresponding **private** pointer variable is assigned NULL.

A pointer-based zero-length array section is convenient when a pointer variable is used in a **target** construct, and the memory it points to was mapped (for example, by an enclosing target data region) before the **target** construct is encountered. The code that uses the pointer variable in the target region might not refer to the length of the pointed-to memory.

Pointer variables referenced in a **target** construct that have an implicit data-mapping attribute are treated as if they had appeared in a **map** clause as the pointer variable in a zero-length array section with a *map-type* of **tofrom**. Some simple examples using zero-length array section are shown in Figure 6.42.

The **map** clause on the **target data** construct on line 11 maps the array **A** and the dynamically allocated memory that **p** points to. The pointer variable **p** is not mapped. Because it appears in an array section, the pointer variable **p** is **private** in the **target** construct starting at line 13. The **private** variable **p** is assigned the corresponding device address of the memory allocated at line 8.

For the **target** construct at line 16, the pointer variable **q** is implicitly treated as if it appeared in a **map** clause in a zero-length array section. At line 17, **q** is a private pointer variable that is pointing at the device address of the mapped array **A**. If you explicitly map a pointer variable as shown in line 19, then you are mapping the value of a host address to the accelerator. The mapped pointer variable does not contain a valid accelerator memory address. The call to **f1()** will possibly de-reference the invalid address stored in **p**.

```
1 #include <stdlib.h>
2 void f()
3 {
4    char *p, *q, A[128];
5    extern void f1(char *);
6    #pragma omp declare target to(f1)
7
8    p = malloc(1024);
9    q = A;
10
11   #pragma omp target data map(p[:1024], A)
12   {
13     #pragma omp target map(p[:0])
14     f1(p);
15
16     #pragma omp target // Implicit map(q[:0])
17     f1(q);
18
19     #pragma omp target map(p)
20     f1(p); // Error
21   }
22   free(p);
23 }
```

Figure 6.42: **Example of C/C++ pointers as zero-length array sections**
– Pointer variables are implicitly treated as pointer-based zero-length array sections in
target regions.

6.7 The Declare Target Directive

The declare target construct is used for both functions and variables. If a function is called from a target region, then the name of the function must appear in
a declare target directive. The declare target directive is used to map global
variables to an accelerator's device data environment for the whole execution of the
program. The declare target construct syntax in C/C++ and Fortran is shown
in Figure 6.43 along with its supported clauses.

The various syntactical forms of the declare target directive result in an
extended-list of variable and function names, or in the case of the link clause,

```
#pragma omp declare target
    declarations-definitions-seq
#pragma omp end declare target
    or
#pragma omp declare target (extended-list)
    or
#pragma omp declare target clause[[[,] clause] ...]
!$omp declare target (extended-list)
    or
!$omp declare target [clause[[,] clause]...]
where clause is:
to (extended-list)
    or
link (list)
```

Figure 6.43: **Syntax of the declare target construct in C/C++ and Fortran** – The various syntactical forms of the directive result in a *extended-list* of variable and function names.

a list of variable names. In describing the functionality, we will refer to a function or variable name that appears in a `declare target` directive.

In C/C++, the `declare target` and `end declare target` directives provide a convenient means to create an *extended-list* of the names of variables and functions that are declared between the two directives, where the variable declarations are at file or namespace scope and the function declarations are at file, namespace, or class scope. An *extended-list* of function and variable names may appear as list items on the directive or in clauses. The `to` clause accepts an *extended-list* of variable and function names. The `link` clause accepts only a list of variable names. In Fortran, the `declare target` directive without clauses or an *extended-list* may appear in the interface specification for a subroutine, function, program or module.

If a function name appears in a `declare target` directive in the same translation unit as the definition of the function, then it is a *mapped function*. A mapped function has a corresponding accelerator-specific version of the function. A function name must appear in a `declare target` directive before the function is called from a `target` construct or another mapped function.

A variable whose name appears in the `declare target` directive must have static storage duration. In C/C++, these are variables that are declared at file, namespace, static-block, or static-class scope. In Fortran, these are named variables and named common blocks.

A variable name that appears in a `declare target` directive in the same translation unit where it is defined is *globally mapped*. If the variable is referenced in a mapped function or device construct, it must appear in a `declare target` directive in the same translation unit as the function or construct.

A variable that is globally mapped is created and initialized in an accelerator's device data environment before a program begins execution. Globally mapped variables have an infinite reference count and are never removed from an accelerator's device data environment. They are permanently mapped for the execution of the whole program. Some examples of the `declare target` directive are shown in Figure 6.44.

The first form of the `declare target` directive on line 3 declares that the variables `Lastpos` and `Buf` are globally mapped. The original `Lastpos` variable on the host and an accelerator's corresponding version of the variable are initialized to 0. The variable `Buf` is declared but not defined in the example. `But` must appear in a `declare target` directive in the place where `Buf` is defined.

The `declare target` directive on line 6 uses the `to` clause to declare that `F()` is a mapped function. The prototype of the function `F()` is declared, but `F()` is not defined in the example. The function name `F` must appear in a `declare target` directive in the place (some other file) where the definition of `F()` occurs.

The `declare target` on line 8 and the `declare end target` on line 20 declare that variable `State` and `search()` and `find_state()` are mapped functions. The host's original variable `State` and an accelerator's corresponding version of the variable are initialized to -1. Like `F`, the function name `search` must appear in a `declare target` directive where it is defined. The function `find_state()` is both declared and defined between the pair of directives, and an accelerator-specific version of it is generated. The call to `find_state()` appears inside a `target` construct at lines $24 - 25$. When an initial thread executes the target region, the accelerator-specific version of the `find_state()` function is invoked.

A variable that is globally mapped will reserve memory in an accelerator's device data environment for the whole program. The `link` clause provides another way to access a global variable in a mapped function without having to globally map the variable. Note that function names cannot appear in a `link` clause. The `link` clause declares that a variable is *globally linked*. A reference to a globally linked variable

```
 1 int Lastpos = 0;
 2 extern char Buf[128];
 3 #pragma omp declare target(Lastpos, Buf)
 4
 5 extern int F(int, int);
 6 #pragma omp declare target to(F)
 7
 8 #pragma omp declare target
 9 int State = -1;
10 extern int search(char *);
11
12 void find_state(char c)
13 {
14    int pos;
15    Buf[Lastpos] = c;
16    pos = search(Buf);
17    Lastpos = pos;
18    State = F(Lastpos, pos);
19 }
20 #pragma omp end declare target
21
22 void process_input(char c)
23 {
24    #pragma omp target firstprivate(c)
25    find_state(c);
26 }
```

Figure 6.44: **Example of the declare target directive** – Various forms of the directive all have the same effect.

can appear in a mapped function with the restriction that before the function is called from a target region, the variable will have been mapped by a map clause.

An example of link clause is shown in Figure 6.45. On line 2 the variable Vector is globally linked by the declare target directive, which declares that the global variable Vector will be mapped before the compute() function is executed on the accelerator. The map clause on the target construct at line 15 maps Vector. The call to compute() in the target region can then find the mapped Vector variable.

```
 1 float Vector[1024];
 2 #pragma omp declare target link(Vector)
 3
 4 #pragma omp declare target
 5 extern float F(float , float);
 6 int compute(float a)
 7 {
 8    for (int i=0; i<1024; i++)
 9       Vector[i] = F(Vector[i], a);
10 }
11 #pragma omp end declare target
12
13 int update_vector(float a)
14 {
15   #pragma omp target map(Vector) firstprivate(a)
16   compute(a);
17 }
```

Figure 6.45: **Example of the link clause on a declare target directive** – Variables appearing in the link clause are *globally linked*. They must be mapped before they are referenced in a mapped function.

6.8   The Data-mapping Constructs

This section describes a group of constructs that map variables and manage the consistency of mapped variables between the host and an accelerator. A map-enter and map-exit phase occurs at the entry and exit of each target region for variables that are mapped in the region. Redundantly mapping a variable in multiple target regions can be detrimental to performance, especially when the host and the accelerator do not share memory. The target data construct described in Section 6.8.1 maps variables across a region of code that encloses multiple target regions. Variables are mapped once and then used in many enclosed target regions. The target enter data and target exit data construct are not associated with a specific code region and perform only the map-enter or map-exit phase, respectively. These two unstructured constructs are described in Section 6.8.3. Once a variable is mapped, the target update construct described in Section 6.8.2 can be used to make its value consistent between the host and the accelerator where it is mapped.

#pragma omp target data *[clause[[,] clause]...]*   *structured block*
!$omp target data *[clause[[,] clause]...]*   *structured block*   **!$omp end target data**

Figure 6.46: Syntax of the target data construct in C/C++ and Fortran – Map variables to a device for the extent of the region.

if *([target data:] scalar-expression)*	(C/C++)
if *([target data:] scalar-logical-expression)*	(Fortran)
map *([[map-type-modifier[,]] map-type:] list)*	
device *(integer-expression)*	(C/C++)
device *(scalar-integer-expression)*	(Fortran)
use_device_ptr *(list)*	

Figure 6.47: Clauses supported by the target data construct – The `if` and `device` clauses are discussed in Section 6.10. The `map` clause is discussed in Section 6.6.1. The `use_device_ptr` clause is discussed in Section 6.11.2.

6.8.1 The Target Data Construct

The `target data` construct maps variables to a device data environment for the extent of the target data region. In other words, when a thread executing on the host device encounters a `target data` construct, variables appearing in `map` clauses on the construct are mapped according to the map-enter phase. However, unlike the `target` construct, the host thread continues executing the code inside the target data region. Once the host thread encounters the end of the target data region, the map-exit phase occurs for the variables that appeared in the `map` clauses on the construct.

In summary, a `target data` construct is like a `target` construct minus the code executing on the accelerator. It only maps variables. The `target data` construct syntax in C/C++ and Fortran is shown in Figure 6.46. Clauses that can appear on the `target data` construct are shown in Figure 6.47.

On entry to and exit from a target data region, map-entry and map-exit phases occur, respectively, for the variables that appear in `map` clauses on the construct. An original variable can have only one corresponding variable in an accelerator's device data environment (See Section 6.6.1). When a variable is mapped by a `target data`

```
1 #define N (1024*1024)
2 double A[N], B[N];
3 extern double F(double * restrict);
4
5 void G(double c, double d)
6 {
7   double e;
8   #pragma omp target data map(B)
9   {
10    #pragma omp target map(B) map(always,from:A) \
11                       firstprivate(c,d)
12    for (int i=0; i<N; i++)
13      A[i] =  B[i] * c + d;
14
15    e = F(A);
16
17    #pragma omp target map(B) firstprivate(e)
18    for (int i=0; i<N; i++)
19      B[i] =  B[i] / e;
20
21  } // End of target data
22 }
```

Figure 6.48: **Example of a target data construct** – The array variable B is mapped once to an accelerator across two target regions.

construct, all device constructs enclosed in the target data region that also map that variable will find a corresponding variable present in the accelerator's device data environment and use it. An example of a **target data** construct that encloses two **target** constructs is shown in Figure 6.48.

The variable B is mapped by the **target data** construct at line 8, which encloses the two **target** constructs at lines 10 and 17. Storage is allocated in the accelerator's device data environment for the corresponding B variable, assigned the value of the host's original B variable, and its reference count is initialized to one.

The host thread that encounters the **target data** construct executes the code inside the target data region. It encounters the **target** construct at line 10, which maps B. During its map-enter phase, B is found to already be present in the accelerator's device data environment and the reference count for B is incremented to two. When the target region completes and during the map-exit phase, the reference count for B is decremented back to one. B is not removed from the accelerator's device data environment.

After the target region spanning lines $10 - 13$ has completed, the host thread continues executing the code in the target data region calling the function F() at line 15 and then encountering the second **target** construct at line 17. The reference count for the variable B is again incremented at the entry to and decremented at the exit from the target region. Because it still has a reference count greater-than zero, B remains mapped.

Finally, the host thread continues execution after the second target region is complete and then completes the target region at line 21. During the map-exit phase for the variable B, its reference count is decremented to zero, the value of the accelerator's corresponding B variable is copied to the host's original B variable, and the storage for B on the accelerator is released.

The variable A may be mapped by a **target data** or **target enter data** construct before the function G() is called, and so it would be present in the accelerator's device data environment with a non-zero reference count. However, the updated value of A is always needed for the call to F() at line 15. The **always** *map-type* in the **map** clause on line 10 ensures that, regardless of the reference count for A, after the associated target region completes, the value of the variable A on the host and the accelerator is always consistent (the same).

6.8.2   The Target Update Construct

If a variable is mapped by the **target data** or **target enter data** constructs or by the **declare target** directive, there are instances when a host thread might need to access the mapped variable. The **target update** construct makes the value of a mapped variable the same on the host as on an accelerator. It either assigns the value of the host's original variable to the accelerator's corresponding variable, or it assigns the value of the corresponding variable to the original variable. It makes the original and corresponding variables consistent. The **target update** construct syntax in C/C++ and Fortran is given in Figure 6.49. The clauses that are available on the **target update** construct are shown in Figure 6.50.

#pragma omp target update *[clause[[,] clause]...]*
!$omp target update *[clause[[,] clause]...]*

Figure 6.49: **Syntax of the target update construct in C/C++ and Fortran** – Make the value of a mapped variable consistent between the host and an accelerator.

if *([target update:] scalar-expression)*	(C/C++)
if *([target update:] scalar-logical-expression)*	(Fortran)
device *(integer-expression)*	(C/C++)
device *(scalar-integer-expression)*	(Fortran)
nowait	
depend *(dependence-type: list)*	
to *(list)*	
from *(list)*	

Figure 6.50: **Clauses supported by the target update construct** – The if and device clauses are discussed in Section 6.10. The map clause is discussed in Section 6.6.1. The **nowait** and **depend** clauses are discussed in Section 6.9. The **to** and **from** clauses are described below.

An example using the **target update** construct is shown in Figure 6.51. At line 4 the array variable B is globally mapped by the **declare target** directive (see Section 6.7). The **target update** construct at line 8 uses the **from** clause to assign the first and last 1 elements of B from the accelerator's corresponding B variable to the same elements in the host's original B variable. It makes the array elements consistent between the host and the accelerator. In this case, it is getting the values from the accelerator's version of B.

Let us assume that the function **update_boundary()** at line 9 reads and then writes only the 1 first and last elements of B. It updates the boundaries of B. When the host writes to the elements in B, those elements are no longer consistent between the host and the accelerator. The **target update** construct at line 10 then uses the **to** clause to assign the first and last 1 elements of B from the host to the sames elements in the accelerator's B variable. It makes the array elements consistent, but this time it is using the values from the host's version of B.

```
 1 #define N (1024*1024)
 2 extern void update_boundary(double *, int, int);
 3 double B[N];
 4 #pragma omp declare target(B)
 5
 6 void G(double *restrict B, double e, int n, int l)
 7 {
 8   #pragma omp target update from(B[0:1],B[n-1-1:1])
 9   update_boundary(B, n, l);
10   #pragma omp target update to(B[0:1],B[n-1-1:1])
11
12   #pragma omp target
13   for (int i=0; i<n; i++)
14     B[i] = B[i] / e;
15 }
```

Figure 6.51: **Example of the target update construct** – The array variable B
is globally mapped. The target update construct is used make elements at the start and
the end the array B consistent between the host and the accelerator.

Notice that the **target update** construct is executed by a host thread. The
construct cannot appear in a target region. This example used a variable that was
globally-mapped, but any mapped variable may appear in a **to** or **from** clause (for
example, one that was mapped by an enclosing target data region).

6.8.3 The Target Enter and Exit Data Constructs

The **target data** construct applies to a subsequent structured block. There is
a map-enter phase that occurs on entry to and a map-exit phase that occurs on
exit from a target data region. However, sometimes the way we want to map
variables does not fit a structured block model. We want to map variables in an
unstructured way. The target enter and exit data constructs provide this capability. These are standalone constructs that are not associated with a statement or
structured block of code. When a host thread encounters the **target enter data**
construct, a map-enter phase occurs for variables that appear in **map** clauses on the
construct. Similarly, a map-exit phase occurs for variables in **map** clauses on the
target exit data construct when it is encountered.

> **#pragma omp target enter data** *[clause[[,] clause]...]*
> **#pragma omp target exit data** *[clause[[,] clause]...]*
> **!$omp target enter data** *[clause[[,] clause]...]*
> **!$omp target exit data** *[clause[[,] clause]...]*

Figure 6.52: **Syntax of the target enter and exit data constructs in C/C++ and Fortran** – Standalone constructs for mapping variables to and from an accelerator's device data environment.

if *([target enter data:] scalar-expression)*	(C/C++)
if *([target exit data:] scalar-expression)*	(C/C++)
if *([target enter data:] scalar-logical-expression)*	(Fortran)
if *([target exit data:] scalar-logical-expression)*	(Fortran)
map *([[map-type-modifier[,]] map-type:] list)*	
device *(integer-expression)*	(C/C++)
device *(scalar-integer-expression)*	(Fortran)
nowait	
depend *(dependence-type: list)*	

Figure 6.53: **Clauses supported by the target enter and exit data constructs** – The **if** and **device** clauses are discussed in Section 6.10. The **map** clause is discussed in Section 6.6.1. The **nowait** and **depend** clauses are discussed in Section 6.9.

The syntax for the **target enter data** and **target exit data** constructs in C/C++ and Fortran is shown in Figure 6.52. The clauses that are available on the constructs are shown in Figure 6.53.

The *map-types* that may appear in a **map** clause on a **target enter data** construct are restricted to **alloc** and **to**. The *map-types* that may appear in a **map** clause on a **target exit data** construct are restricted to **release**, **from**, and **delete**. An explicit *map-type* must be specified in **map** clauses on these constructs. A **tofrom** *map-type* is not legal in a **map** clause on either construct.

The **delete** *map-type* may appear only in a **map** clause on a **target exit data** construct. It sets the reference count of a corresponding variable to zero and removes it from an accelerator. Its purpose is to force the removal of a variable from an accelerator's device data environment no matter what its reference count is.

A C++ class declaration is shown in Figure 6.54 with two member functions **allocate()** and **release()**. At line 9, the **target enter data** construct executes a map-enter phase for a pointer-based array section. The pointer variable in the

```
1  class myArray {
2    int length;
3    double *ptr;
4
5    void allocate(int l) {
6      double *p = new double[l];
7      ptr = p;
8      length = l;
9      #pragma omp target enter data map(alloc:p[0:length])
10   }
11
12   void release() {
13     double *p = ptr;
14     #pragma omp target exit data map(release:p[0:length])
15     delete[] p;
16     ptr = 0;
17     length = 0;
18   }
19 };
```

Figure 6.54: **C++ Example of the target enter and exit data constructs**
– The `allocate()` method will execute a map-enter phase for the dynamically allocated
memory pointed to by `p`. The `release()` method will execute the corresponding map-exit
phase.

array section is `p`, and it contains the address of the memory that was dynamically
allocated at line 6. The `alloc` *map-type* indicates that the corresponding memory
for the array section on the accelerator is not initialized with any value.

At line 16, in the `release()` member function, the `target exit data` construct
executes a map-exit phase for a pointer-based array section. It is expected that
the class member `ptr` is still pointing at the memory allocated in the `allocate()`
member function. The locally scoped pointer variable `p` is assigned the value of `ptr`
and then used in the pointer-based array section. The `release` *map-type* in the
`map` clause frees the corresponding storage for the array section in the accelerator's
device data environment. The corresponding array section is not copied back to
the original host memory.

```
1 void G(char S[128], int v)
2 {
3   extern int mutate(char *s, int);
4   while (!v) {
5     #pragma omp target enter data map(to:S)
6     v = mutate(S, v);
7   }
8   #pragma omp target exit data map(delete:S)
9 }
```

Figure 6.55: **Example of the delete map-type** – Regardless of its reference count, remove S from an accelerator's device data environment.

Notice that the array sections in both **map** clauses are examples of pointer-based array sections where only the pointed-to memory is mapped and not the pointer variable itself. The locally scoped **p** variables are required because the C++ **this->ptr** is an lvalue expression, not a pointer variable. The variable that appears in an array section must be an array name or a pointer variable.

An example using the **delete** *map-type* is shown in Figure 6.55. Line 5 is executed zero or more times depending on the value of the variable **v**. Each time a host thread executes the **target enter data** construct, a map-enter phase occurs for **S**. The first map-enter phase allocates storage, initializes the corresponding variable **S** with the value of the host's original **S** variable, and sets the corresponding variable's reference count to one. Each subsequent map-enter phase increments the reference count. The **map** clause on the **target exit data** construct on line 8 uses the **delete** *map-type* to set the reference count of **S** to zero. The variable **S** is then removed from the accelerator's device data environment. The value of **S** on the host after line 9 is undefined since the **delete** *map-type* does not copy the corresponding variable back to the original host variable.

When a variable appears in a **map** clause on a **target exit data** construct and that variable is not present in the accelerator's device data environment, then it is ignored by the construct. For example, in the case where the variable **v** is 0 on entry to the function, the **target exit data** construct at line 8 does nothing.

The `target enter data` and `target exit data` constructs have another potential benefit. Using the `nowait` clause, the constructs may execute as deferrable tasks.
This enables the possibility of asynchronously executing map-enter and map-exit
data transfers while the host thread continues executing other tasks in parallel.

6.9 The Nowait Clause on Device Constructs

To execute code in parallel on both the host and an accelerator the host thread must
not be blocked waiting for a device construct to finish. Section 6.2.4 discussed the
target task, which is an explicit task that is generated by a `target`, `target enter
data`, `target exit data` or `target update` construct. Because these constructs
generate a task, the parallel execution features of OpenMP tasking, covered in
detail in Chapter 3, are now available to the device constructs.

By default the target task is included and executed immediately. The host thread
that generated the target task cannot continue executing the code after the device
construct until the target task completes. The `nowait` clause changes the target
task into a deferrable task. This means that after generating the target task, the
host thread may immediately continue executing the code after the device construct.
An explicit parallel region is not required to execute a host task in parallel with
a target task. A single host thread may execute a host task, while in parallel, the
device construct is executed in by an accelerator.

The code example in Figure 6.56 uses the `nowait` clause to allow the host thread
to continue past the `target` construct at lines $7-9$. A target task is generated that
encloses the execution of the target region. A thread on the accelerator executes
the target region. In parallel, the host thread executes the loop at lines $11-12$. It
then encounters the `taskwait` construct at line 13 and waits there until the target
task generated at line 7 is complete. The host thread then executes the remainder
of the function.

Similar to the `task` construct, the `depend` clause may be used to express target
task dependences. If a `depend` clause appears on a device construct then the generated target task cannot be scheduled to execute until the dependences in the clause
are satisfied.

A target task's `private` and `firstprivate` variables are created and initialized
when the task is generated. However, map-enter phase assignments for mapped
variables occur when the target task executes, and map-exit phase assignments
occur when the task completes.

```
1 extern int max(int,int);
2 #pragma omp declare target(max)
3 void F(char *v, short *restrict s, int n)
4 {
5    int i;
6
7    #pragma omp target nowait map(v[0:n])
8    for (i=0; i<n; i++)
9      v[i] = max(v[i],0);
10
11   for (i=0; i<n; i++)
12     s[i] = max(s[i],0);
13   #pragma omp taskwait
14
15   for (i=0; i<n; i++)
16     s[i] = s[i] - v[i];
17 }
```

Figure 6.56: **Example using the nowait clause** – Execute the target region on an accelerator in parallel with the code executing on the host.

Tasks may be used to overlap computation with data transfers between the host and accelerator. There can be dependences between target tasks and other tasks generated by the **task** constructs. In Figure 6.57, the **nowait** and **depend** clauses are used to execute target tasks in parallel with other tasks.

At line 7 a parallel region is started with two threads. Because of the **single** construct, one host thread executes the region and generates a sequence of tasks. In the following discussion, the tasks are labeled (*taskname*), when the are generated.

A deferrable target task (*t0*) is generated for the **target enter data** construct at line 10. When it executes, the *t0* task performs a map-enter for the memory pointed to by a. A host task (*h0*) is generated that encloses the call to the function h0() at line 14. The *h0* host task and the *t0* target task may execute in parallel. A deferrable target task (*t1*) is generated that encloses the call to the function t1() at line 18. Because of the task dependences expressed in the **depend** clauses at line 17, the *t1* target task cannot be scheduled to execute until the *t0* and *h0* tasks have completed. A host task (*h1*) is generated that encloses the call to the function h1() at line 21. The *h1* task cannot be scheduled to execute until the dependence

```
 1 extern void h0(int*, int);
 2 extern void h1(int*, int);
 3 extern void t1(int*, int*, int);
 4 #pragma omp declare target(t1)
 5 void F(int *a, int *b, int n)
 6 {
 7    #pragma omp parallel num_threads(2)
 8    #pragma omp single
 9    {
10    #pragma omp target enter data map(to:a[:n]) \
11                nowait depend(out:a[:n]) // t0
12
13    #pragma omp task depend(out:b[:n])
14    h0(b, n);
15
16    #pragma omp target map(to:b[:n]) \
17                nowait depend(in:b[:n]) depend(inout:a[:n])
18    t1(a, b, n);
19
20    #pragma omp task depend(in:b[:n])
21    h1(b,n);
22
23    #pragma omp target exit data map(from:a[:n]) \
24                depend(in:a[:n]) // t2
25    }
26 }
```

Figure 6.57: **Example using the nowait and depend clauses** – Use the depend
and nowait clauses to execute target tasks in parallel with other host tasks.

on b[:n] is satisfied, which occurs when the $h0$ task completes. Notice that the $t1$
and $h1$ tasks may execute in parallel and that the $h1$ task may start before $t1$.

An included target task ($t2$) is generated for the target exit data construct at
line 23, and when it executes, it performs a map-exit phase for the memory pointed
to by a. A nowait clause does not appear on the construct, but there is a depend
clause. The target task $t2$ cannot be scheduled to execute until the dependence
on a[:n] is satisfied by the completion of the $t1$ task. The host task (and thus

the host thread) that generated $t2$ cannot be resume execution until $t2$ completes. Finally, there is a task synchronization point at the implicit barrier at line 25.

6.10   Selecting a Device

OpenMP provides support for multiple accelerators. Devices are enumerated such that each one has a unique device number. The actual number for a specific accelerator is implementation-defined. A device number for an accelerator must be non-negative and less than the value returned by the `omp_get_num_devices()` runtime function.

There is currently no support in OpenMP to determine the characteristics of a particular accelerator device. The only distinction made between devices is that there is a host device where the program begins execution and an optional set of accelerator devices.

You can find the device number for the host device using the `omp_get_initial_-device` routine. The host device number has some odd restrictions. If it is not greater than or equal to zero and less than the value returned by the `omp_get_-num_devices` runtime function, then it may be used only in certain device memory runtime functions (see Section 6.12).

Programs using the OpenMP device constructs should be portable, to systems that do not have accelerators. OpenMP supports *host fall back*, which is the concept that a target region can always be executed by the host device. If you take an OpenMP program that contains device constructs and compile and run that program on a system without accelerators, then the device constructs are executed on the host device.

6.10.1   The Default Device and the Device Clause

The device number determines to which device a construct applies. The `device` clause is used to specify a device number. When there is no `device` clause, the device number for a `target`, `target data`, `target update`, `target enter data` or `target exit data` construct is the *default-device-var* ICV. There may be only one `device` clause on a construct, and the expression in the clause must be non-negative. If the device number specified for a device construct does not correspond to any devices in the system where the program is running, then the construct falls back to the host device.

```
1 #include <omp.h>
2 extern int a[1024]; int Work(int *, int, int);
3 #pragma omp declare target to(a, Work)
4
5 void F()
6 {
7   int defdev = omp_get_default_device();
8   int numdev = omp_get_num_devices();
9
10  for (int i=0; i<numdev; i++) {
11    omp_set_default_device(i);
12    #pragma omp target update to(a) nowait
13  }
14  omp_set_default_device(defdev);
15  #pragma omp taskwait
16
17  for (int i=0; i<numdev; i++) {
18    #pragma omp target device(i) nowait
19    Work(a,i,numdev);
20  }
21
22  if (numdev == 0) Work(a,0,1);
23  #pragma omp taskwait
24 }
```

Figure 6.58: **Example of the device clause and related runtime functions**
– The variable a is updated with the host's value on all devices and then the function
Work() is executed by all devices.

When a program begins execution, the *default-device-var* ICV is initialized to
the value of the OMP_DEFAULT_DEVICE environment variable. If the environment
variable is not set, then the *default-device-var* is implementation-defined. During program execution you may determine the default device using the omp_-
get_default_device function or change the default device using the omp_set_-
default_device function.

An example using the device clause and related runtime functions is shown in
Figure 6.58. The example first copies the value of the array a from the host to all

of the accelerators and then starts a target region on all devices. Tasks are used to execute the operations in parallel.

The assignments on lines $7-8$ use runtime functions to find the current default device and the number of devices. Each time through the loop spanning lines $10-13$, the default device number is changed. The **target update** construct makes the variable **a** consistent between the host and the default device using the value of **a** from the host. Because of the **nowait** clause, the target update executes as a deferrable target task (see Section 6.9). The host thread does not wait for the target update region to complete.

The default device is restored at line 14. The host thread waits at the **taskwait** at line 15 until all of the tasks started at line 12 have finished. In the loop spanning lines $17-20$, the **device** clause is used to select a specific device where the target region executes. Again, because of the **nowait** clause a deferrable target task is generated that encloses the target region. The host thread executing the loop does not wait for the target region to complete before continuing. The conditional call to the function **Work()** at line 22 is there just in case **omp_get_num_devices()** returns 0. The **taskwait** at line 23 ensures that all of the tasks started at line 18 have completed before returning from the function.

6.10.2 The If Clause on Device Constructs

An **if** clause may appear on a **target**, **target data**, **target update**, **target enter data** or **target exit data** construct.

Except for the **target update** construct, when the expression in an **if** clause evaluates to *false*, then host fall back occurs and:

- The device for the construct is the host.

- The execution of the region occurs on the host device.

- Variables appearing in **map** clauses are mapped to the host's device data environment.

- If a **device** clause appears on the construct, it is ignored.

When the **if** clause expression evaluates to *false* on a **target update** construct, then assignments resulting from the construct do not occur. The **if** clause is useful for setting a threshold on the amount of computation in a target region versus the

```
1 #define MB (1024*1024)
2 extern void Work(float*, int);
3 #pragma omp declare target(Work)
4 void F(float * restrict a, int n)
5 {
6    #pragma omp target if(n > MB) map(a[:n])
7    Work(a,n);
8 }
```

Figure 6.59: **Example of an if clause on the target construct** – If n is greater than a threshold, execute the target region on the default accelerator. Otherwise, execute the region on the host device.

expected overhead of launching the target region on an accelerator device. A simple code example using the if clause is shown in Figure 6.59.

Be careful when using the if clause on constructs that map variables or effect the value of mapped variables. For example, if an if clause evaluates to false on a target update construct and a target construct is dependent on the execution of the target update, then a program error may occur.

6.11   The Device Pointer Clauses

The clauses described in this section are used to refer to device pointers. Recall from Section 6.3.3 that a device pointer is a pointer variable on the host whose value is an object that represents an address in device memory.

Assignments to a device pointer are restricted to values that arise from the following cases:

- The return value of the omp_target_alloc() function.

- The address of a variable referenced in the lexical scope of a target data construct when that variable appeared in a use_device_ptr clause on the construct.

- The return value of an implementation-defined device memory allocation function.[7]

---

[7]For example, CUDA's cudaAlloc[19] or OpenCL's BufferAllocate[12] functions.

```
1 #include <omp.h>
2 void *init(int n, int dev)
3 {
4   char *dptr = omp_target_alloc(dev, n);
5
6   #pragma omp target is_device_ptr(dptr) device(dev)
7   for (int i=0; i<n; i++)
8     dptr[i] = i;
9
10  return (void*)dptr;
11 }
```

Figure 6.60: **Example of the is_device_ptr clause** – The device pointer variable dptr must appear in the is_device_ptr clause to de-reference it in the target region.

The operations on a device pointer variable on the host are restricted as follows:

- A device pointer variable cannot be de-referenced.

- Pointer arithmetic cannot be performed on a device pointer variable.

6.11.1   The Is_device_ptr Clause

The purpose of the is_device_ptr clause is to provide a way for a device pointer to be accessed in a target region. The is_device_ptr clause accepts a list of device pointer variable names and may only appear on a target construct.

When a device pointer appears in an is_device_ptr clause on a target construct, the corresponding variable in the region is private. On entry to the target region, the corresponding private variable is initialized with the device's representation of the address stored in the original device pointer.

A simple example of a target construct with an is_device_ptr clause is shown in Figure 6.60. In line 4, a device address on the dev device is assigned to dptr. The device pointer dptr is listed in the is_device_ptr clause at line 6 indicating that dptr is private in the target region. On entry to the target region, the private instance of dptr is initialized with the dev device's representation of the device address that corresponds to the variable's original value.

```
1 int A[1024];
2 #pragma omp declare target to(A)
3 extern int AccelFunc(void *);
4
5 int Func()
6 {
7   int err;
8   #pragma omp target data map(err) use_device_ptr(A)
9   err = AccelFunc(A); // Requires device address of A
10   return err;
11 }
```

Figure 6.61: **Example of the use_device_ptr clause** – Replace the reference to the host address of A in the lexical scope of the `target data` construct with the device address of A.

6.11.2   The Use_device_ptr Clause

The purpose of the `use_device_pointer` clause is to provide a way to refer to the device address of a mapped variable, so that it may be passed to a function as a device pointer argument. Some vendors implement optimized functions that expect device pointers as arguments. These optimized functions, called by a host thread, offload their execution to an accelerator, either using a `target` construct with an `is_device_ptr` clause or some other vendor-specific mechanism.

The `use_device_ptr` clause accepts a list of variable names. The clause valid only on a `target data` construct. The clause applies to the lexical scope of its associated `target data` construct. In the construct, references to variables that appear in a `use_device_ptr` clause must be to the address of the variable. In the lexical scope of the `target data` construct, a reference to the address of a variable that appears in a `use_device_ptr` clause is replaced with the corresponding device address.

In Figure 6.61, the variable A is globally mapped by the `declare target` construct at line 2. Because of the `use_device_ptr` clause on the `target data` construct at line 8, the reference to the address of A in the call to `AccelFunc()` at line 9 is replaced with the device address of A.

6.12   Device Memory Functions

OpenMP provides a set of runtime functions for creating, copying, and mapping dynamically allocated device memory. They use device pointers (see Section 6.3.3 on page 265) and provide advanced users with capabilities to share complex data structures across devices. These device memory functions are described in detail in Section 2.3.4 starting on page 70. In this section, some simple examples using the functions are presented and discussed.

Copy a Linked List To Device Memory   The example code in Figure 6.62 uses the `omp_target_memcpy()` function to copy a linked list from the host to the default device. Storage for the linked list is allocated in the default device's memory using the `omp_target_alloc()` function.

After counting the number of elements in the list, the `omp_target_alloc()` function is called at line 14 to allocate memory for the linked list in the accelerator's address space. The variable `dst` is assigned the device pointer returned by `omp_target_alloc()`. In lines 16 − 19, each list item is copied from the host to the device using the `omp_target_memcpy()` function. The destination device is the default device, and the source device is the host.

A host thread cannot perform pointer arithmetic on an accelerator's device pointer. Fortunately, the `omp_target_mempcy()` function has offset arguments for the source and destination addresses. The destination accelerator address is calculated by adding the `i*sizeof(item_t)` offset expression to the `dst` device pointer.

Finally, in lines 21 − 26, the `next` pointers in the copied list items are initialized by running a short target region on the destination device. The `is_device_ptr` clause indicates that `dst` is a device pointer in the target region.

Associate Host Memory with Device Memory   Host memory may be associated with device memory using the `omp_target_associate_ptr()` function. The function performs a map-enter phase for host memory without allocating associated storage in device memory. Instead, the device address of the associated storage is passed as an argument to the function. The `omp_target_disassociate_ptr()` runtime function performs a map-exit phase for host memory, but does not free the associated storage in device memory.

```
1 #include <omp.h>
2 #include <stdlib.h>
3 typedef struct item {struct item *next; int v; } item_t;
4 void *copy_list2dev(item_t *list)
5 {
6   int i, count=0;
7   int dev  = omp_get_default_device();
8   int host = omp_get_initial_device();
9   item_t *src = NULL, *dst = NULL;
10
11  if (list == NULL) return NULL;
12  for (src=list; src; src=src->next)
13    count++;
14  dst = omp_target_alloc(count*sizeof(item_t), dev);
15
16  for (src=list, i=0; src; src=src->next, i++)
17    omp_target_memcpy(dst, src, sizeof(item_t),
18                      i*sizeof(item_t), 0,
19                      dev, host);
20
21  #pragma omp target is_device_ptr(dst)
22  {
23    for (i=0; i<count-1; i++)
24      dst[i].next = &dst[i+1];
25    dst[i].next = NULL;
26  }
27  return (void*)dst;
28 }
```

Figure 6.62: **Copy a linked list to device memory** – Copy a linked list from the host to dynamically allocated device memory.

Figure 6.63 shows an example that uses these functions to stream sections of a large buffer stored in host memory through a smaller buffer allocated in device memory. At line 5, the pointer variable devptr is assigned the device address of a chunk-sized buffer of type float allocated in device memory. The pointer variable a points to a buffer of size n float elements. For simplicity, assume that $n\%chunk = 0$ and $n >= chunk$. The loop starting on line 7, iteratively maps a chunk-sized section

```
1 #include <omp.h>
2 void stream(float *restrict a, int n, int chunk, int dev)
3 {
4   int size = sizeof(float)*chunk;
5   float *devptr = omp_target_alloc(size, dev);
6
7   for (int i=0; i<n; i+=chunk)
8   {
9     omp_target_associate_ptr(&a[i], devptr, size, 0, dev);
10
11    #pragma omp target map(always,tofrom:a[i:chunk]) device(dev)
12    for (int j=i; j<i+chunk; j++)
13      a[j] = 1/(1+a[j]);
14
15    omp_target_disassociate_ptr(&a[i], dev);
16  }
17  omp_target_free(devptr, dev);
18 }
```

Figure 6.63: **Map host memory to dynamically allocated device memory**
– Iteratively associate a smaller device memory buffer with a section of a larger **a** buffer.

of the **a** buffer to the **devptr** buffer and executes a target region that operates on the section. The call to `omp_target_associate_ptr()` at line 9 performs a map-entry phase for the section, adding it to the device data environment. The associated storage for the section is the device memory pointed to by **devptr**.

The section appears in the **map** clause as the array section `a[i:chunk]` in order to specify its offset and size in the associated target region at lines 11 − 13. Because the section has a non-zero reference count, the **always** *map-type-modifier* is required to force the map-entry phase assignment of the section from the host to the device. Likewise, during the map-exit phase, the **always** *map-type-modifier* ensures that the assignment of the section from the device to the host occurs. Note that, instead of the **always** *map-type-modifier*, **target update** `to(a[i:chunk])` and **target update** `from(a[i:chunk])` constructs may be used before and after the target region.

The call to `omp_target_disassociate()` at line 15 performs a map-exit phase for the section and removes it from the device data environment but does not

```
1 #include <stdio.h>
2 #include <omp.h>
3 int copy_2d(void *dst, void *src, int dst_dev, int src_dev,
4             int sz, int vol_sz, int offset)
5 {
6    const int num_dims = 2;
7    const int vol_dims[2] = {vol_sz, vol_sz};
8    const int dst_dims[2] = {sz, sz};
9    const int src_dims[2] = {sz, sz};
10   const int dst_offset[2] = {offset, offset};
11   const int src_offset[2] = {0, 0};
12
13   return omp_target_memcpy_rect(dst, src, sizeof(char),
14        num_dims,
15        vol_dims,
16        dst_offset, src_offset,
17        dst_dims, src_dims,
18        dst_dev, src_dev);
19 }
```

Figure 6.64: **Copy a sub-matrix from a source matrix to a destination matrix - part 1** – Two-dimensional square matrices are assumed. Copy a sub-matrix from `src[0][0]` to `dst[offset][offset]`.

free the associated device memory. Finally, after the loop completes, the call to `omp_target_free()` at line 17 frees the `devptr` buffer.

Copy a Sub-matrix Between Two Matrices An example program is presented below that demonstrates the `omp_target_memcpy_rect` function. The program copies a 4x4 sub-matrix between two 8x8 matrices. The source matrix is allocated in the device memory of the default accelerator device, and the destination matrix is in host memory. The first part of the program is shown in Figure 6.64.

The `copy_2d()` function assumes that the matrices and the sub-matrix have two dimensions and are square. The arrays initialized at lines 6−9 define the dimensions of the matrices and the sub-matrix. The offset arrays initialized at lines 10−11 are indexes into the matrices and, along with the `dst` and `src` pointer variables, are used to determine the starting source and destination addresses. The call to the

```
21 #define N 8
22 void main()
23 {
24   int dst_dev = omp_get_initial_device();
25   int src_dev = omp_get_default_device();
26   unsigned char DST[N][N];
27   unsigned char (*SRC)[N] = omp_target_alloc(N*N, src_dev);
28
29   #pragma omp target is_device_ptr(SRC) nowait
30   for (int i=0; i<N; i++)
31     for (int j=0; j<N; j++) SRC[i][j] = 1;
32
33   for (int i=0; i<N; i++)
34     for (int j=0; j<N; j++) DST[i][j] = 0;
35
36   #pragma taskwait
37   copy_2d(DST, SRC, dst_dev, src_dev, N, 4, 2);
38
39   omp_target_free(SRC, src_dev);
40
41   for (int i=0; i<N; i++) {
42     for (int j=0; j<N; j++) printf("%d" , DST[i][j]);
43     printf("\n");
44   }
45 }
```

Figure 6.65: **Copy a sub-matrix from a source matrix to a destination matrix - part 2** – Allocate and initialize an $8x8$ SRC matrix on an accelerator and fill it with 1. Initialize an $8x8$ DST matrix on the host and fill it with 0. Copy a $4x4$ sub-matrix from SRC[0][0] to DST[2][2].

omp_target_memcpy_rect() function at lines $13 - 18$ copies a vol_sz by vol_sz sub-matrix from the source device address starting at src[0][0] to the destination host address starting at dst[offset][offset]. The second part of the program is shown in Figure 6.65. The SRC matrix is dynamically allocated in the default device's memory by the call at line 27 to the omp_target_alloc() function. The elements in the $8x8$ SRC matrix are initialized to 1 in the target region, and the elements in the $8x8$ DST matrix are initialized to 0 on the host device.

```
00000000
00000000
00111100
00111100
00111100
00111100
00000000
00000000
```

Figure 6.66: **Example output from the sub-matrix copy program** – This
is the output from the program in Figure 6.64 and Figure 6.65. A 4x4 sub-matrix from
the SRC matrix was copied into the center of the DST matrix.

The `is_device_ptr` clause is necessary on the `target` construct at line 29, because SRC is a device pointer. Due to the `nowait` clause, the execution of the target
region is enclosed in a deferrable target task, and the initialization of the SRC and
DST matrices may execute in parallel. The host thread cannot continue past the
`taskwait` construct until the target task has completed. After this point, both
matrices have been initialized.

The call to the function `copy_2d()` at line 37 copies a 4x4 sub-matrix from the
device address starting at `SRC[0][0]` to the host address starting at `DST[2][2]`.
The call to `omp_target_free` at line 39 frees the memory allocated for the SRC
matrix. Lines $41-43$ print the DST matrix after the copy has occurred. The output
of the program is shown in Figure 6.66.

6.13   Concluding Remarks

This chapter has covered how to use the OpenMP device constructs to program
heterogeneous systems composed of a host device and one or more accelerator devices. The execution model is host-centric; the program starts on the host device,
and during its execution, target regions may be executed by threads running on
accelerator devices. Because the host and accelerator memories may be in different
address spaces, there are restrictions on how variables are shared across devices.

The device constructs fall into two general categories: 1) constructs that are used
to manage sharing variables between devices, and 2) constructs that are used to

·

select on which device code executes. Following are guidelines to consider when using the device constructs.

There is overhead involved with executing a target region on an accelerator. Consider that there should be enough computation in the target region to justify the overhead.

To share a variable among threads executing on different devices, the variable is mapped. Very often the key to getting good performance using the device constructs is correlated with the strategy used for mapping variables.

The overhead from mapping variables is especially a concern for those heterogeneous systems where the host and accelerator do not share memory. Minimize the potential for copying data between the host and accelerator devices. Use a *map-type* in `map` clauses to eliminate unnecessary copies. Use the data-mapping constructs to map variables in a way that encloses target regions where the variables are used.

Except for the `target data` construct, the device constructs generate tasks. Use the asynchronous features of tasks so that host and accelerator code regions may execute in parallel. Use tasks to hide the overhead of mapping variables by overlapping data mapping constructs with computation.

Consider the dual-nature of mapped variables. Treat mapped variables like shared variables when determining how two threads on different devices can safely access a variable when it is mapped.

Do not assume that mapping a variable will always update its value with an assignment. If it was already mapped by a target data-mapping construct, then the map simply increments its reference count If an assignment is always required, then use the `always` *map-type* or the `target update` construct.

Consider carefully whether a scalar variable is `firstprivate` or mapped in a target region. The best way to be sure is to always list variables in explicit clauses. Be careful when mapping pointer variables, and use array sections to ensure that the pointed-to memory is mapped. The pointer variable in an array section is not mapped, and it is private in a target region. Remember that if a pointer variable does not appear in a clause on a `target` construct, then it is implicitly treated as if it had appeared in one as the base of a zero-length array section.

When using the accelerated worksharing constructs, first start with the `target teams distribute` construct, and then as needed, gradually add the more prescriptive worksharing constructs and clauses that fix the number of teams, threads, and SIMD lanes. See how far you can get with letting the compiler make these determinations.

7 What is Next?

As this book is being printed, the OpenMP language committee is actively working on the next version of the specifications. Although the release number is subject to change, it probably will be called "OpenMP 5.0."

Some of the future directions of OpenMP may be determined from the Technical Reports that are being released by the Language Committee. These can be found at [21]. Until these proposals for extending OpenMP have passed the user feedback process, and have been approved by the OpenMP Architecture Review Board (ARB), nothing is final, but these are the topics and features most likely included:

- Memory model.

- Support for Fortran 2003 and the latest C/C++11 standards.

- Interoperability with other parallel programming models.

- APIs to enable better debug and profiling tools.

- The `depend` clause on the `taskwait` construct.

- Affinity support for tasks.

- An environment variable to display affinity information at runtime.

- Support for reductions with tasks.

- Enhancements to task dependences.

- Memory management.

- Heterogeneous architectures.

The last two topics, memory management and heterogeneous architectures, are discussed in more detail in the following sections.

7.1 Memory Management

The memory subsystems of modern computing devices have a deep hierarchy, employing a variety of memory technologies, including main memory, high-bandwidth memory, texture memory, scratchpad memory, and multiple levels of cache. The hierarchy found in future systems is expected to become even deeper, following the introduction of non-volatile RAM and other developments. The particular challenge for the user is that each of these technologies has a different programming interface, and distinct performance characteristics. Addressing these differences becomes increasingly critical for all types of computing where performance is tied to memory bandwidth.

Under the term *Memory Management*, the OpenMP Language Committee is currently working on concepts and constructs to support the use of these memory types from within OpenMP. In January 2017, the OpenMP Technical Report 5 – Memory Management Support for OpenMP 5.0 – was released [21], describing the current approach to this topic. A detailed description is provided in [23]. These are the three new concepts proposed in this paper:

- Memory spaces and allocators - A *memory space* refers to a memory resource available in the system, at the time the OpenMP program is executed. Memory spaces are differentiated by their characteristics, which are expressed by *traits*. An *allocator* is an object that allocates and frees memory from an associated memory space.

- Memory allocation API - The `omp_alloc()` and `omp_free()` API routines are provided for C/C++ to allocate and deallocate memory using an allocator.

- The `allocate` directive and clause - The new `allocate` directive and clause allow for the allocation of variables, without the explicit use of the aforementioned API and, in consequence, support Fortran. Both offer several modifiers to impact their behavior.

Memory management and affinity are related. While OpenMP 4.0 introduced the thread affinity model, the concept of memory management may build the foundation to provide support for data affinity in OpenMP. Data affinity refers to the association of data with computation. Managing data affinity to threads is possible by leveraging the functionality provided by the Operating System. The best approach to provide data affinity to tasks in OpenMP is still an open (research) question, however. This is of high interest, because task scheduling remains opaque and may lead to performance variations on NUMA architectures.

Given the complexity of this topic, it remains to be seen how far, and in which form, these concepts find their way into OpenMP 5.0, and subsequent releases.

7.2   Heterogeneous Architectures

Accelerators and general-purpose processors are becoming more tightly coupled. In particular in the memory subsystem, there is a trend toward a single, virtual memory address space among all devices in a compute node. What this means for OpenMP is that mapped variables might evolve to be more akin to shared variables, and it will become easier to map (or share) complex data structures across devices.

In some ways, general-purpose and accelerator processors are becoming more similar. For example, new generations of both types have wider SIMD instructions, and more cores, and thus more available threads. Both types of processors might ultimately converge back into one. There might be subsets of processors in a node that are more tightly coupled and the device constructs could be used to target code and data to such processor domains.

The work improve the support in OpenMP for heterogeneous architectures is ongoing. Some of the improvements that have been worked on are:

- Implicitly map functions - Remove the requirement that a function called from a target region, or another mapped function, must appear in a `declare target` directive. The compiler can infer that a function is mapped when it is called from a target region, or another mapped function.

- Provide better C++ support - Allow C++ class variables to be mapped when the class includes static members, or virtual member functions. The first step is to allow the variable to be mapped. It remains an open question as to whether an implementation may support invoking a virtual member function of a mapped class variable on the accelerator.

- Map complex data structures - Map complex data structures, such as linked lists, arrays of pointers, or structures and classes with pointer members. On heterogeneous systems, where the host and accelerator do not share the same address space, copying complex data structures requires systematically dereferencing pointers, which is a process referred to as deep-copy.

- Add device types - New syntax enables conditionally selecting the clauses on a construct for a specific device type. New routines and clauses are able to target any device of a certain type.

- Workshare loops across devices - Distribute the iterations of a loop across either multiple accelerators, or the host device, plus one or more accelerators.

- Support for device-specific environment variables - Extend the syntax of OpenMP environment variables to indicate that their values are applied to devices other than the host. The method of initializing ICVs with environment variables is currently implementation-defined for accelerator devices.

Given the popularity of heterogeneous architectures across all types of computing, it is expected that, in some form, many of these new features will be included in OpenMP 5.0, or a later release.

Glossary

Address space The set of all legal addresses in memory for a process. It constitutes the amount of memory available to it. The OpenMP programming model assumes a shared address space for all threads in a process.

API Application Programming Interface. An API consists of a well-defined set of language features, library routines, annotations, or directives that may be employed by a programmer to solve a programming problem, often in a system-independent manner. An API often serves to hide lower-level implementation details from the user. OpenMP is an API for shared memory parallel programming.

ARB Architecture Review Board. An organization to maintain specifications and continue to evolve these to follow trends in the market.

Array section A subset of the elements of an array. Pointer-based array sections describe the size of pointed to memory. A zero-length pointer-based array section is used in `map` clauses on `target` constructs to find the corresponding accelerator address of the original pointed-to host address.

Atomic operation As suggested by the name, an atomic operation cannot be subdivided into smaller operations and it is uninterruptible, that is, only one thread at a time can execute such an operation.

An example is the "atomic add" which performs an operation of the type `a_val += new_value`. Atomic operations are used to correctly read and write shared variables.

They have been introduced to take advantage of highly efficient atomic instructions many processors support. OpenMP uses the `atomic` construct to support atomic operations.

Atomic read This guarantees that the read (or better, memory load instruction) of a variable is an atomic operation. It means that the value cannot change while the read/load is in progress.

Atomic write This guarantees that the write (or better, memory store instruction) of a variable is an atomic operation. It means that the value cannot change while the write/store is in progress.

Bandwidth For memory system transfer rates, the peak speed expressed in the number of bytes that can be transferred per second. There are different bandwidth rates between different parts of the memory system. For example, the transfer rate between a cache and CPU may be higher than the bandwidth between main memory and the cache. There may be multiple caches and paths to memory with different rates.

Barrier A synchronization point in the code where all threads in a team have to wait. No thread reaching the barrier can continue until all threads have reached the barrier. OpenMP provides explicit barriers as well as implicit barriers at the end of parallel loops, sections, single constructs, and parallel regions. The user has the option of removing barriers at the end of worksharing constructs to achieve better performance. Barriers at the end of parallel regions cannot be removed.

Cache A relatively small, very high speed memory buffer between main memory and the processor. A cache contains data, instructions or both. In case of the latter it is called a unified cache. Data (or instructions) is copied from main memory to cache and back in blocks of contiguous data called a "cache line." The size of the line depends on the machine. A line may be evicted from cache if another data block needs to be stored in the same line. The strategy for replacing data in cache is system-dependent. Since cache is usually built from very high speed, but expensive memory components, it is substantially smaller than main memory. However, cache sizes tend to increase over time and on some platforms, small data sets might fit entirely into cache. Without cache, a program would spend the vast majority of its execution time waiting for the arrival of data, since processor speeds are significantly faster than memory access times. Computers may have several levels of cache, with those closest to the CPU being smaller, faster, and more expensive than those closer to main memory. The cache with the shortest access time is usually called an "L1 cache." The one with the second shortest access time is referred to as an "L2 cache," etc. Data is copied between levels. A different type of cache is called "Translation Lookaside Buffer" (TLB). It contains addresses mapping information.

Cache coherence The ability of a multi-processor (or multi-core) system to maintain the integrity of data stored in local caches of shared memory. On uniprocessor systems, data written into cache typically remains there until the cache line is replaced, at which point it is written back to a higher level cache or main memory. Multiprocessor systems share memory and caches. Without a mechanism for maintaining coherency between memory and cache, a load instruction executing on one processor might not have access to a value recently updated by other processors. With cache coherence, a processor is informed that data it needs is in a cache line that is stale or invalid, requiring a fetch of the updated value. The cache coherence protocol is architecture specific and implemented in various ways on different systems.

Cache line A level of cache is subdivided into lines, each of which may be filled by a block of data from main memory. The cache line size thus determines the unit of data transfer between the cache and memory, as well between the various levels of a specific cache type. The size of the line is system dependent and may differ from one level to another. For instance, a level-1 cache line could be smaller than a level-2 cache line. There is no unique best size for a cache line. A long line, for example, increases bandwidth but also increases the chance that false sharing occurs.

cc-NUMA cache coherent Non-Uniform Memory Access. These are NUMA systems where coherence is supported across all caches of the individual cores in the system. Maintaining cache coherence across shared memory is costly, but systems without this feature are extremely difficult to program. Therefore, shared memory NUMA systems available today generally provide some form of cache coherence and are really cc-NUMA systems. Thanks to cache coherence, data access is transparent throughout the entire system, but just as with a NUMA system, there is a notion of "local" and "remote" memory. For good scalability one had better take this into account and make sure a thread primarily accesses data in its local memory. Note that the existence of cache coherence does not prevent the user from introducing race conditions into OpenMP programs as a result of faulty programming.

Ceiling function The description can be found under "Floor function."

Compiler directive A source-code comment in Fortran or pragma in C/C++ that provides the compiler with additional information and guidance. In OpenMP, directives are used to identify parts of the code the compiler should parallelize, define shared and private data, thread synchronization, and more.

Composite construct A construct that is composed of two other constructs and has functionality that cannot be expressed by nesting one of the constructs immediately inside the other construct.

Computing the number of threads per subset With thread affinity support, threads are distributed over OpenMP places. If the number of threads T and the number of places P do not evenly divide, the distribution of threads over the sets of threads, the number of threads per place, or the number of places per subpartition, is not equal. Below we show the recipe how to compute this for one specific case. It is trivial to apply this to other scenarios.

Assume there are $T = 7$ threads and $P = 4$ places. If we use the `close` affinity policy, there are five sets with threads, but some sets contain $floor(7/4) = 1$ thread, while the remaining sets contain $ceiling(7/4) = 2$ threads. If we define the number of sets with one or two threads to be N_1 and N_2 respectively, the question is what their values are.

This problem is simply expressed in terms of two linear equations and then solved: $1 * N_1 + 2 * N_2 = 7$ and $N_1 + N_2 = 4$. It is easy to see that $N_1 = 1$ and $N_2 = 3$ is the unique solution.

In other words, there is one set with 1 thread and three sets contain 2 threads.

Conditional compilation This is a Fortran-only feature to deal with OpenMP specific run time functions in case the source is not compiled with the recognition of OpenMP directives enabled, or if the compiler does not support

OpenMP. Without special precautions, usage of OpenMP run time functions leads to unresolved references when linking the object files. The solution is to start the source line that uses the run time function with `!$` (or `C$/*$` in case old style fixed format Fortran is used). The specifications guarantee that these two characters are replaced by two spaces in case OpenMP is supported and enabled at compile time. This means the comment line is expanded to an executable statement, but only in an OpenMP context. For more details we refer to the specifications. An example can be found in [2].

Contention group An initial thread and all its descendent threads. An initial thread is not a descendent of another initial thread.

Core A component of a microprocessor that is able to load/store data and execute instructions. Beyond this generic description there are significant implementation differences. Depending on the architecture, hardware resources, and components may be shared among, or specific to, a core. Examples are the register file, caches (for both data and instructions), functional units, and paths to other components. In some designs, an individual core is able to execute multiple independent threads.

CPU Central Processing Unit. The CPU is also referred to as the "processor." The circuitry within a computer that executes the instructions of a program and processes the data. Current designs often contain multiple cores.

Data race A data race occurs if multiple threads simultaneously modify the same (and therefore shared) memory location. The outcome of such an update is undetermined and most likely varies from run to run. The result is also affected by the number of threads used. After a data race has occurred, the behavior of the program is undefined. Note that by definition, a data race also causes false sharing, usually resulting in a performance impact. There are ways to avoid data races. The critical section is probably the most commonly used OpenMP construct to prevent data races from happening.

Deadlock A situation where one or more threads are waiting for a resource that will never become available. There are various ways to introduce such deadlock situations into an OpenMP application. For example, a barrier inserted at a point not encountered by all threads, or improper calls to OpenMP locking routines, will result in deadlocks.

Device A processing element that executes program code. A device has access to a memory that may or may not be shared with other devices.

Device data environment Referred to in the context of an accelerator, the set of variables and ICVs that are available to a device. It includes the set of variables that are currently mapped to an accelerator. A variable is present on the accelerator if it is in its device data environment

Device pointer A pointer variable on the host device whose value is an object that represents an address in an accelerator's address space.

Directive sentinel A special sequence of characters that indicates that the line is to be interpreted as a compiler directive. OpenMP directives in Fortran must begin with a directive sentinel. The format of the sentinel differs between fixed and free-form source files.

Doacross loop A loop-carried dependence inhibits straightforward parallelization of a loop. In case of a doacross loop however, code transformations and/or additional synchronization(s) result in a loop that can be parallelized after all. The run time benefit depends on the details because sometimes an additional overhead is introduced, or the parallelism is limited even after the transformation(s).

DSP Digital Signal Processor. It is an example of a hardware accelerator. DSPs can be found in many embedded devices, cell phones being a case in point. They are specialized to efficiently execute signal, vision and image processing applications.

DTrace DTrace stands for "Dynamic Tracing." Initially available on the Oracle Solaris^{TM}operating system, it has since then been ported to Mac OS X^{TM}and Oracle Linux^{TM}.

A full description of DTrace as well as examples can be found at [7]. There is also a DTrace website [6] and several books cover this tool in great detail [17, 11, 10].

DTrace is a tool that allows one to trace activities in the operating system kernel, as well as user applications if they have been instrumented for this. The main use is to follow what happens in the kernel though. A very powerful feature is that the kernel is ready to be instrumented at any time, but if instrumentation is not requested, there is no overhead at all. There is also no need to use a special kernel. DTrace is there and ready to go.

Although one can use DTrace at the command line, most users prefer to write a script to do this. DTrace comes with its own language "D." The syntax is very easy to learn for those with programming experiences in C/C++, awk, perl, etc.

In Chapter 4 starting on 151 it is shown how DTrace is used to verify the thread affinity policies and see where threads end up running in the system.

There is a related tool for Linux. It is called SystemTap [25].

Environment variable A Unix shell variable that may be set by the user to influence some aspect of a program's execution behavior. The OpenMP API includes a set of environment variables to control aspects of the program's execution, including the number of threads to use, the default work schedule, and the use of nested parallelism.

False sharing A situation where multiple threads update the same cache line. Since the granularity of information used by cache coherence mechanisms is a cache line, the system cannot distinguish whether there is true sharing, or if independent updates happen to be on different chunks of the same cache line. False sharing results in poor performance, but it is not an error affecting correctness of the numerical results.

First touch This is a common page placement policy and the default on most, if not all, Operating Systems. Under this policy, the thread that touches the data first, owns the data. Technically, this is controlled through the D-TLB. The first time an entry in this cache is created, ownership and location are determined. With this policy, the page resides in the memory connected to the socket where the thread executes. Unless there is a capacity issue and some data needs to be placed elsewhere.

Floor function This mathematical function maps a floating point number to an integer. For a floating point number x, $floor(x)$, or $\lfloor x \rfloor$, returns the largest integer not exceeding x. For example, $floor(2.3) = \lfloor 2.3 \rfloor = 2$.

A related function is the ceiling function: $ceiling(x)$, or $\lceil x \rceil$, returns the smallest integer not less than x. For example, $ceiling(2.3) = \lceil 2.3 \rceil = 3$.

Generating task A task that generates another task.

Globally linked variable A variable that is linked to all accelerators for the whole program. A globally linked variable can be accessed in a mapped function as long as it is present in the device data environment of the accelerator where the mapped function is being executed.

Globally mapped variable A variable that is mapped to all accelerators for the whole program. A globally mapped variable has an infinite reference count, is never removed from a device data environment, and is initialized on all devices when a program starts.

GPGPU General Purpose Graphics Processing Unit. Nowadays the term "GPU" is more commonly used. See the description for GPU.

GPU Graphics Processing Unit. A GPU is an accelerator for graphics operations. The original GPU was extremely fast on specific (graphics) operations only, but this is no longer the case. The strength of a GPU lies in the massive parallelism it offers. Each node in the GPU is not very powerful, but there are many of such nodes. GPUs can be used for all sorts of floating-point intensive computations. An issue with this type of hardware is the programming model. Since the GPU is connected to the main processor it is an example of a hardware accelerator, but with a different instruction set, memory architecture, etc. Various programming models are available for GPUs.

Hardware thread To start with, there are many different implementations of this concept. The differences can be substantial and the description below is a generalization.

A *hardware thread*, or "strand," is not one entity. It is the combination of one or more pipelines (that execute the instructions) and "state."

With "state" we mean additional hardware resources to execute the instructions coming from a software thread, or process. For example, there could be multiple Register Files (RF). When a software thread starts executing instructions in the pipeline it gets assigned one of these register files and while executing it has its own dedicated RF. This is a good thing because other threads executing cannot interfere with its register values. Another example is an Instruction Buffer (IB) for each hardware thread.

In general, the more dedicated hardware resources (a richer "state"), the more efficient the hardware threads execute.

Nowadays, many cores have this kind of dedicated hardware support to efficiently execute multiple threads within the same pipeline(s). It is as if each instruction executing in the pipeline is tagged with an identifier to distinguish the various threads. Although there are significant implementation details, at a sufficiently high level it appears as if multiple threads are executing simultaneously. This is why this kind of technology is known under various other names like "Virtual threading" or "Simultaneous threading."

Home node The home node is the location where the data resides in memory. On a flat memory system, this is irrelevant, but on a cc-NUMA architecture it is an important concept. All pages in the system have a home node. The placement policy dictates where this is. See also the entry for *First Touch*.

Host device The initial device where program execution begins.

Host fall back The concept that a device construct may fall back and execute on the host device.

ICV Internal Control Variable. This is OpenMP specific terminology for certain variables that are used to store information used by the run time system. For example, the number of threads is stored in ICV `nthreads-var`. Prior to program execution, this variable is set to the default number of threads used, which is implementation defined. At run time, this value may change. The application can never access ICVs directly, but through run time functions the value can be read and possibly modified.

Idle thread A software thread that is not performing any work is said to be *idle*. By default the Operating System decides what to do with such a thread. Keeping it busy ("spinning") in the core is usually good for performance, but wastes cycles. Putting it to sleep frees up resources for other threads, but waking up a sleeping thread is relatively costly Through environment variable `OMP_WAIT_POLICY` an OpenMP can specify a preference for this.

Initial thread A thread that starts the execution of an OpenMP program. A thread that starts the execution of a target region. One of the threads in a league that, in parallel, start the execution of a target teams region. An initial thread starts a contention group.

Latency This is the time spent waiting for a response. Memory latency is the time it takes for data to arrive after the initiation of a memory reference. A data path with high memory latency would be inappropriate for moving small amounts of data.

LCD See Loop-carried dependence.

League The set of initial threads, each in their own team, that is started by a `teams` construct. Each team is a contention group.

Lexical If used in the context of (parallel) programming, the informal way to describe this is that a construct, or other source code element, is directly visible in the program source. For example, "tasks can be lexically nested" means that a tasking directive can be included within another tasking directive.

Lock A mechanism for controlling access to a resource in an environment where there are multiple threads of execution. Locks are commonly used when multiple threads need to perform some activity, but only one at a time is allowed to do so. Initially, all threads contend for the lock. One thread gets exclusive access to the lock and performs the task. Meanwhile, the other threads wait for the lock to be released. When that happens, a next thread takes ownership of the lock, and so forth. There may be a special data type for declaring locks. In a C/C++ OpenMP program, this is the `omp_lock_t` type. In Fortran, it must be an integer variable of `kind=omp_lock_kind`.

Lock contention In case multiple threads access the same lock simultaneously, or very shortly after each other, the lock is said to be "contended." Such a situation can greatly degrade parallel performance. The cache line containing the lock variable needs to be acquired by the threads and quickly this can become the bottleneck.

One approach to make things go smoother is to use a backoff algorithm. If a thread fails to obtain the lock, it waits for a while. Upon successive failures to acquire the lock, this delay time increases either linearly, or exponentially. This often helps to improve the performance, but if the lock is not so heavily contended, may take somewhat more time.

This is why OpenMP supports a hint to be specified when initializing the lock variable. Through this hint, the developer can indicate whether a lock is contended, or not, for example.

Loop overhead This is the cost associated with the execution of the instructions related to the mechanics of executing a loop. For example, the loop iteration variable needs to be incremented and a branch instruction is required to either terminate the loop or proceed to the next iteration. All such instructions are collectively called the "loop overhead." For a short loop with little work performed per iteration this cost can dominate the total execution time. On longer loops, or more work per iteration, this cost is less important.

Loop-carried dependence This is a loop where the result for a loop iteration depends on an earlier iteration, or iterations. For example, a statement like this has a loop-carried dependence: `a[i] = a[i-1] + 1`. For a given loop iteration `i`, result `a[i-1]` has to be computed first, before `a[i]` can be computed.

Mapped function A function that can be called from code running on an accelerator.

Mapped variable A variable that is shared between a host device and one or more accelerator devices. A mapped variable must have a type that is bitwise copyable. Pointer variables may be mapped, but what they point to is not mapped.

The original variable on the host is mapped to a corresponding variable in the accelerator's device data environment. Depending on the underlying memory system, the original and corresponding variable may or may not share the same memory location. An original variable may have only one corresponding variable in an accelerator's device data environment.

Mapped variables have map-enter and map-exit phases that occur at the entry to or exit from a device construct that maps the variable. A corresponding variable has a reference count that is incremented in the map-exit phase and decremented in the map-enter phase.

A mapped variable has a map-type that determines how the consistency of the original and corresponding variables is managed. The map-type is used to minimize the performance overhead of copying values between a host device and an accelerator.

Mflop/s This is an abbreviation of "million floating-point operations per second." Mflop/s is a performance metric that can be calculated if the number of floating-point operations (flops) is known. Dividing flops by the execution time in seconds and scaling by 10^6 gives Mflop/s. Related metrics are Gflop/s (gigaflop/s), Tflop/s (teraflop/s) and Pflop/s (petaflop/s).

MPI Message Passing Interface. This is a de facto standard API that was developed to facilitate programming for distributed-memory architectures. MPI consists of a collection of library routines. In an MPI program, multiple processes operate independently and communicate data via messages that are inserted by the programmer. The MPI API specifies the syntax of the functions and format of the messages. MPI is increasingly mixed with OpenMP to create a program that is tailored to exploit both the distributed memory and shared memory, as supported in a cluster of shared-memory nodes. This model can also be used to take advantage of hierarchical parallelism in an application.

MPI Forum An open group with representatives from many organizations that define and maintain the MPI standard. The official website is at [18].

Multi-core A microprocessor design with multiple cores integrated onto a single processor die. Just as with the individual cores, there are vast differences between the various designs available on the market. Among others, there are differences in cache access and organization, system interface, and support for executing more than one independent thread per core.

NUMA Non-Uniform Memory Access. What it means is that there is a notion of "local" versus "remote" memory. This is because a processor is only directly connected to a portion of the total memory, but through an interconnect can also access the memory connected to other processors. Typically, cores that are part of the same processor have the same access time to their own memory, but a longer access time to a memory further away. Historically, the word "NUMA" was reserved for clustered systems connected through a conventional network like Ethernet or Infiniband. Neither of these support cache coherence and the cost of accessing memory on another node in the network is relatively costly. Depending on the topology of the network, the remote cost need not be the same either. A memory can either be close by ("one hop"), or further away ("multiple hops"). The typical way to program such systems was, and still is, with a distributed memory programming model like MPI. If the interconnect supports cache coherence, a system consisting of multiple compute nodes is referred to as "cc-NUMA." Although there is a distinct difference in terms of performance and ease of use with a NUMA cluster architecture, nowadays, *NUMA* and *cc-NUMA* are often used interchangeably, but in practically all cases the latter is meant.

OpenMP ARB The ARB was created to maintain the OpenMP specifications and keep OpenMP relevant to evolving computer architectures, programming languages, and multiprocessing paradigms. Members of this ARB are organizations, not individuals. The website is at http://www.openmp.org.

OpenMP region This is all code encountered during a specific instance of the execution of a given OpenMP construct or library routine. A region includes any code in called routines, as well as any implicit code introduced by the OpenMP implementation.

Operating system page The Operating System (or OS for short) manages data at the *page* level. A page is a relatively large block of memory. The typical size for a default page size is 4 or 8 Kbyte. Even if an application uses a single byte element only, the OS allocates a page to contain this element. All actions on pages are under control of the OS. It is at the page level that data is placed and possibly moved around. As one can imagine, conflicts may arise if on a cc-NUMA system multiple threads execute in a different socket, but access the same page. This degrades performance and should be avoided. This is why it is best to allocate per-thread data on page boundaries.

There is a link with the TLB. Each page needs to have a mapping in the TLB before it can be used. In case only a small fraction of the data in a page is used, more TLB misses than necessary may occur. In such a situation, changing the page size (if supported of course) can improve performance.

Parallel overhead Parallel execution comes with a cost. A sequential program needs to be transformed into a parallel program. Typically this is achieved by inserting calls to an underlying parallel run time system. This system performs a variety of tasks, including the creation and management of the threads, but it may also need to handle data transfer, communication and synchronization of the threads. These are all activities one does not have in a serial program. The cost of all of this is usually referred to as "parallel overhead."

Parallel programming model A set of rules and features to express and control parallelism in an application. Examples are Posix Threads, Java Threads, OpenMP, MPI, and OpenCL.

Parallel scalability The behavior of an application when an increasing number of threads are used to solve a problem of constant size. Ideally, increasing the number of threads from 1 to P yields a parallel speed-up of P.

Parallel speed-up The ratio of the wall-clock time measured for the execution of the program by one thread to the wall-clock time measured for execution by multiple threads. Theoretically, a program run on P threads should run P times as fast as the same program executed on only one thread.

Perfectly nested loop In a perfectly nested loop the individual loops are back to back. That is, there is no other code in between the loop statements.

Pointer aliasing A pointer in an application points to an address in memory. A pointer alias exists if different pointers share the same memory address. If this is the case, a change made through one pointer, affects the value pointed to by another pointer. Programming languages all have their own default rules in how far aliasing is (not) allowed. Pointer aliasing can have a profound effect on the performance. The number one goal of any compiler is to produce correct results. Pointer aliasing may force the compiler to generate slower code than necessary. If the compiler knows that different pointers cannot be aliased, much more efficient code may be generated. This is why the C99 `restrict` keyword is important to consider and apply where relevant. Compilers also often support various options to specify the extent of the aliasing.

Process An entity created by the Operating System to execute an application. A process has its own state information code and data. At runtime, it has its private set of registers, address space, program counter, and stack pointer.

A process can have multiple threads of control and instructions, which is the basis for the OpenMP programming model.

Processor A physical resource that may be used to execute programs. Many different processors have been built, some of which are designed for a special purpose. A general-purpose processor is typically able to execute multiple instructions simultaneously, because it has functional units that can operate independently. A conventional processor executes multiple processes via time slicing, in which each gets some share of the overall CPU time. To achieve this, the state of a program including the values in its registers, is saved and the state of another process loaded. This is known as context switching. Context switching is considerably faster for threads, as they share some of their state. The processes or threads appear to be executing in parallel. A single processor may also be able to execute multiple instruction streams simultaneously by interleaving their instructions or by permitting two or more threads to issue instructions. Machines with this capability appear to the user to be a shared memory parallel computer.

Race condition A programming fault that produces unpredictable program behavior due to unsynchronized concurrent executions. Race conditions are hard to find with conventional debugging methods and tools. Most common is the *data race condition* that occurs when two or more threads access the same shared variable simultaneously with at least one thread modifying its value. Without the appropriate synchronization to protect the update, the behavior will be indeterminate, and the results produced by the program will differ from run to run. Other, more general race conditions are also possible.

Register file The register file is part of a core. Its entries are called "registers." Values in registers are immediately accessible. Registers are what instructions use as their operands. For example, (pseudo) instruction `add %r1,%r2,%r3` adds two values stored in registers `%r1` and `%r2` respectively. The result is stored in register `%r3`. Data is fetched from memory and stored back through load and store instructions. These instructions use an address in memory and a destination register to load a value into or store from.

Scoping In an OpenMP program, each variable is of a certain memory type. It is basically either a private, or a shared variable. There are default rules for this data environment, but one can also explicitly specify the nature of a variable. This is often referred to as "scoping a variable."

Semaphore A semaphore is a synchronization object used in parallel programming to control access to a shared resource. It can be used to arbitrate access and avoids conflicts between multiple threads.

Sequential consistency Defined by Leslie Lamport [16], a (shared memory) parallel program implementation conforms to this property if it guarantees that "the result of any execution is the same as if the operations of all the processors were executed in some sequential order, and the operations of each individual processor appear in this sequence in the order specified by its program." If applied to an OpenMP program, this requires a memory update after each operation that modifies a shared variable and, potentially, before each use of a shared variable.

Side effect A side effect in the context of programming is said to occur if a variable changes as the result of a modification to a seemingly unrelated variable. This can happen because of pointer aliasing for example. In such a situation, two different pointers point to the same memory location. Changing one pointer affects the others. Another example is a function that modifies global data. Since global data is (potentially) used by other functions, this can wreak havoc in a parallel program and care needs to be taken to handle this situation.

SIMD Single Instruction Multiple Data. A SIMD instruction performs the same operation (like an addition) on multiple data elements and does so simultaneously. It is another example of parallel execution, but at a fairly low level. The instructions are typically generated by the compiler and works best on vector type of operations. This is why it is also called "micro-vectorization."

SIMD instruction An instruction that operates on multiple data elements simultaneously, also referred to as vector instruction.

SMP Symmetric Multi-Processor. This is a computer system whose individual processors share memory in such a way that each of them can access any main memory location in the same amount of time. Until about a decade ago, many small shared-memory machines had an SMP architecture, while larger systems often had a cc-NUMA architecture. are symmetric in this sense, larger systems do not necessarily satisfy this definition. On such non-symmetric systems, the physical distance between a CPU and memory will determine the length of time it takes to retrieve data from memory. Memory access times do not affect the OpenMP programming model, but can have a significant impact on the performance of the application. The term can also refer to other kinds of shared-memory computers. In this book, we use the acronym SMP broadly to refer to all platforms where multiple processes share memory.

Socket This is a word that has become more popular with the advent of multi-core architectures. In the context of computer architecture, a "socket" is physical location on the motherboard of a computer system. It is where the chip with the processor is placed. The processor may or may not have multiple cores and optionally each core could have support for multiple hardware threads. The socket typically has connections to the rest of the system, including memory. In case of a cc-NUMA architecture, each socket is connected to a portion of the total memory available and the sockets are connected through a cache coherent interconnect.

Stack memory This is often abbreviated to "the stack." It is a region of memory that is used as a scratchpad when executing a function or subroutine. It is used to manage variables local to the function for example. Unless one writes assembly code directly, managing the stack is under control of the compiler. The Operating System defines a default size for the stack, but the user can change this. For example, on Unix systems with the Bourne or Bash shell, one can use the `ulimit` command. Check the documentation of your OS how to do this.

Unfortunately, OpenMP users get confronted with the stack more easily than others. This is because most, if not all, compilers use "outlining" that pushes regular code into a function body. Private variables are then local variables to the function, but that means stack space is needed to manage them. If not enough space is available, the program may crash and environment variable `OMP_STACKSIZE` needs to be used to increase the size of the stack for the threads.

Strand This word is often used by computer architects to denote what we call a "hardware thread" in this book. Please check this entry for a description.

Structured block For C/C++ programs, an executable statement with a single entry at the top and a single exit at the bottom. In Fortran code, it refers to a block of executable statements with a single entry at the top and a single exit at the bottom. An alternate name for this is *basic block*.

Synchronization Synchronization is used to coordinate the actions of multiple threads. It is essential in order to ensure correctness of the application. By default, an OpenMP program has barrier synchronization points at the end of parallel work-sharing constructs and parallel regions, where all threads have to wait until the last thread has finished its work. Synchronization may be expressed in many ways. OpenMP provides several constructs for explicit thread synchronization that should be used if accesses to shared data need to be ordered or if interference between multiple updates is to be avoided. These include critical regions, atomic updates, lock routines, and barriers. Memory synchronization, where thread-local shared data is made consistent with the process-wide values, is achieved via flushing.

Target task A task that is generated by a device construct. By default it is an included task, but if a `nowait` clause appears on the construct, it is a deferrable task.

Thread An Operating System entity that executes a stream of instructions. A process is executed by one or more threads and many of its resources (e.g., page tables, address space) are shared among these threads. However, a thread has some resources of its own, including a program counter and an associated stack. Since so few resources are involved, it is considerably faster to create a thread or to context switch between threads than it is to perform the same operation for processes. Sometimes threads are known as lightweight processes. In Unix environments, a thread is generally the smallest execution context.

Thread affinity This controls where in the system a thread should run and allows the application to leverage the system hardware characteristics. For example, if an application requires a significant amount of bandwidth, it may be beneficial to place the threads across the socket. If on the other hand, threads communicate very frequently, placing them on the same socket may be the best thing to do for performance. Often, thread affinity is combined with thread binding to re-schedule the thread on the same hardware thread, after a context switch.

Thread binding With thread binding, a thread is pinned down to a specific core or even hardware thread. If the Operating System supports this, the thread will never be rescheduled onto another core or hardware thread. This provides the optimal thread affinity and is supported in OpenMP. Be aware though that binding may slow down an application in case other applications are running as well, or if there are no hardware threads left for the OS to run on. In case of the latter, the OS will claim the resources it needs, potentially slowing down one or more application level threads.

Thread ID A means to identify a thread. In OpenMP the thread IDs are consecutive integer numbers. The sequence starts at zero, which is reserved for the master thread, and ends with $P - 1$, if P threads are used. The `omp_get_thread_num()` function call enables a thread to obtain its thread ID.

Thread-safe A property that guarantees software will execute correctly when run on multiple threads simultaneously. Programs that are not thread safe can fail due to race conditions or deadlocks when run with multiple parallel threads. Particular care has to be taken when using library calls or shared objects and methods within OpenMP parallel regions.

TLB Translation Lookaside Buffer. The TLB buffer, or cache, is an important part of the memory system. It is a relatively small cache that maintains information on the physical pages of memory associated with a running process. If the address of data needed by a thread is loaded but not covered through the TLB, a TLB miss occurs. Setting up a new entry in the TLB is an expensive operation that should be avoided where possible.

Transactional memory With this, a lock is initially ignored and the code in the locked region is executed unconditionally. Only afterwards it is checked if there was a lock collision, or not. In case of the former, a rollback mechanism is triggered to ensure correct results. The advantage is that handling a lock that is not contended is really fast. If however, the lock is heavily contended, the cost of executing the rollback part can reduce, or even ruin, any performance benefit and ultimately handling the lock may be more expensive.

Several research and commercial implementations have become available in recent years. There are significant variations between the various architectures, including hybrid versions augmenting the hardware support with software features to enhance the efficiency.

Vector instruction An instruction that operates on multiple data elements simultaneously, also referred to as SIMD instruction.

Vector width The number of vector operations executed simultaneously in a vector, or SIMD, instruction.

Vectorization This is hardware acceleration first found in mainframes in the late 60's. Soon after, special vector machines were designed and built. The main idea is to perform the same basic operation, like an add, on a series of operands, the "vectors." Much later, this technology was implemented in micro-processors. Nowadays it is usually referred to as "SIMD." Refer to SIMD entry for more information.

Wall-clock time A measure of how much actual time it takes to complete a task, in this case a program or part of a program. Wall-clock time is also referred to as "elapsed time." It is an important metric for parallel programs. Although the aggregate CPU time most likely goes up, the wall-clock time of a parallel application should decrease when an increasing number of threads is used to execute it. Care needs to be taken when measuring this value. If there are more threads than processors or cores on the system, or if the load is such that a thread will not have a processor or core to itself, there may be little or no reduction in wall-clock time when adding a thread.

References

[1] Eduard Ayguadé, Nawal Copty, Alejandro Duran, Jay Hoeflinger, Yuan Lin, Federico Massaioli, Xavier Teruel, Priya Unnikrishnan, and Guansong Zhang. *The Design of OpenMP Tasks. IEEE Trans. Parallel Distrib. Syst.*, 20(3):404–418, March 2009.

[2] Barbara Chapman, Gabriele Jost, and Ruud van der Pas. *Using OpenMP—Portable Shared Memory Programming*. The MIT Press, Cambridge, MA, 2007.

[3] James C. Beyer, Eric J. Stotzer, Alistair Hart, and Bronis R. de Supinski. *OpenMP for Accelerators*. In Barbara M. Chapman, William D. Gropp, Kalyan Kumaran, and Matthias S. Müller, editors, *IWOMP 2011*, volume 6665 of *Lecture Notes in Computer Science*, pages 108–121. Springer, Berlin, Heidelberg, 2011.

[4] The C11 Standard. `http://www.iso.org/iso/iso_catalogue/catalogue_tc/catalogue_detail.htm?csnumber=57853`.

[5] The C++11 Standard. `http://www.open-std.org/jtc1/sc22/wg21`.

[6] DTrace website. `http://dtrace.org`.

[7] Oracle Solaris Dynamic Tracing Guide. `http://docs.oracle.com/cd/E53394_01/html/E53395/index.html`, 2017.

[8] Alexandre E. Eichenberger, Christian Terboven, Michael Wong, and Dieter an Mey. *The Design of OpenMP Thread Affinity*. In Barbara M. Chapman, Federico Massaioli, Matthias S. Müller, and Marco Rorro, editors,

IWOMP 2012, volume 7312 of *Lecture Notes in Computer Science*, pages 15–28. Springer, Berlin, Heidelberg, 2012.

[9] M. J. Flynn. Some Computer Organizations and Their Effectiveness. *IEEE Transactions on Computing*, C-21:948–960, 1972.

[10] Brendan Gregg. *Systems Performance: Enterprise and the Cloud*. Pearson Education, Inc, 2013.

[11] Brendan Gregg and Jim Mauro. *DTrace: Dynamic Tracing in Oracle Solaris, Mac OS X and FreeBSD*. Prentice Hall, 2011.

[12] Khronos Group. *OpenCL*^{TM} Open Computing Language. `http://www.khronos.org/opencl`.

[13] J.L. Hennessy and D.A. Patterson. *Computer Architecture: A Quantitative Approach*. Morgan Kaufmann Publishers, Inc., San Francisco, CA, 5th edition, 2011.

[14] Jim Jeffers, James Reinders, and Avinash Sodani. *Intel Xeon Phi Processor High Performance Programming –Knights Landing Edition*. Morgan Kaufmann, Elsevier, Cambridge, MA, 2016.

[15] Michael Klemm, Alejandro Duran, Xinmin Tian, Hideki Saito, Diego Caballero, and Xavier Martorell. Extending OpenMP* with Vector Constructs for Modern Multicore SIMD Architectures. In Barbara M. Chapman, Federico Massaioli, Matthias S. Müller, and Marco Rorro, editors, *IWOMP 2012*, volume 7312 of *Lecture Notes in Computer Science*, pages 59–72. Springer, Berlin, Heidelberg, 2012.

[16] L. Lamport. *How to Make a Multiprocessor Computer That Correctly Executes Multiprocess Programs*. *IEEE Trans. on Software Engineering*, C-28(9):690–691, 1979.

[17] Richard McDougall, Jim Mauro, and Brendan Gregg. *Solaris Performance and Tools: DTrace and MDB Techniques for Solaris 10 and OpenSolaris*. Sun Microsystems Press, 2006.

[18] MPI Forum website. `http://www.mpi-forum.org`.

[19] Nvidia. CUDA^{TM} programming model. `http://docs.nvidia.com/cuda`.

[20] OpenMP website. `http://www.openmp.org`.

[21] OpenMP Active Technical Report Drafts and Proposals. `http://www.openmp.org/specifications`.

[22] Quicksort Wikipedia website. `http://en.wikipedia.org/wiki/Quicksort`.

[23] J. Sewall, S. J. Pennycook, A. Duran, C. Terboven, X. Tian, and R. Narayanaswamy. *Developments in Memory Management in OpenMP. To appear in IJHPCN.*

[24] Jun Shirako, Priya Unnikrishnan, Sanjay Chatterjee, Kelvin Li, and Vivek Sarkar. *Expressing DOACROSS Loop Dependences in OpenMP.* In Alistair P. Rendell, Barbara M. Chapman, and Matthias S. Müller, editors, *IWOMP 2013*, volume 8122 of *Lecture Notes in Computer Science*, pages 30–44. Springer, Berlin, Heidelberg, 2013.

[25] SystemTap website. `http://sourceware.org/systemtap/wiki`.

[26] Xinmin Tian, Hideki Saito, Milind Girkar, Serguei Preis, Sergey Kozhukhov, and Alejandro Duran. *Putting Vector Programming to Work with OpenMP SIMD.* `https://goparallel.sourceforge.net/putting-vector-programming-to-work-with-openmp-simd/`, 2015.

Subject Index

Scientific and Engineering Computation

William Gropp and Ewing Lusk, editors; Janusz Kowalik, founding editor

Using MPI: Portable Parallel Programming with the Message-Passing Interface, third edition, William Gropp, Ewing Lusk, and Anthony Skjellum, 2015

Using Advanced MPI: Beyond the Basics, Pavan Balaji, William Gropp, Torsten Hoefler, Rajeev Thakur, and Ewing Lusk, 2015

Scientific Programming and Computer Architecture, Divakar Viswanath, 2017

Cloud Computing for Science and Engineering, Ian Foster and Dennis B. Gannon, 2017

Using OpenMP—The Next Step : Affinity, Accelerators, Tasking and SIMD, Ruud van der Pas, Eric Stotzer, and Christian Terboven, 2017

Printed in the United States
by Baker & Taylor Publisher Services